Empirically Supported Cognitive Therapies

Current and Future Applications

William J. Lyddon, PhD, is professor of psychology and director of training of the APA-accredited counseling psychology program in the Department of Psychology at the University of Southern Mississippi. He received his PhD from the University of California, Santa Barbara in 1989. He is a licensed psychologist and Founding Fellow of the Academy of Cognitive Therapy, has served on the editorial board of several scholarly journals, and is currently an executive board member of the International Association of Cognitive Psychotherapy, Consulting Editor of the *Counselling Psychology Quarterly*, and the Assistant Editor of the *Journal of Cognitive Psychotherapy*, published by Springer Publishing. Dr. Lyddon has published over 70 journal articles and book chapters, mostly in the areas of adult attachment, cognitive and constructivist therapies, and conceptual and philosophical issues in psychotherapy.

John V. Jones, Jr., PhD, LPC, NCC, ACT, graduated from the University of North Texas with a PhD in counselor education in 1996. Currently, he is an associate professor at South Dakota State University where he trains master's level counselors for mental health counseling. He has authored several articles on cognitive therapy, and is a member of the Academy of Cognitive Therapy. Dr. Jones received training in cognitive therapy at the Beck Institute of Cognitive Therapy through both the intramural and extramural programs offered by the Institute. His particular interests lie in working with social phobia, theoretical integration, and the history of counseling and psychology.

Empirically Supported Cognitive Therapies

Current and Future Applications

William J. Lyddon, PhD
John V. Jones, Jr., PhD, LPC, NCC, ACT
Editors

 Springer Publishing Company

Springer Publishing Company, Inc.
536 Broadway
New York, NY 10012-3955

Acquisitions Editor: Sheri W. Sussman
Production Editor: Elizabeth Keech
Cover design by Susan Hauley

00 01 02 03 04 / 5 4 3 2 1

Library of Congress Cataloging-in-Publication Data

Empirically supported cognitive therapies : current and future applications / William J. Lyddon, John V. Jones, editors.
  p. m.
  Includes bibliographical references and index.
  ISBN 0-8261-2299-X
  1. Congnitive theraphy. I. Lyddon, William J. II. Jones, John V.

  RC489.C63 .E46 2001
  616.89'142—dc21

                                                                      2001020070

Printed in the United States by Maple-Vail.

CONTENTS

Part III NEW DIRECTIONS AND DEVELOPMENTS

Contributors

Monica Ramirez Basco, PhD
University of Texas Southwestern
  Medical Center
Dallas, Texas

**Ivy-Marie Blackburn, PhD, MA,
Dip Clin Psychol, C Psychol**
Newcastle Cognitive and
  Behavioural Therapies Centre
Newcastle Upon Tyne, United
  Kingdom

Anne E. Blackhurst, PhD
Counseling and Student Personnel
  Department
Minnesota State University,
  Mankato
Mankato, Minnesota

David K. Chatkoff, MA
Department of Psychology
University of Southern Mississippi
Hattiesburg, Mississippi

Eric R. Dahlen, PhD
Department of Psychology
University of Southern Mississippi
Hattiesburg, Mississippi

Jerry L. Deffenbacher, PhD
Department of Psychology
Colorado State University
Fort Collins, Colorado

E. Thomas Dowd, PhD, ABPP
Department of Psychology
Kent State University
Kent, Ohio

Deborah R. Fahr, MA
Department of Psychology
Kent State University
Kent, Ohio

Sherry A. Falsetti, PhD
National Crime Victims Research
  and Treatment Center
Department of Psychiatry and
  Behavioral Sciences
Charleston, South Carolina

Laura D. Hanish, PhD
Department of Family Resources
Arizona State University
Tempe, Arizona

**Steve Moorhead, MB, ChB,
MRC Psych**
University of Newcastle Upon Tyne
Newcastle Upon Tyne, United
  Kingdom

Simon A. Rego, PsyM, MA
Department of Clinical Psychology
Graduate School of Applied and
  Professional Psychology
Rutgers University
Piscataway, New Jersey

Heidi S. Resnick, PhD
National Crime Victims Research
  and Treatment Center
Department of Psychiatry and
  Behavioral Sciences
Charleston, South Carolina

William C. Sanderson, PhD
Department of Clinical Psychology
Graduate School of Applied and
  Professional Psychology
Rutgers University
Piscataway, New Jersey

Patrick H. Tolan, PhD
Institute for Juvenile Research
Department of Psychiatry
University of Illinois at Chicago
Chicago, Illinois

Sabine Wilhelm, PhD
Obsessive Compulsive Disorder
Massachusetts General Hospital
Charlestown, Massachusetts

Nona L. Wilson, PhD
College of Education and
  Counseling
South Dakota State University
Counseling and Human Resources
  Development
Brookings, South Dakota

Foreword

Empirically Supported Cognitive Therapies: Current and Future Applications, will be a valuable reference tool for clinicians interested in learning about the most up- to-date empirically supported treatments available for a wide range of disorders. The editors, William J. Lyddon and John V. Jones, have gathered together leading cognitive therapy researchers and clinicians in this collection. Clinicians and students alike will find this book to be a very helpful clinical tool for many of the most common disorders seen in practice.

Each chapter provides some background on the historical, conceptual, and empirical contexts of the cognitive model. The authors provide the reader with clear clinical guidelines, examples, and treatment recommendations. The first section on mood disorders covers both unipolar depression and bipolar depression. The chapter by Blackburn and Moorhead on unipolar depression reviews the evidence of the efficacy of cognitive therapy for this disorder and provides a short case study to illustrate the application of the therapeutic model. The chapter by Basco on the treatment of bipolar disorder offers a particularly helpful treatment manual. The section on anxiety disorders covers phobias (Fahr and Dowd), panic (Sanderson and Rego), obsessive-compulsive disorder (Wilhelm) and post-traumatic stress disorder (Falsetti and Resnick). These authors provide information on diagnostic practices, theoretical issues, and clinical application, along with case examples that will assist the reader in utilizing their recommendations.

I found the section on "New Directions" quite interesting, because the authors of these chapters provide useful clinical guidelines for anger management (Dahlen and Deffenbacher), antisocial behavior in children and adolescents (Hanish and Tolan), and eating disorders (Wilson and Blackhurst). Of course it seems quite ironic that anger is not a separate diagnostic category in the DSM—perhaps reflecting the distortion in our cultural values whereby anxiety is viewed as more problematic than hostility. The angry patient, as Dahlen and Deffenbacher correctly illustrate, can be quite difficult for the clinician. Their chapter will be helpful to therapists who must confront these issues on a regular basis. Hanish and Tolan provide a comprehensive approach to the treatment of antisocial minors—a population group that has substantial social and economic costs in our society. Wilson and Blackhurst provide an integrative cognitive-behavioral-feminist perspective on eating disorders—a set of problems disproportionately affecting women than men. Their creative suggestion of addressing the internalization of self-defeating cultural values within a cognitive model is a much needed recommendation. Finally, Lyddon and Chatkoff provide a balanced discussion of both the promise and current limitations of the empirically supported treatment (EST) movement as well as offering suggestions for improving EST research and the effectiveness of ESTs. Taken together, the selections in this volume will be a significant tool for therapists interested in expanding their knowledge and repertoire of empirically supported cognitive therapies.

Robert L. Leahy
Editor, Journal of Cognitive Psychotherapy:
An International Quarterly

Director, The American Institute for
Cognitive Therapy, New York City

Preface

During the past 2 to 3 decades the field of psychotherapy has experienced a tremendous amount of differentiation and growth. To be sure, the current psychotherapy landscape is represented by a diverse, and sometimes overwhelming, array of theoretical models and practices. Paralleling this differentiation and diversification, however, has been a trend toward convergence and integration of psychotherapy approaches, exemplified by the common factors approach, systematic eclecticism, and theoretical integration. A more recent and significant integrative force in contemporary psychotherapy is the empirically supported treatment (EST) movement, which has a primary goal of identifying and consolidating treatments that "work" for particular types of disorders based on empirical criteria of efficacy. While the contemporary EST movement has been galvanized by a number of political and professional forces—including managed health care, the ascendance of biological psychiatry, and changing accreditation guidelines for doctoral training programs in applied professional psychology—a significant but often underemphasized justification for the EST movement is related to the ethical issues of public trust and accountability. Psychologists, psychiatrists, and other mental health professionals have an ethical obligation to the public they serve to ensure, as much as possible, that the treatments they offer are fundamentally sound. As a result, researchers and practitioners are obligated to use empirically supported treatments to guide their work as a matter of ethical accountability.

When Aaron Beck began reporting on the efficacy of cognitive therapy in the treatment of depression, the groundwork was being laid to establish an empirical basis for the practice of cognitive therapy. Today cognitive therapy is at the forefront of the EST movement and has been demonstrated in over 325 research studies to be efficacious for a wide range of psychological problems. Empirically supported treatments derived from the cognitive model are increasingly being applied across the full spectrum of psychological disorders. The present volume brings together leading researchers and clinicians in the field in order to summarize the most current empirical developments in cognitive therapy for the treatment of mood disorders, phobias, panic, obsessive-compulsive disorder, and posttraumatic stress disorder. Recent developments in empirically based extensions and elaborations of the cognitive model in the treatment of anger, antisocial behavior in children and adolescents, and eating disorders are also presented. The overarching principle for each of these contributions is that clinical research should play an important role in guiding clinical practice. As a result, the authors of each chapter summarize the empirical literature bearing on the treatment of the particular disorder under consideration and then offer relevant practice guidelines suggested by clinical research. Case examples and clinical protocols are employed to further illustrate how the practice of cognitive therapy may be informed by empirical outcomes. From this standpoint, the contributors to this volume have all significantly advanced cognitive therapy's increasingly prominent role in the EST movement.

William J. Lyddon

Acknowledgments

I want to extend appreciation to my colleagues and mentors, Mike Mahoney and Tom Dowd, who have supported me both personally and professionally over the years. I am particularly indebted to my parents for their consistent support, and to my wife and life companion, Darlys Alford, for her daily encouragement and enthusiasm for life's simple pleasures.

—WJL

I would like to thank my parents who over the years influenced my education, on one hand, and who patiently put up with my journeys on the other hand. Additionally, I owe gratitude to the counseling department at South Dakota State University (SDSU) for supporting faculty research efforts. I also appreciate those students in the counseling program at SDSU who have a thirst for knowledge and who continually charge me with the responsibility of providing for them the kind of learning environment they deserve.

—JJJr

1

Empirically Supported Treatments: An Introduction

William J. Lyddon and John V. Jones, Jr.

In 1952, the British psychologist Hans Eysenck published a review of 24 psychotherapy outcome studies and concluded that there was no evidence to support the effectiveness of psychotherapy (Eysenck, 1952). Most historiographers of psychotherapy point to Eysenck's review as a provocative challenge to psychotherapy researchers to demonstrate the effectiveness of psychotherapy over and above various estimates of natural recovery, or so-called spontaneous remission (Bergin & Garfield, 1994; Nathan & Gorman, 1998; Roth & Fonagy, 1996). Although Eysenck's data and methods were brought into question by several researchers (cf. Bergin, 1971; Lambert, 1979; McNeilly & Howard, 1991), the debate over Eysenck's claims has persisted over the years (Rachman & Wilson, 1980; Stiles, Shapiro, & Elliot, 1986). Furthermore, in recent years, various groups have brought increased pressure upon psychotherapists to demonstrate that what they do actually works. Such pressures have come from health maintenance organizations, insurance companies, consumer activist groups, and from practitioners and researchers within the field. All of these forces continue to converge on two prominent questions: (a) Is psychotherapy effective? and, if so (b) Are some forms of psychotherapy more effective than others for particular kinds of problems and disorders?

In an attempt to address the above questions, the purpose of this volume is to review and disseminate information on the current status of empirically supported cognitive therapies for particular psychological disorders. In this introductory chapter we will provide a brief historical overview of research on the effectiveness of psychotherapy since Eysenck's (1952) challenge, discuss some of the issues and debates surrounding the empirically supported treatment movement, and finally, provide a brief sketch of the organization of and contributions to this volume.

1

POST–EYSENCK REACTIONS

Following Eysenck's (1952) critique of the effectiveness of psychotherapy, many people within the field understandably became incensed. Indeed, those who disagreed with Eysenck believed that his claim took on the stature of a myth (Smith & Glass, 1977). However, Eysenck persuaded others that the field of psychotherapy could not live up to its claims of being an effective treatment for psychological disorders. In fact, 17 years after his original challenge to the field, Eysenck (1969) published a book, *The Effects of Psychotherapy*, in which he came to the same conclusions as in his 1952 work. Consequently, for a period of approximately 20 years, the field of psychotherapy was essentially divided into two camps—those who endorsed and those who disagreed with Eysenck's claims.

Researchers and practitioners did not begin to authoritatively respond to Eysenck (1952) until the 1970s. Bergin (1978), for example, explicated some of the methodological flaws in Eysenck's (1952) research, identifying such problems as the lack of comparable cases across the 24 studies, the lack of equivalent outcome criteria, large variations in the amount and quality of treatment received, and imprecise definitions of psychological disorder and criteria for improvement. Smith, Glass, and Miller (1980) provided evidence of psychotherapy's effectiveness through a meta-analytic study of 475 investigations. Comparing treated and untreated groups, these researchers reported an effect size of 0.85—suggesting that the average person who received psychotherapy was better off than 80% of the people who had not received psychotherapy. In addition, around this time the organizers of the third edition of the *Diagnostic and Statistical Manual for Mental Disorders* (*DSM-III*; American Psychiatric Association [APA], 1980) sought to solidify the descriptions and discussions of psychological disorders with more empirical data. The organizers and team researchers of the *DSM-III* hoped the manual could provide a standardized diagnostic system for use in outcome studies (Nathan & Gorman, 1998). With such a system in place, the field could move beyond general descriptions about the effectiveness of psychotherapy to more specific conclusions related to the treatment of specific psychological problems.

However, not all researchers and practitioners were convinced that the responses during the decade of the 1970s had adequately countered Eysenck's (1952, 1969) claims. For example, based on his own analysis of psychotheray research, Rachman (1971) concurred with Eysenck's conclusions. In a follow-up volume, however, Rachman and Wilson (1980) were somewhat more optimistic, but guarded about the effects of psychotherapy. Consequently, by the end of the 1970s there was still considerable debate among researchers and practitioners concerning the benefits of psychotherapy.

In 1986, the American Psychological Association published a special issue on psychotherapy outcome research in the *American Psychologist* (VandenBos, 1986). At least two major themes were evident in this special issue. First, researchers correlated the positive benefits of psychotherapy with the amount of treatment undertaken (Nathan & Gorman, 1998). Second, echoing the findings of Smith, Glass, and Miller (1980), the special issue continued to support the notion that most major forms of psychotherapy are relatively equivalent. Hence, a second myth about psychotherapy surfaced. Not only was it difficult to demonstrate the effectiveness of psychotherapy as a whole, but it was equally difficult to demonstrate that one therapeutic approach was necessarily superior to another. For example, Smith and associates (1980) found no significant effect size differences among Gestalt therapy, rational-emotive therapy, behavioral therapy, transactional analysis, psychodynamic therapies, and humanistic approaches. As late as 1986, many researchers and practitioners still believed that these approaches were relatively equivalent (Nathan & Gorman, 1998). More recently, Persons (1995) argued that the belief that the major forms of psychotherapy were equivalent influenced practitioners to not attend to research designed to test the empirical support of particular treatments for particular disorders.

RECENT DEVELOPMENTS

Nathan and Gorman (1998) pointed out that over the last decade, psychotherapy has faired better than Eysenck's (1952, 1969) original assessment may have predicted. Perhaps one of the most significant trends in the past 10 to 15 years has been the growth of empirical research designed to evaluate the effectiveness of specific therapeutic interventions for particular disorders. This trend has produced at least two significant developments in the field. First, compilations of edited works have emerged demonstrating the effectiveness of treatments for particular disorders. Examples of such works include *Sourcebook of Psychological Treatment Manuals for Adult Disorders* (Van Hasselt & Hersen,1996), *What Works for Whom? A Critical Review of Psychotherapy Research* (Roth & Fonagy, 1996), and *A Guide to Treatments that Work* (Nathan & Gorman,1998). In the last decade numerous empirically based research articles have emerged in the clinical literature along with debates about and criticisms of empirically supported treatments.

A second development stemming from the empirically supported treatment movement is the generation of therapeutic protocols, practice guidelines, and standards of care. Because researchers have identified a number of empirically supported treatments for particular psychological disorders, psychotherapists have become expected to provide such treatments. Consequently, specific practice guidelines for the treatment of particular problems have emerged in recent years. Examples of such guidelines include *Practice Guideline for Major Depressive Disorder in Adults* (APA, 1993); *Practice Guideline for Treatment of Patients with Substance Use Disorders: Alcohol, Cocaine, Opioids,* (APA, 1995); and *Practice Guideline for the Treatment of Patients with Panic Disorder* (APA, 1998). The format of each guideline entails an empirical description of the disorder for which the guideline has been developed, a section on general treatment principles and alternatives, and a section on directions for further research. Each guideline also includes a summary of recommendations regarding treatment (Nathan & Gorman, 1998). Although many practitioners have welcomed the innovations that have stemmed from empirical research in the field, empirically supported treatments and practice guidelines have not escaped criticism.

Debate and Criticism

While many clinicians have welcomed and embraced the development of empirically supported treatments, treatment protocols, and practice guidelines, others view such innovations with doubts, philosophical skepticism, and even hostility. Persons (1995) suggested a number of reasons why clinicians have failed to fully adopt and integrate empirically supported treatments into clinical practice. The reasons she delineated revolve around three major issues: (a) philosophical differences underpinning different psychotherapeutic approaches, (b) difficulties associated with translating research into practice, and (c) shortcomings both in training students and disseminating results of empirically supported interventions.

Philosophical Differences

Many theorists and clinicians believe that empirically supported treatments and practice guidelines that prescribe them are theory driven and intended to support particular theoretical approaches (Kohlenberg, 1995). Opponents of empirical research and manualized protocols argue that while behavioral and cognitive therapies value symptom reduction, other approaches such as psychodynamic therapies value insight and increased understanding. Consequently, the question is left open as to which dependent measure to use in defining effectiveness (Kohlenberg, 1995). Others argue that protocols and guidelines ignore such parameters as therapist and client variability (Garfield, 1996; Hubble, Duncan, & Miller, 1999; Kovacs, 1995; Smith, 1995). Theorists claim that factors common to all psychotherapies play a major role in treatment effectiveness. Hence, many of the questions and debates regarding practice guidelines revolve around the relevance of theory to standards of practice (Adams, 1995; Ghezzi, 1995).

Hubble and colleagues (1999) have recently suggested that empirically supported treatments are designed to support particular theoretical models over others. Such a claim, however, may miss the point that empirically supported evidence is not exclusively about theoretical models. Although a specific intervention may be derived from a particular theoretical model, it can be integrated into a different theoretical framework. For example, while clinicians and theorists such as Persons (1995) and Wilson (1995, 1996) fall within the cognitive camp, both have pointed to the efficacy of other approaches, such as interpersonal psychotherapy (Klerman, Weissman, & Rounsaville, 1984). Indeed, Persons suggests more attention be given to training in interpersonal psychotherapy because the approach has proven efficacious for depression. Wilson (1995) similarly endorses a combination of cognitive-behavioral therapy and interpersonal therapy for eating disorders. Hence, the claim that clinicians who value empirically supported treatments may be theory biased may not be accurate. Furthermore, Sanderson (1997) has argued that the field of psychotherapy cannot wait for theoretical debates to be settled. He suggests that if the field of psychotherapy does not develop some type of standard of care, then someone else will develop the standards for the field. Indeed, pharmaceutical companies have done just that—research on medication for psychological disorders has been more widely disseminated than research of effective psychotherapy treatments (Persons, 1995; Sanderson, 1997).

Research Efficacy and Clinical Effectiveness

The gap between psychological research and clinical practice has had a long history. One shortcoming associated with clinical trials concerns their generalizability to clinical practice. Persons (1995), for example, points to the relatively high subject exclusion rate associated with many research projects. Sometimes inclusion criteria are so stringent that those who are screened for research participation are significantly different from the clients who typically walk into a therapist's office. In addition, protocols developed on the basis of research projects may be difficult to implement in clinical practice. Wetzler and Sanderson (1997) have called for more clinical researchers to employ diagnostically comorbid samples in order to improve the generalizability to actual clinical practice settings. Although recognizing the gap between research and practice, Wilson (1996) suggests that the differences between clients involved in research and those seen in practice might be overemphasized. He pointed to the fact that many clients involved in research projects enter such programs because of long-standing difficulties.

While it is important for researchers to provide practical and cost-effective results for clinicians, it is equally important for clinicians to realize that part of the art of doing scientific therapy involves finding ways to effectively translate research findings into clinical practice. Along this line, Persons (1995) recommended that researchers make their results user-friendly for practitioners; otherwise, clinicians will continue to avoid research literature. In addition, both Persons and Sanderson (1997) argue for both better dissemination of research knowledge of empirically supported treatments and improved graduate-student training in such treatments. Persons recommended that training of graduate students should also involve learning how to interpret and use research results.

Dissemination of Knowledge and Training of Graduate Students

Many university training programs would have to undergo dramatic changes if they began to train students in empirically supported treatments and practice guidelines (Persons, 1995). As suggested above, such training would also involve philosophical as well as practical changes for many in the field. Indeed, many professors are not trained in up-to-date interventions, and many graduate programs train students in a particular theoretical approach. Moreover, psychotherapists have not matched the aggressiveness of pharmacotherapists in disseminating research results. Persons challenged psychotherapy organizations to disseminate knowledge of empirically supported treatments. She also called for the American Psychological Association (APA) to base continued education credits on training in empirically supported treatments and to assess graduate programs on whether students receive training in such treatments. If the field of psychotherapy does not disseminate knowledge gleaned from research to practitioners in ways that practitioners can understand and use, then practice guidelines will fall significantly short of their potential impact.

Cognitive Therapy and Empirically Supported Treatments

In the last 10 to 15 years, empirical research has not only answered Eysenck's (1952, 1969) original charge, but has also responded to Smith and colleagues' claim (1980) that most major forms of psychotherapies are generally equivalent. Cognitive therapy, in particular, has faired well among empirically supported treatments. Following Beck's (1967, 1976; Beck, Rush, Shaw, & Emery, 1979) seminal work, empirical support for cognitive therapy of depression continues to emerge (Clark & Beck, 1999; Williams, 1997). Several researcher-clinicians have built upon Beck and Emery's (1985) original work on cognitive therapy for anxiety disorders and phobias. Bruce and Sanderson (1998), for example, have developed evidenced-based cognitive treatments for specific phobias. Clark (1997) has provided evidence for an empirically based cognitive therapy for anxiety disorders and social phobia. Fairburn (1997) developed research-based treatment protocols in cognitive therapy for eating disorders. Basco and Rush (1996) produced a manualized approach for working with bipolar disorder. In the treatment of personality disorders, Linehan's (1993) cognitive-behavioral treatment for borderline personality disorder has also generated empirical support. Cognitive models for particular disorders continue to be researched and developed (Clark & Fairburn, 1997), and cognitive therapy continues to emerge as an efficacious treatment for particular psychological disorders.

THE PRESENT VOLUME

In the spirit of disseminating some of the most recent research on empirically supported treatments, the present volume brings together several distinguished researchers and scholars in the field who use a cognitive model as the basis of their research and practice. The contributions to this book are organized into three sections that tend to reflect the evolution of empirical developments in the application of the cognitive model to the treatment of particular psychological disorders and problems. Because formative developments in the field were directed toward the amelioration of depression, Part I is devoted to the topic of mood disorders. In chapter 2, Ivy-Marie Blackburn and Steve Moorhead discuss the continued evolution of cognitive therapy for depression. They examine new theories inspired by cognitive science, and report the results of major meta-analyses of controlled outcome studies, as well as examine recent outcome and follow-up studies. Current controversies regarding the efficacy of cognitive therapy for depression and the role of process variables are evaluated. In order to illustrate the structure and process of cognitive therapy, the authors provide a case study of a depressed patient who also exhibits two personality disorder syndromes.

Continuing with research in cognitive therapy for mood disorders, Monica Ramirez Basco (chapter 3) focuses on the treatment of bipolar I disorder. She reviews interventions developed to (a) improve patient compliance with pharmacotherapy and (b) provide patients with skills for controlling symptoms. Toward this end, Ramirez Basco reviews the empirical literature on patient compliance and then provides a cognitive behavioral treatment manual for bipolar I disorder, illustrating its application through a case study.

The four chapters in Part II focus on recent empirical developments in the treatment of anxiety disorders. In their chapter on phobias (chapter 4), Deborah R. Fahr and E. Thomas Dowd note that empirical evidence has shown cognitive behavior therapy to be the treatment of choice for specific and social phobias. The authors discuss diagnostic issues and criteria related to different types of phobias, review empirical evidence supporting cognitive behavior therapy as the treatment of choice for phobias, and provide a case study to illustrate fundamental treatment issues and concepts.

William C. Sanderson and Simon A. Rego have conducted extensive research on the application of the cognitive model to the treatment panic disorder. In chapter 5, they discuss various treatment components that have been shown to be effective (either alone or in combination) in the treatment of panic disorder, review pivotal experiments designed to study the efficacy of cognitive behavioral therapy for panic disorder, and illustrate the application of core treatment components with a case example.

In chapter 6, Sabine Wilhelm suggests that cognitive therapy for obsessive-compulsive disorder (OCD) may be at least as effective (and less stressful) as the current psychological treatment of choice—exposure and response prevention (ERP). She reviews studies on cognitive therapy for OCD and provides a case example to illustrate specific cognitive treatment techniques.

Sherry A. Falsetti and Heidi S. Resnick have done extensive research on trauma at the National Crime Victims Research and Treatment Center at the Medical University of South Carolina. In chapter 7 they review issues related to the assessment and cognitive behavioral treatment of patients with civilian posttraumatic stress syndrome disorder (PTSD). Several empirically supported treatments are described and extant treatment outcome literature is reviewed. A case example designed to highlight cognitive strategies within cognitive behavioral therapy is presented.

The final part of the book, "New Directions and Developments," emphasizes the extension of the cognitive model into new areas as well as the expansion of current empirically supported treatments to include more contextual and cultural variables. In chapter 8, Eric R. Dahlen and Jerry L. Deffenbacher describe an empirically supported cognitive-behavioral approach to anger management. The authors discuss the absence of anger in the diagnostic nomenclature, offer suggestions for diagnostic criteria, present a cognitive-behavioral model for understanding anger, review empirically supported treatments for anger, and provide a treatment protocol (illustrated through a case example). Dahlen and Deffenbacher conclude their chapter by offering suggestions to practitioners regarding the delivery of interventions to angry clients.

In chapter 9, Laura Hanish and Patrick H. Tolan argue for the viability of expanding traditional child-focused cognitive approaches in the treatment of antisocial behavior to include more contextually sensitive interventions. The authors review the critical aspects of antisocial behavior, focusing on important contextual dimensions of the disorder, such as child behavior and family interactions. The authors offer data that support the efficacy and effectiveness of an integrated model that includes cognitive, behavioral, family, and contextual intervention components for treating antisocial behavior in youths.

Nona L. Wilson and Anne E. Blackhurst (chapter 10) argue for an integration of established cognitive-behavioral principles with feminist perspectives on eating disorders. They present a unified conceptual framework linking the layers of individual cognition emphasized in cognitive-behavioral therapy with layers of cultural values emphasized in feminist models. They demonstrate how the latter give rise to and reinforce the former. Following from this conceptual integration, the authors offer guidelines for (a) assigning and processing media-based interventions with clients and (b) assisting clients in using enhanced cultural criticism skills for relapse prevention.

William J. Lyddon and David K. Chatkoff conclude the volume with a critical discussion of empirically supported treatments and ideas for future directions. Following a brief review of recent converging economic, political, and professional forces that continue to shape the empirically supported treatment (EST) movement, Lyddon and Chatkoff highlight the issue of ethical accountability as a significant benefit of this movement. They point out, however, that while psychologists and other professionals have an ethical obligation to ensure that the treatments they offer are fundamentally sound, they also have an ethical obligation to accurately present the limitations of such treatments. As a result, the authors discuss two perceived limitations of the EST movement: (1) its emphasis on treatment efficacy over treatment effectiveness data and (2) its adoption of the randomized clinical trials methodology used in drug research. Following a review of the sources of error associated with these limitations, Lyddon and Chatkoff offer a recommendation for improving EST research and the effectiveness of ESTs. They point out that one very important component of the clinical drug trials approach to research that has not been incorporated into psychotherapy research is a feedback mechanism for monitoring the effectiveness of ESTs in actual clinical practice. They suggest that the addition of this crucial component would not only allow for the continual improvement and refinement of ESTs but that it would also represent an important additional step toward ensuring greater ethical accountability to the public trust.

Over the last 3 to 4 decades, treatments based on the cognitive model have evolved from an intervention for depression and have expanded to include treatments for many psychological problems and disorders. We believe this volume continues the effort of exploring and expanding conceptualizations and applications of the cognitive therapies. Science never offers final answers, and the destiny of any scientific discipline should be not to remain static, but to evolve. The contributions to this volume offer additional testimony to the fact that the field of cognitive therapy continues to abound in scientific research and, rather than standing still, continues to evolve. As editors of this volume, we commend all the authors for their outstanding contributions to the field and wish to thank Springer Publishing for its commitment to the dissemination of research on empirically supported cognitive therapies.

REFERENCES

Adams, H. E. (1995). The relevance of psychological theories to standards of practice. In S. C. Hayes, V. M. Follette, R. M. Dawes, & K. E. Grady (Eds.), *Scientific standards of psychological practice: Issues and recommendations* (pp. 251–260). Reno, NV: Context Press.

American Psychiatric Association (1980). *Diagnostic and statistical manual for mental disorders* (3rd ed.). Washington, DC: Author.

American Psychiatric Association (1993). *Practice guideline for major depressive disorder in adults.* Washington, DC: Author.

American Psychiatric Association (1995). *Practice guideline for treatment of patients with substance use disorders.* Washington, DC: Author.

American Psychiatric Association (1998). *Practice guideline for the treatment of patients with panic disorder.* Washington, DC: Author.

Basco, M. R., & Rush, A. J. (1996). *Cognitive-behavioral therapy for bipolar disorder.* New York: Guilford Press.

Beck, A. T. (1967). *Depression: Causes and treatment.* Philadelphia: University of Pennsylvania Press.

Beck, A. T. (1976). *Cognitive therapy and the emotional disorders.* New York: New American Library.

Beck, A. T., & Emery, G. (1985). *Anxiety disorders and phobias: A cognitive perspective.* Delran, NJ: Basic Books.

Beck, A. T., Rush, A. J., Shaw, B. F., & Emery, G. (1979). *Cognitive therapy of depression.* New York: Guilford Press.

Bergin, A. E. (1971). The evaluation of therapeutic outcomes. In A. E. Bergin & S. L. Garfield (Eds.), *Handbook of psychotherapy and behavior change: An empirical analysis* (pp. 217–270). New York: Wiley.

Bergin, A. E. (1978). The evaluation of therapeutic outcomes. In A. E. Bergin & S. L. Garfield (Eds.), *Handbook of psychotherapy and behavior change* (pp. 217–270). New York: John Wiley & Sons.

Bergin, A. E., & Garfield, S. L. (Eds.). (1994). *Handbook of psychotherapy and behavior change* (4th ed.). New York: Wiley.

Bruce, T. J., & Sanderson, W. C. (1998). *Specific phobias: Clinical applications of evidenced-based psychotherapy.* Northvale, NJ: Jason Aronson.

Clark, D. M. (1997). Panic disorder and social phobia. In D. M. Clark & C.

G. Fairburn (Eds.), *Science and practice of cognitive behavioral therapy* (pp. 119–154). Oxford: Oxford University Press.

Clark, D. M., & Beck, A. T. (1999). *Scientific foundations of cognitive theory and therapy of depression*. New York: Wiley.

Clark, D. M., & Fairburn, C. G. (Eds.). (1997). *Science and practice of cognitive-behavioral therapy*. Oxford: Oxford University Press.

Eysenck, H. J. (1952). The effects of psychotherapy: An evaluation. *Journal of Consulting Psychology, 16*(5), 319–324.

Eysenck, H. J. (1969). *The effects of psychotherapy*. New York: Science House.

Fairburn, C. G. (1997). Eating disorders. In D. M. Clark & C. G. Fairburn (Eds.), *Science and practice of cognitive behavior therapy*. Oxford: Oxford University Press.

Garfield, S. L. (1996). Some problems associated with "validated" forms of psychotherapy. *Clinical Psychology: Science and Practice, 3*(3), 218–229.

Ghezzi, P. M. (1995). Science, theory, and practice. In S. C. Hayes, V. M. Follette, R. M. Dawes, & K. E. Grady (Eds.), *Scientific standards of psychological practice: Issues and recommendations* (pp. 261–264). Reno, NV: Context Press.

Hubble, M. A., Duncan, B. L., & Miller, S. D. (1999). *The heart and soul of change: What works in therapy*. Washington DC: American Psychological Association.

Klerman, G. L., Weissman, M. M., & Rounsaville, B. J. (1984). *Interpersonal psychotherapy for depression*. New York: Basic Books.

Kohlenberg, B. S. (1995). Dissemination of what, and to whom? In S. C. Hayes, V. M. Follette, R. M. Dawes, & K. E. Grady (Eds.), *Scientific standards of psychological practice: Issues and recommendations* (pp. 158–161). Reno, NV: Context Press.

Lambert, M. J. (1979). *The effects of psychotherapy* (Vol. 1). New York: Eden Press.

Linehan, M. M. (1993). *Cognitive-behavioral treatment of borderline disorder*. New York: Guilford Press.

McNeilly, C. L., & Howard, K. I. (1991). The effects of psychotherapy: A reevaluation based on dosage. *Psychotherapy Research, 1*, 74–78.

Nathan, P. E., & Gorman, J. M. (Eds.). (1998). *A guide to treatments that work*. New York: Oxford University Press.

Persons, J. B. (1995). Why practicing psychologists are slow to adopt empirically-validated treatments. In S. C. Hayes, V. M. Follette, R. M. Dawes, & K. E. Grady (Eds.), *Scientific standards of psychological practice: Issues and recommendations* (pp. 141–157). Reno, NV: Context Press.

Rachman, S. (1971). *The effects of psychotherapy*. Oxford: Pergamon Press.

Rachman, S., & Wilson, G. T. (1980). *The effects of psychological therapy* (2nd ed.). Oxford: Pergamon Press.

Roth, A., & Fonagy, P. (1996). *What works for whom? A critical review of psychotherapy research.* New York: Guilford Press.

Sanderson, W. C. (1997). The importance of empirically supported psychological interventions in the new healthcare environment. In L. VandeCreek, S. Knapp, & T. L. Jackson (Eds.), *Innovations in clinical practice: A sourcebook, 15*(pp. 387–400). Sarasota, FL: Professional Resource Press.

Smith, E. W. L. (1995). A passionate rational response to the manualization of psychotherapy. *Psychotherapy Bulletin, 30*(2), 36–40.

Smith, M. E., & Glass, G. V. (1977). Meta-analysis of psychotherapy outcome studies. *American Psychologist, 32,* 752–760.

Smith, M. E., Glass, G. V., & Miller, T. I. (1980). *The benefits of psychotherapy.* Baltimore: Johns Hopkins University Press.

Stiles, W. B., Shapiro, D. A., & Elliot, R. K. (2986). Are all psychotherapies equivalent? *American Psychologist, 41,* 165–180.

VandenBos, G. R. (1986). Psychotherapy research: A special issue. *American Psychologist, 41,* 111–112.

Van Hasselt, V. B., & Hersen, M. (Eds.). (1996). *Sourcebook of psychological treatment manuals for adult disorders.* New York: Plenum Press.

Wetzler, S., & Sanderson, W. C. (Eds.). (1997). *Treatment strategies for patients with psychiatric comorbidity.* New York: Wiley.

Williams, J. M. G. (1997). Depression. In D. M. Clark & C. G. Fairburn (Eds.), *Science and practice of cognitive behavior therapy* (pp. 259–284). Oxford: Oxford University Press.

Wilson, G. T. (1995). Empirically validated treatments as a basis for clinical practice: Problems and prospects. In S. C. Hayes, V. M. Follette, R. M. Dawes, & K. E. Grady (Eds.), *Scientific standards of psychological practice: Issues and recommendations* (pp. 163–195). Reno, NV: Context Press.

Wilson, G. T. (1996). Empirically validated treatments: Reality and resistance. *Clinical Psychology: Science and Practice, 3*(3), 341–344.

Part I
Mood Disorders

2

Depression

Ivy-Marie Blackburn and Steve Moorhead

Depressive illness remains the most common mental disorder (World Health Organization [WHO] 1998, 1999) and is reported to be on the increase. The prevalence of major depression over a 12-month period is reported at 10.3% (men 7.7% and women 12.9%) (Kessler et al., 1994) and it is estimated that as many as a third of the population suffer from an episode of mild depression at some point in their lives (Paykel & Priest, 1992). Depression is a costly illness, in terms of days away from work, bed occupancy in hospitals, treatment, state benefits and degree of distress to the sufferers and their family. The direct health service cost for depression in England is estimated to be $710 (£420) million per year (Kind & Sorensen, 1993) and the indirect cost may be twice or three times as much. By the year 2020 clinical depression is likely to be second only to chronic heart disease as an international health burden, as measured by cause of death, disability, incapacity to work and medical resources used (Hartley, 1998; WHO, 1998).

In this chapter, recent advances in the cognitive theory and cognitive therapy of depression will be reviewed, and a case example will be given to illustrate current methods of treatment.

DIAGNOSTIC CRITERIA

It is now standard for outcome studies to specify the diagnostic criteria used in the selection of patients. The most commonly used criteria are those from *Diagnostic and Statistical Manual of Mental Disorders* (4th ed.) (*DSM-IV*; American Psychiatric Association, 1994) or from the International

We would like to thank Lucy Daley for preparing the manuscript and Nicola Belsham for the literature search.

Classification of Diseases (*ICD 10*). Since *major depression* will be the sub-category most often referred to in this paper and is the subcategory represented in most outcome studies, the relevant criteria are reproduced below in Tables 2.1 and 2.2.

As can be seen, the criteria from the two sources are nearly identical. Other subcategories include *endogenous* and *non-endogenous depression; minor depression, situational depression, psychotic and non-psychotic depression, dysthymia.* The term *melancholia* has also made a comeback from the 19th and 20th century literature. Klein (1974) considers that the criteria for endogenicity are too overinclusive and may or may not include the "melancholia" subtype, in which biological dysfunction has been shown to be particularly implicated and which may be resistant to psychotherapy. This is a moot point, as some of the current controversies in cognitive therapy for depression will indicate later in this chapter. Currently most studies use the Research Diagnostic Criteria (RDC; Spitzer, Endicott, & Robins, 1978) to define the presence of endogenous symptoms. Some studies (for example, Blackburn & Moore, 1997), in particular in the U.K., have used the Newcastle Diagnostic Criteria (NDI; Carney, Roth, & Garside, 1965) to diagnose endogenous depression. These criteria are far more strict and less overinclusive than the RDC. Blackburn and Moore (1997), in a sample of 124 patients with major depression, found that 31 satisfied NDI criteria for endogenicity whereas 73 satisfy RDC criteria, kappa between the two scales being negligible at 0.19. The corresponding criteria are listed in Table 2.3 below.

It is evident that subcategories of depressive disorder as defined by *DSM-IV* or other classificatory methods, fulfill a useful role in ensuring that outcome studies are concerned with comparable groups of patients. However, this author believes, as Costello (1992), that as well as using categorical systems, future progress lies in the study of the response of key symptoms to different treatment approaches. Symptoms such as retardation and anhedonia, for example, may respond differently to cognitive therapy and pharmacotherapy. Such an approach may resolve the current heated debates relating to the severity of depression and differential response to psychotherapy or medication (Elkin, Gibbons, Shea, & Shaw, 1996; Jacobson & Hollon, 1996; Klein, 1996).

COGNITIVE THEORY OF DEPRESSION

The Early Theory and Criticisms

Since the first descriptions of a cognitive theory of depression by Beck (1963, 1964, 1967) a number of theoretical modifications and advances have been proposed, mostly backed by experimental studies. The original theory, based primarily on careful and astute clinical observation, has been

TABLES 2.1 Criteria for Major Depressive Episode (DSM–IV)

A. Five (or more) of the following symptoms have been present during the same 2-week period and represent a change from previous functioning; at least one of the symptoms is either (1) depressed mood or (2) loss of interest or pleasure.

Note: Do not include symptoms that are clearly due to a general medical condition, or mood-incongruent delusions or hallucinations.

(1) depressed mood most of the day, nearly every day, as indicated by either subjective report (e.g., feels sad or empty) or observation made by others (e.g., appears tearful). **Note:** In children and adolescents, can be irritable mood.

(2) markedly diminished interest or pleasure in all, or almost all, activities most of the day, nearly every day (as indicated by either subjective account or observation made by others).

(3) significant weight loss when not dieting or weight gain (e.g., a change of more than 5% of body weight in a month), or decrease or increase in appetite nearly every day. **Note:** In children consider failure to make expected weight gains.

(4) insomnia or hypersomnia nearly every day.

(5) Psychomotor agitation or retardation nearly every day (observable by others, not merely subjective feelings of restlessness or being slowed down).

(6) Fatigue or loss of energy nearly every day.

(7) Feelings of worthlessness or excessive or inappropriate guilt (which may be delusional) nearly every day (not merely self-reproach or guilt about being sick).

(8) Diminished ability to think or concentrate, or indecisiveness, nearly every day (either by subjective account or as observed by others).

(9) Recurrent thoughts of death (not just fear of dying), recurrent suicidal ideation without a specific plan, or a suicidal attempt or a specific plan for committing suicide.

B. The symptoms do not meet criteria for a Mixed Episode (see p. 335).

C. The symptoms cause clinically significant distress or impairment in social, occupational, or other important areas of functioning.

D. The symptoms are not due to the direct physiological effects of a substance (e.g., a drug of abuse, a medication) or a general medical condition (e.g., hypothyroidism).

E. The symptoms are not better accounted for by bereavement, i.e., after the loss of a loved one, the symptoms persist for longer than 2 months or are characterized by marked functional impairment, morbid preoccupation with worthlessness, suicidal ideation, psychotic symptoms, or psychomotor retardation.

TABLE 2.2 Criteria for Major Depressive Episodes ICD-10

Mild depression: at least two symptoms from group 1 and at least two from group 2.
Moderate depression: at least two symptoms from group 1 and at least three from group 2.
Severe depression: all three symptoms of Group 1 and at least four from group 2, some of severe intensity.

1   (a)   Depressed mood
    (b)   Loss of interest and enjoyment
    (c)   Reduced energy leading to increased fatiguability and diminished activity
2   (a)   Reduced concentration and attention
    (b)   Reduced self-esteem and self-confidence
    (c)   Ideas of guilt and unworthiness
    (d)   Bleak and pessimistic views of the future
    (e)   Ideas or acts of self-harm or suicide
    (f)   Disturbed sleep
    (g)   Diminished appetite

---

enriched by a closer association with basic cognitive science (Stein & Young, 1992) which itself has developed sharply in the last 10–15 years.

The original cognitive description of the development and maintenance of depression by Beck was a relatively straightforward model, whereby all the symptoms of depression were seen as maintained by a general negative content of thought relating to the self, the environment and the future. This negative content of thought was the result of a style of negative bias in information processing, for example, magnification of the negative aspects of information and minimization of the positive aspects. The negative content of thought and biased information processing were deemed to be understandable in terms of underlying stable cognitive structures or schemata which represent the individual's past learning history. These might be rules of behavior ("I must always do everything perfectly"), basic assumptions ("If I make a mistake, people will lose respect for me"), or core beliefs ("I am incompetent"). Schemata would be dormant for long periods of time, but could be activated by particular triggering events, such as real or perceived loss of a loved one or loss of status. Once triggered the underlying schemata would be applied to more and more situations and events and depressed mood would escalate into the full depressive syndrome. This psychological description had immediate clinical appeal and led to a system of therapy, cognitive therapy (Beck, Rush, shaw, & Emery,

TABLE 2.3 The Diagnosis of Endogenous Depression Using the
Newcastle Diagnostic Index (NDI) and Research Diagnostic Criteria (RDC)

Research Diagnostic Criteria (RDC) for Endogenous Major Depression (Spitzer et al., 1978)	Newcastle Diagnostic Index (Carney et al., 1965)	
A1. Distinct quality of depressed mood	Adequate personality	+1
2. Lack of reactivity to environmental changes	No precipitating event	+2
3. Mood regularly worse a.m.		
4. Pervasive loss of interest or pleasure	Quality of mood change	+1
	Waking early	+2
B1. Feelings of self-doubt, self-reproach or excessive or inappropriate guilt	Previous episodes	+1
2. Early morning wakening or middle of night insomnia.	Psychomotor	+2
3. Psychomotor retardation or agitation	Delusions	+2
4. Poor appetite		
5. Weight loss (1kg a week over several weeks or 9kg in a year, when not dieting)	Guilt	+1
	Anxiety	−1
6. Loss of interest or pleasure (may not be pervasive) in usual activities or decreased sexual drive	Blames others	−1
Probable: 4 symptoms from groups A and B		Cut off: ≥6
Definite: 6 symptoms with at least one from group A		

1979), which was quickly applied and tested successfully (Blackburn, Bishop, Glen, Whalley, & Christie, 1981; Murphy, Simon, Wetzel, & Lustman, 1984; Rush, Beck, Rkovacs, & Hollon, 1977; Teasdale, Fennell, Hibbert, Amies, 1984).

Criticisms of the original model came from several quarters both theoretical and experimental.

(1) Coyne and Gotlib (1983) criticized Beck's approach for not paying
    enough attention to environmental factors, in particular to real neg-
    ative events, rather than to negatively distorted thinking.

(2) The processing "errors" identified in depression do not differ nec-
    essarily from the type of processing errors made by non-depressed
    individuals (labeled heuristics by Kahneman, Slovic, & Tversky,
    1982). The difference between depressed and non-depressed think-
    ing is the direction of the bias which is primarily positive in non-
    depressed (Taylor & Brown, 1988; Schwartz, 1986) and negative in
    the depressed individuals.

(3) The unidirectional effect of cognition on mood was also challenged
    (Bower, 1981; Ingram, 1984; Teasdale, 1983) and a reciprocal rela-
    tions demonstrated experimentally (Blaney, 1986; Clark & Teasdale,
    1982; Miranda & Persons, 1988).

(4) Cognitive therapy of depression which directly targets negative cog-
    nitions was not found to be uniquely effective at changing negative
    thinking. Antidepressant medication also changes negative cogni-
    tion (Simons, Garfield, & Murphy, 1984).

(5) The hypothesized stable cognitive patterns (schemata, basic assump-
    tions and attitudes) proved to be elusive when assessed in recovered
    depressed patients (Blackburn, Roxborough, Muir, Glabus, &
    Blackwood, 1990; Simons et al., 1984).

(6) The theory was also criticized for being too positivist and assuming
    that there is a reality and that therapy consisted of educating patients
    in rational and "reality-based" thinking (Mahoney & Lyddon, 1988).

(7) Finally, the theory and cognitive therapy were criticized for overem-
    phasising conscious thoughts at the expense of unconscious pro-
    cessing. Teasdale (1993) comments that cognitive therapists use the
    term cognition in a restricted way which "clearly diverges from the
    much wider use of the term in cognitive psychology. There, it is
    assumed that the majority of cognitive processing is not experienced
    as consciously accessible thoughts or images" (p. 340).

Recent Developments in Cognitive Theory of Depression

The implication of Beck's original model (Beck, 1967; Beck et al., 1979)
was that there is a causative link between cognitions and emotions, and that
cognitions are primary. This was probably an overinterpretation or misinterpretation of the model, which was nonetheless challenged vigorously by
Zajonc (1980) and Rachman (1981, 1984). Beck (1987) clarified his point
of view, pointing out that negative cognitions are inherent to depression,

in the same way as delusions are inherent to psychosis, and that therefore, negative cognitions cannot be conceptualised as causing depression. Negative cognitions are one side of the coin and emotional and biological changes the other side. Bower (1981) presented his associative network theory, derived experimentally, to explain the relationships between cognition and mood. The associative network theory postulates that emotions, cognitions and events are represented in the brain by discrete nodes or units which are interlinked in a network. An emotion can, therefore, be triggered by an appropriate external stimulus or by the activation of other linked nodes in the associative network, for example, a sad memory, an internal sensation or a sensory input. Once activated a depressed mood influences information processing by the spreading of activation through the associative network, so that situations are more likely to be interpreted negatively. This reciprocal relationship between mood and cognition explains mood state-dependant retrieval (superior recall of material retrieved in the same mood state as was present during learning) and mood-congruent retrieval (increased ease of recall of sad memories when in a depressed mood state (Clark & Teasdale, 1982; Lloyd & Lishman, 1975; Miranda & Persons, 1988; Teasdale & Fogarty, 1979). Because not all of the predictions from the associative network theory were supported (Ucros, 1989), Bower (1987, 1992) revised his theory and proposed that emotions may activate not only isolated semantic concepts, but wider rule-based action plans. This brings his thinking nearer to more recent revisionists (Power & Dalgleish, 1997; Teasdale, 1993, 1996, 1997; Teasdale & Barnard, 1993).

In the Interacting Cognitive Subsystems approach (ICS), Teasdale (1997) attempts to address some of the problems encountered in cognitive therapy as outlined above, by applying principles from cognitive science. He considers that "simple construct accessibility accounts cannot do justice to the phenomena of mood-related cognitive biases, and accounts focusing on higher levels of representation need to be developed" (Teasdale, 1997, p. 74). He borrows from cognitive neuroscience (Fodor, 1983) the idea that human beings have a number of distinct "minds," each specialized for certain functions and having its own evolutionary and developmental history. The ICS approach attempts to take into account all aspects of information processing and depression is seen as a shift in schematic models. Dysfunctional schematic models in depression encode more global negative views of self and imply a close dependence of personal worth on approval or success. Teasdale and Barnard (1993) differentiate between two different "meaning codes" associated with two highly different levels of meaning. The *propositional code* encodes specific meanings, discrete concepts, and the relationship among them. This code is similar to Bower's (1981) semantic network, for example, "Mary has freckles." The *implication code* encodes generic, holistic levels of meaning which are not easily expressed in language; it represents recurring very high order regularities across the nine information codes that they describe. Importantly, only the implication code is linked directly to emotion, with implicit meaning content. So, a patient might say "I know that I have achieved a number of things" (propositional code) "but I feel like a failure" (implicational code).

According to ICS, cognitive therapy of depression can only be successful by changing patients' dysfunctional schematic models or mind sets to alternative schematic models and mind sets. This shift of perspective occurs through decentering, for example, by reevaluating negative automatic thoughts and by behavioral tasks. The alternative schematic model incorporates a different view of depression and its symptoms—say, from "I am worthless" to "I see myself as worthless." The use of methods, such as reviewing the evidence for and against a self-schema addresses the propositional, but not the implicational meaning of the belief. While the application of such cognitive methods may help the patient in reexperiencing success experiences and hence achieve change in affect related models, the use of experiential or enactive procedures either in reality or in experience are recommended.

Power and Dalgleish (1997) similarly criticize the original cognitive theory of depression for its rationalistic view of human beings and its apparent proposal that the self-concept is "monolithically" negative in depressed patients and "monolithically" positive in normal individuals. Brewin and associates (1992), among others, have demonstrated that depressed individuals can have access to positive self-descriptors. Power and Dalgleish (1997), as Teasdale, propose a multilevel model of emotion, labeled SPAARS (Schematic, Propositional, Analogical and Associative Representational Systems), which also includes subsystems representing higher order meaning and basic propositional meaning. All stimuli are first processed through the analogical representation system which includes all sensory modalities. The output from the analogical system then feeds into three semantic systems in parallel, the associative, propositional and schematic systems.

Their model is useful in pointing out that "therapeutic techniques for working successfully with the emotional disorder may vary according to the primary route involved in the disorder" (Power & Dalgleish, 1997, p.432). The fast direct methods are exemplified in panic disorder, where the patient is taught an alternative schematic model for the hyper-arousal symptoms that he/she experiences. Where the emotional disorder is based on associative learning mechanisms, they suggest that exposure methods are indicated. In depression, they consider that overinvestment in one or two domains creates vulnerability and therapy should attempt to explore and develop underinvested roles.

Related to multilevel cognitive theories and schematic models, several theorists, (Papageorgiou & Wells, 1999; Teasdale, 1999; Wells & Matthews, 1996) now use the term *metacognition* (Flavell, 1979) to refer to the aspect of information processing that evaluates, interprets and regulates the contents and processes of thought. Thus, the depressed or anxious patient's beliefs about his/her own thoughts (for example, "I must be mad to think these thoughts" or "These thoughts indicate that I am a bad person") will have emotional consequences beyond those associated with the content of the original cognitions and these metacognitions need to be addressed in cognitive therapy or metacognitive therapy. In depression, metacognitions are characterized as thoughts "*about* the self, *about* depression-related thoughts and feelings and *about* how to understand what is going on" (Teasdale 1999, p.151). They tend to be self-focused (Pyszczynski & Greenberg, 1987) ruminative (Nolen-Hoeksema, 1991) and related to generalized rather than specific negative autobiographical memories (Brittlebank, Scott, Williams, & Ferrier, 1993). Teasdale (1999) and Wells and Matthews (1996, p.886) recommend mindfulness-based cognitive therapy as a method of decentering from metacognitions. Mindfulness (Kabat-Zinn, 1994) teaches individuals to relate to thoughts as events in the mind rather than as direct reflections of oneself or of reality.

Similar to the cognitive models described above, which are derived from cognitive science, several other developments of Beck's model inspired by information processing theory have been usefully described by Ingram (1990), Brewin (1996), Hollon and Shelton (1991) and Eysenck (1991). These theoretical developments have usually produced a wealth of experimental work. Although they have not led to revolutionary changes in the process of cognitive therapy, they have, nonetheless, inspired some newer methods for accessing implicational and metacognitive processes and for accessing and changing emotions. These have been mentioned above.

Early criticisms of Beck's theory as underemphasizing *interpersonal processes* have also been addressed, in particular, by Safran and Segal (1990). These authors state that "the individual must always be understood as part of the interpersonal system in which he or she is participating. Thus, one cannot understand the patients in therapy independently on the therapist" (Safran & Segal, 1990, p. 5). Core dysfunctional interpersonal schemata can be revealed through the therapeutic relationship. The interpersonal schema is defined as a generic cognitive representation of interpersonal events which derives from interactions with attachment figures of the past and serves to predict future interactions with these figures and with others.

This approach has led to more emphasis on the therapeutic relationship and more attention to developmental factors in the conceptualization of cases. Issues which might have been considered as stumbling blocks in therapy, for example, lack of trust, aggressivity or lack of compliance, are now used directly to guide questioning and formulation.

The constructivist approach (Guidano & Liotti; 1983; Mahoney, 1993; Neimeyer, 1993) has also facilitated an evolution of the style of cognitive therapy, although many of the contrasts between constructivism and "Beckian cognitive therapy" are again, in the view of this author, an over-interpretation or misinterpretation of Beck's original stance. Constructivism adopts the epistemological stance that all knowledge is proactive and that reality is a construction. Constructivists emphasize the operation of tacit or unconscious processes, the complexity of human experiences, and the need for a developmental, process-focused approach to knowing. Neimeyer (1993) considers constructivism to be predicated on a post-modern epistemology which is contrasted with the logical positivism and rationalism in Beck and colleagues (1979) and Ellis's rational-emotive approach (Ellis, 1962). Kelly is considered to epitomize constructivism when he states "What we think we know is anchored only in our assumptions, not in the bedrock of truth itself, and that world we seek to understand remains always on the horizons of our own thoughts" (Kelly, 1977, p.6). Ellis (1993) has argued that even rational-emotive therapy has never been truly rationalistic and Beck (Beck et al., 1979) has always stressed the functionality, rather than the rationality, of non-depressed thinking, through, for example, therapy methods of examining the advantages and disadvantages of thinking in certain ways. Moreover, several research studies have shown that depressed subjects do not have the exclusive right to "illogical" thinking (Alloy & Abramson, 1979; Kahneman, Slovic, Tversky, 1982). To correct these misinterpretations, cognitive therapists now use the term "alternative responses" instead of "rational responses" when attempting to help patients "re-evaluate" instead of "challenge" their negative automatic thoughts. Other possible influences of the constructivist school on cognitive therapy are a greater emphasis on conceptualization, on schematic models of the self and the world and on developmental and interpersonal processes.

This section indicates that several theoretical influences have combined, in a not too dissimilar fashion, in shaping the development of cognitive therapy.

OUTCOME STUDIES

Cognitive therapy for depression has been to date the most researched aspect of cognitive therapy, both for its short- and long-term efficacy. There have been several reviews of these studies (Blackburn, Twaddle, & Associates, 1996; Williams, 1992) which will not be repeated here. Instead, the main conclusions of meta-analytical studies, and some more recent studies and controversies will be reviewed with a view to assessing current state of knowledge in this area.

Since the first controlled outcome study of Rush and associates (1977) comparing cognitive therapy with imipramine, there has been a regular flow of studies of increasing sophistication comparing cognitive therapy with antidepressant medication or other psychotherapies. Dobson (1989) reviewed 28 studies and concluded that CT in depression was superior to waiting list control, drug treatment, behavior therapy and miscellaneous therapies. Of the 10 studies comparing CT with no-treatment or a waiting list control, the mean effect size of 2.15 indicated that the average patient treated with CT did better than 98% of the control subjects. Of the nine studies comparing CT and behavior therapies, the average effect size was 0.46, indicating the average CT patient did better than 67% of behavior therapy patients. Of the eight studies contrasting CT and antidepressants, the mean effect size was 0.53, indicating a superior outcome for the average CT patient to 70% of drug-treated patients. Dobson found no relationship between outcome and length of therapy or patients' gender, but younger patients did significantly better.

The effect of therapists' allegiance on effect size for CT of depression was forcefully put by Robinson, Berman, and Neimeyer (1990) in their comprehensive review of controlled outcome studies of psychotherapy for depression. Gaffan, Tsaouis, and Kemp-Wheeler (1995), for example, investigated the effect of therapist allegiance in a meta-analytic study of CT for depression. Their study included the 28 studies of Dobson (1989) published between 1976 and 1987 and a further set of 37 studies published between 1987 and 1994. This meta-analysis, therefore, includes two important recent studies (Elkin et al., 1989; Hollon et al., 1992). In their re-analysis of Dobson's studies, using slightly different groupings, Gaffan and colleagues (1995) confirmed Dobson's conclusions that CT was more effective than control conditions, behavior therapy, other psychotherapies or pharmacotherapy, although they obtained smaller effect sizes and only the differences with waiting list control and attention control groups were significant. Comparisons with larger effect sizes were associated with relatively higher allegiance to CT. Looking at pre-post outcome within treatment groups, the contribution of allegiance was positive, but not significant. In their analysis of the 37 later studies, Dobson's (1989) results were replicated in that CT was superior to waiting list, attention control and psychotherapy (all three significantly) and to pharmacotherapy (non-significantly), but behavior therapy was non-significantly superior, although the data are based on only a few studies. Generally, in these later studies, effect sizes were smaller and allegiance effect was non-significant. This decline in effect size of CT and of allegiance effect over time raises important issues. Several possibilities are mentioned by Gaffan and associates (1995): (1) with the widespread use of CT, therapists involved in outcome studies are less expert. However, there was no relationship between effect size and experience; (2)

more complex cases are now included in studies. No relationship was found with categories of patients; (3) other therapies, including pharmacotherapy are now better developed; (4) early results reflected higher enthusiasm from therapists who were pioneers in CT; (5) earlier studies reflected selective publication, that is, only studies showing strong effects for CT were published. The decline over time in effect-size of CT and in allegiance effect reflects a historical phenomenon which may represent "Pygmalion effects" (Shapiro et al., 1994) or, more likely, may be due to the interaction of all the factors mentioned above.

The most recent meta-analytical study of CT in depressed patients (Gloaguen et al., 1998) reviewed 78 outcome trials published between 1977 and 1996. Thirty trials, including four that had been included by Dobson (1989) and 14 by Gaffan and associates (1995), were excluded for methodological reasons. These included no control group, no Beck Depression Inventory (BDI) as an outcome measure, no randomization or absence of major depression or dsythymia according to set criteria. The results indicated that CT was highly significantly superior to waiting list or placebo control ($p < .0001$), the average CT patient being better off by 29% than the average control patient. CT was superior to antidepressants ($p < .0001$), equal to behavior therapy ($p = 0.95$) and superior to miscellaneous psychotherapies ($p < .01$). There was no association between effect size and BDI at baseline, gender, or age. Thus, the results replicate to a large extent the findings of Gaffan and colleagues (1995). The authors comment that the equivalence of CT and behavior therapy may not be surprising in view of the fact that CT (Beck et al., 1979) uses a large number of behavioral methods and behavior therapy advocates "disputing your non-constructive self-talk" (Lewinsohn, Clarke, Hops, & Andrews, 1990), which is not dissimilar from the evaluation of negative automatic thoughts in CT.

Since this last meta-analytical study was published, two recent series of studies need to be considered, relating to short-term and long-term outcome of CT in depression. Fava and his colleagues (1994) examined the efficacy of CT in patients with major depression who had residual or prodromal symptoms after treatment with antidepressant medication for 3–5 months. Forty-three patients were randomly allocated to pharmacotherapy and CT or pharmacotherapy plus clinical management. Medication was tapered every other week and then withdrawn completely. Three patients could not be taken off their medication.. Treatment consisted of 10 sessions of 40 minutes every other week. At the end of treatment, the group receiving CT showed a significant decrease in residual symptoms ($p < .0001$) and there were no significant changes in the clinical management group. During a 2-year follow-up, 15% of the CT group and 35% of the clinical management group relapsed. In a second study, Fava and colleagues (1998) tested the same approach in 40 patients with recurrent major depression

(≥ 3 episodes of depression). During a 2-year follow-up, no antidepressant drugs were used unless a relapse or recurrence occurred. CT (supplemented by lifestyle modification and well-being therapy) was found to bring about a reduced relapse rate (25%) as compared with clinical management (80%). Lifestyle management involved instructing patients in reducing life stress and interpersonal friction; not indulging in excessive work and taking appropriate rest. Well-being therapy involved methods based on Ryff's and Singer's (1996) model of well-being as the result of self-acceptance, positive relations with others, autonomy, environmental mastery, purpose in life, and personal growth. Lifestyle management and well-being therapy appear, to us, to be common methods used in CT for relapse prevention.

Blackburn and Moore (1997) reported a controlled acute and follow-up trial of CT versus pharmacotherapy in 75 depressed patients with recurrent depression. One group received antidepressant medication during acute treatment (16 weeks) and antidepressant medication as maintenance treatment during the 2 years (at reduced, but acceptable doses); one group received the same regime of medication during acute treatment, but changed over to CT for maintenance treatment for 2 years (medication tapered off over a period of 4 weeks); the third group received CT during acute treatment and as maintenance treatment for 2 years. Maintenance CT took place three times in the first month, twice in the second month and monthly thereafter. The three groups had equivalent mean number of previous episodes of depression (3.2, *SD* = 2.2; 4.1, *SD* = 3.4; 3.0, *SD* = 1.4). After acute treatment all three groups improved significantly, with no difference in level of improvement or in pattern of response over time (as measured every 4 weeks). During the maintenance phase, patients in all three groups continued to improve over time and there was no significant differences between groups. CT was marginally superior to medication both in the acute and follow-up phases. The equivalence of effect of CT and antidepressants in acute treatment has been found in several studies (Gaffan et al., 1995), but the equivalence of maintenance CT and maintenance antidepressants is a new finding. The results support the findings of Fava and associates (1998). Moreover, Moore and Blackburn (1997) looked at patients who had not responded to antidepressants during the acute phase and who were maintained on antidepressants (N = 7) or on maintenance CT (N = 6). Although caution is needed in interpretation of the results, because of the small numbers, CT patients improved significantly more on two measures, the BDI (Beck et al., 1961)and the HRSD (Hamilton, 1960). On the other hand, Stewart and colleagues (1993) randomly allocated 17 of 36 outpatients with depressive disorder, who had not responded to 16 weeks of CT, to 6 weeks of imipramine (to a maximum dose of 300mg daily) or placebo for 6 weeks. Of the 12 patients who completed the double blind trial, the 5 assigned to imipramine had a clear-cut response and none of the 7 benefited from placebo. The authors concluded, as did Moore and Blackburn (1997), that medication and CT may be effective for different groups of patients.

Regarding the prophylactic effect of cognitive therapy, a number of naturalistic studies have indicated, in follow-ups of 1 to 2 years, that CT appears to be effective long term (for reviews, see Blackburn, Twaddle, & Associates, 1996, Gloaguen, Cottraux, Cucherat, & Blackburn, 1998;). Shea and colleagues (1992) and Evans and colleagues (1992) represent the most recent naturalistic studies while the studies discussed above (Blackburn & Moore, 1997; Fava et al., 1994, 1998; Moore & Blackburn, 1997) are the only controlled comparative studies to date. Thase and Simons (1992) did recommend that, as in pharmacotherapy, a longer period of continuation treatment for patients at risk of relapse, that is, those with a history of recurrent episodes, may be indicated. Although relapse prevention methods (Wilson, 1992) are now routinely incorporated in short-term therapy, continuation or maintenance CT appears strongly advisable, and may even be extremely cost-effective (Antonuccio, Thomas, & Danton, 1997).

In conclusion of this section, mention must be made of the ongoing controversies which have followed the NIMH Treatment of Depression Collaborative Research Program (TDCRP; Elkin et al. 1989; Shea et al., 1992). This multicenter study is by far the largest and most methodologically scrupulous controlled study of CT versus other treatments to date. The results are well known and have been included in reviews and meta-analytic studies mentioned above (Gaffan et al., 1995; Gloaguen et al., 1998). To recap briefly, 239 depressed patients, satisfying criteria for major depressive disorder, were randomly allocated to 1 of 4 16-week treatment conditions: CT, Interpersonal Psychotherapy (IPT), Imipramine plus Clinical Management (ICM) or Placebo plus Clinical Management (PCM). Follow-up was naturalistic and lasted 18 months. Essentially, the results indicated that at outcome, patients in all treatment groups showed significant improvement, ICM generally doing best and PCM doing worst, with CT and IPT being nearer ICM than PCM in efficacy. The two psychotherapies did not differ significantly from each other or from ICM. There was some evidence that IPT and ICM were superior to PCM, but CT was not. In secondary analyses, patients with severe depression (HRSD ≥ 20) did better on ICM or IPT than on CT or PCM, and there was no difference between treatments for less severe depression. In the follow-up study, there was no difference in sustained recovery over the 18-month period among the four treatments (30% CT, 26% IPT, 19% ICM, 20% PCM). In those recovered at the end of acute treatment, rates of major depression relapse were 36% CT, 33% IPT, 50% ICM, and 33% PCM.

Several criticisms have been levelled at these studies, for example, the stringent criterion of recovery—scores of 6 or less on the HRSD and 9 or less on the BDI compared to the usual 50% reduction required in most drug studies (Klein, 1990). Also, the differential effect of severity on response was apparently found at only one of the three sites and has not been replicated (Blackburn & Moore, 1997; Hollon et al., 1992; McLean & Taylor, 1992; Thase, Simon, Calahance, McGreary, & Harden, 1991). Three recent articles have reported heated controversies related to these topics. Jacobson and Hollon (1996) concede that later analyses (Elkin, Gibbons, Shea, & Shaw, 1996; Klein & Ross, 1993) confirm that pharmacotherapy was superior to psychotherapy, in particular CT, in the more severely depressed or acutely impaired patients, at least in the acute response. However, in view of the acknowledged differences among the three sites, there could be an allegiance effect, with CT being more competently applied at one of the sites. However, as the actual locations of the discrepant results have not been revealed, Jacobson and Hollon (1996, p. 76) state, "Until we see the data, we are left with science by rumour as our only recourse." Moreover, the higher than usual rate of relapse in patients recovered on CT (36% as compared with the usual 20%–25%) may indicate that CT was not adequately implemented at one or more sites. Jacobson and Hollon also take issue with Klein's (1990) opinion that previous studies that did not include pill placebo are invalid, as it is not possible to infer that pharmacotherapy was adequately implemented or that there were enough potentially drug-responsive patients. They argue that without a pill placebo control, it can still be ascertained whether pharmacotherapy was adequately implemented and what the patients' characteristics are.

Klein (1996) in the same issue made an impassioned reply to Jacobson and Hollon: "They fail to assert the finding that CBT was not only worse than medication but that it was never superior to pill placebo-case management (PLA-CM) at the .05 level. Thus, it is not simply that imipramine is better, faster and cheaper than CBT, but that the whole basis for the belief that cognitive therapy is doing anything specific has been placed in jeopardy" (p. 82). Moreover, Klein and Ross (1993) performed treatment by site analysis and found no significant interaction. Klein recommends multicenter studies where both pharmacotherapy and psychosocial treatments are supervised by experts and pill- and psychotherapy-placebo controls are included.

Elkin and associates (1996), again in the same journal, replied to the two above papers. They cogently summarize all their data to date and specify that the analyses using random regression models (RRMs) (Elkin et al., 1995) did have more power to detect significant differences. IMI-CM was significantly superior to CT, IPT, and PLA-CM in more severely depressed and impaired patients in reducing depression. Both IM-CM and IPT were significantly or nearly significantly superior to CT and PLA-CM in these patients on the HRSD and BDI. IMI-CM was also more rapid in its effect.

On the other hand, CT and IPT were not superior to IMI-CM or PLA-CM in less severely depressed or less impaired patients. Elkin and associates (1996) counteract the possibility that TDCRP CT therapists were perhaps lacking in competence by comparing their results with those of Hollon and colleagues (1992) study. The differences in relative response to medication or CT in the more severely depressed patients were not due to poorer response to CT, but to superior response to medication in the TDCRP. Regarding the interaction of treatment by site, therapists use the empirical Bayesian approach to plot each patient's personal trendline. Both on the HRSD and Global Assessment Scale (GAS; Endicott, Spitzer, Fleiss, & Cohen, 1976), there was a large overlap of distributions, indicating that a number of severely depressed and functionally impaired patients did show considerable improvement on both CT and IPT. However, IMI-CM did generally better. There was an indication of one site doing better on CT and another on IPT. However, an analysis of competence level across sites showed no significant interaction between site and level of competence, and no significant main effects for site or severity level. When comparing relapse rates with those reported in other studies, it is also clear that the TDCRP did not show worse results than previous studies, as stated by Jacobson and Hollon (1996). Elkin, and associates (1996) recommend drawing a line under all these controversies and that new questions be investigated from the wealth of data provided by the TDCRP.

To conclude this section, it can be said that regarding the efficacy of CT in the short and long term, the jury is not out yet. The above controversies indicate that we need: multisite studies; trained therapists who are supervised and monitored by experts in the field; an acknowledgment on initial allegiance; well validated competence scales which can measure competence as well as adherence; and better descriptions of patients than simply global measures of severity or diagnosis. Such studies would answer questions of efficacy, while effectiveness of CT, that is, how effective it is in the treatment of depression when administered under non-controlled clinic conditions, remains a moot point.

PROCESS FACTORS

As has been seen in the previous section, in spite of current debates, the efficacy of cognitive therapy in unipolar depression is well established, both for short-term and long-term outcome. However, there is a paucity of data on what constitutes the critical components of cognitive therapy in effecting change. Whisman (1993) and Robins and Hayes (1993) examined this issue in terms of mediators and moderators of change. Mediators are the mechanisms or the patients' characteristics that are changed by treatment and that precede change in depression, whereas moderators are the variables that predict outcome, for example, therapists' competence level or patients' age, sex, and personality traits.

Mediators of Change

Although a large number of studies have demonstrated change in cognitive variables following cognitive therapy (DeRubeis et al. 1990; Rush, Beck, Kovacs, Weissenburger, & Hollon, 1982; Seligman et al. 1988; Simons, Garfield, & Murphy, 1984) and that the degree of change in cognitive variables is related to degree of change in depression (Garamoni, Reynolds, Thase, Frank, & Fasiezka, 1992), the precedence of change in cognition over change in depression has not been firmly established. Rush and associates (1981), using cross-lagged correlations, found that during the first 4 of 11 weeks of cognitive therapy, improvement in hopelessness, in view of self and in mood preceded changes in vegetative and motivational symptoms of depression, whereas no specific pattern of change was found in patients treated with pharmacotherapy. An interesting study by DeRubeis and colleagues (1990) indicated that changes in three cognitive variables (attributional style, dysfunctional attitudes and hopelessness) at midtreatment predicted overall improvement at the end of treatment with cognitive therapy, but not with pharmacotherapy. This study needs replication and may indicate an important difference between the mode of action of the two treatments; cognitive change early in treatment with cognitive therapy is necessary for response to cognitive therapy, but this change is not sufficient for improvement, as pharmacotherapy can be equally effective without early cognitive change.

The second confounding issue is that change in cognitive variables occurs equally with pharmacotherapy, which does not target cognitions (Oei & Free, 1995; Simons et al., 1984). A number of recent studies have also indicated that changes in biological variables occur with cognitive therapy, as well as with pharmacotherapy. Abnormal non-suppression of cortisol level in plasma after the ingestion of dexamethasone, the dexamethasone suppression test (DST) is generally considered to be a test dysfunction of central neuronal and endocrine systems associated with major depression. The normalization of the DST response is considered as indicative of response to treatment (APA Task Force, 1987) and the treatment of choice in patients with abnormal DST responses, mostly suffering from endogenous depression, has been considered to be medication (Arana, Baldessarini, & Ornsteen, 1985). A normalization of DST responses was found in outpatients with major depression treated with cognitive therapy, as well as with tricyclic antidepressants (McKnight, Nelson, Grey, & Barnhill, 1992) and untreated in-patients treated with cognitive therapy (Thase et al., 1996). Similarly, following CT other authors have reported a decrease in urinary MHPG (3-methoxy-4-hydroxyphenylglycol), a norepirephrine metabolite, which is associated with abnormalities, types of neurotransmitters and their receptors in depression (Garvey, Hollon, & Evans, 1992); and changes in electroencephalographic sleep profiles (Thase et al., 1998; Nofzinger et al., 1994).

If cognitive therapy is not uniquely effective in depression, nor in changing key aspects of depression, be they symptoms, biological or cognitive variables, which aspects of the treatment can be considered critical for its efficacy? When cognitive therapy has been broken down into its components in an attempt to answer the above question, the results have been inconclusive. McNamara and Horan (1986) found that cognitive procedures reduced depressive cognitions and improved social skills more than behavioral procedures. Jarrett and Nelson (1987) divided the treatment package into three components: self-monitoring, logical analysis and hypothesis testing, the latter representing presumably behavioral methods and behavioral experiments. The results indicated that self-monitoring did not bring about a change in symptoms, but the other two components, logical analysis and hypothesis testing decreased depressive symptoms and level of negative automatic thoughts, as well as bringing about improvement in interpersonal relationships and increase in engagement in pleasurable activities. The two active components were more effective in combination than singly. However, Jacobson and colleagues (1996), in a dismantling exercise, randomly allocated 150 outpatients with major depression to three aspects of cognitive therapy and found no evidence for any difference. One treatment group only received the behavioral component; a second group received the behavioral component and the teaching of skills to modify automatic thoughts; and a third group received the full CT package, that is, the above two aspects and methods for schema identification and change. There was no difference in outcome at the end of a maximum of 20 sessions of therapy or at six months follow-up on self-reported or observer-rated depression level or in depressive symptoms. There was also no difference in outcome on cognitive measures, the Automatic Thoughts Questionnaire (Hollon & Kendall, 1980) and The Expanded Attributional Style Questionnaire (Peterson & Villanova, 1988). Gortner, Gollan, Dobson, Jacobson, (1998) reported follow-ups of 6,12,18, and 24 months of the same patients. Long-term effects of the three approaches were evaluated through relapse rates, number of weeks with no or minimal symptoms and survival times. They found that full CT was no more effective than its components.

Thus, although there is a wealth of experimental studies indicating the association of negative cognitions with depression (Haaga et al., 1991) and the change in negative cognitions with improvement (Persons & Burns, 1985; Teasdale & Fennell, 1982), the mode of action of cognitive therapy is far from being clearly understood (Barber & DeRubeis, 1989; Persons, 1993), nor is the specific effect of different components of cognitive therapy yet established.

Moderators of Change

The quality of the therapeutic relationship in CT has received a lot of attention recently. Castonguay and colleagues (1996), DeRubeis and associates (1990), Persons and Burns (1985) found that the quality of the therapeutic realtionship, a non-specific factor or an element common to all therapies, predicts outcome. DeRubeis and Feeley (1990) found that the "facilitative" aspects of cognitive therapy (empathy, warmth and understanding) and a measure of the helping alliance did not predict change in depression level after the sessions in which they were rated. However, ratings of the helping alliance made during later sessions of therapy were related to prior change in cognitive therapy. Blatt, Zuroff, Quinlan, and Pilkionis, (1996), in an analysis of the NIHM TDCRP, also reported that the quality of the therapeutic relationship reported early in treatment predicted therapeutic change at outcome between therapeutic alliance ratings during early sessions of cognitive therapy and outcome. In contrast, Beckham (1989) found no relationship between therapeutic alliance ratings during early sessions of cognitive therapy and outcome in the treatment of depression.

A current issue of importance is the level of competence of therapists and outcome. The current measure of competence is the Cognitive Therapy Scale (CTS; Young & Beck, 1980, 1988) which has been validated in its earlier version by Dobson, Shaw, and Vallis (1985) and Vallis, Shaw, and Dobson, (1986). This scale has been revised and validated by Blackburn and colleagues (1999). Several studies have found a positive relationship between level of competence and outcome (Beckham, 1990; Burns & Nolen-Hoeksema, 1992; Hollon et al., 1990) and a recent study (James, Blackburn, Milne, & Reichelt, 1999) found that, in a specialized training program in cognitive therapy, the competence of trainees increased significantly and was related to previous experience of cognitive therapy, but not of therapy in general. One study examined the relationship between adherence to different aspects of CT and outcome (DeRubeis & Feeley, 1990). These authors found that "concrete" and "symptom focused" procedures were associated with a positive outcome, but "abstract" discussions were not. Compliance with homework (Burns & Auerbach, 1992), a CT method, has also been found to be associated with a better outcome. Training programs in CT have mushroomed over recent years in view of the increasing demand for evidence-based clinical practice and for short-term therapies (Roth & Fonagy, 1996) and it is of the utmost importance that competence be reliably and systematically assessed across centers.

In terms of patients' characteristics which may predict response to CT, the literature is also increasing, but remains inadequate. The debate regarding the response of patients with an endogenous pattern of symptoms and with more severe depression was mentioned above. From the NIMH TDCRP, Blatt and associates (1996) found that pretreatment high levels of perfectionism, as rated by the Dysfunctional Attitudes Scale (DAS; Weissman & Beck, 1978), had a significant negative effect on treatment outcome in patients treated with CT as with other treatments (IPT, antidepressants or placebo). High learned resourcefulness (Rosenbaum, 1980) was found to predict good outcome to CT but not to medication (Simons, Lustman, Wetzel, & Murphy, 1985). However, this finding has not been reliably replicated (Beckham, 1989; Jarrett, Giles, Gullion, & Rush, 1991b; Kavanagh & Wilson, 1989.. Counter-intuitively, patients with high levels of cognitive dysfunction (Jarrett, Eaves, Granneman, & Rush, 1991a; Sotsky et al., 1990; Keller, 1983) have been found to have a poorer response to CT. Crews and Harrison (1995) propose a neuropychological explanation of these findings. Low cognitive dysfunction, in the form of biased automatic thoughts and dysfunctional beliefs, may indicate few or no neuropsychological dysfunctions, especially over the frontal regions. Low cognitive dysfunction may also indicate a better balance between left and right hemisphere activation in the brain. In depression, the left frontal region has been found to be hypoactive relative to the right frontal region, in EEG studies (Henriques & Davidson, 1991) and PET scan studies (Baxter et al., 1989). Cognitive therapy methods may be more effective in depressed patients with a normally active left frontal region, which is associated with logical thoughts and reasoning (Luria, 1973).

Finally, as for mediating variables, several biological variables which were considered as indicative of more severe depressions which could only respond to biological treatments, have been found not to be negative predictors of response to CT. These include 24-hour urinary MHPG (Garvey et al., 1992) and increased rapid eye movement (REM) latency (Jarrett, Rush, Khatami, & Roffwarg, 1990; Simons & Thase, 1992; Thase et al., 1994). On the other hand, Thase and colleagues (1996) found that depressed patients with higher severity of depression and/or an abnormal electronencephalographic sleep profile were relatively less responsive to CT.

In conclusion of this section, and in view of the conclusions drawn at the end of the earlier section, CT is an effective treatment in depression and offers a viable alternative for some patients. However, we still need more information about which particular aspects of CT are the active ingredients of the treatment package, and what particular aspects of patients' and therapists' characteristics are critical in predicting good outcome.

CASE DISCUSSION

Identifying Information and Diagnosis

Louise, a 31-year-old housewife living with her architect husband Martin and 2-year old son Paul, was preparing to become qualified to work as a part-time social worker and was referred by her general practitioner for cognitive therapy of depression. This had begun 3 weeks after her son's birth and, although she had delivered a healthy boy by a normal, full-term delivery, she reported herself disappointed with the degree of happiness she felt. After discharge from the maternity unit, she experienced isolation as her husband was working away, her relationships with her mother and mother-in-law were poor, and her friends either worked or had children of their own. She became depressed and sought help from her general practitioner.

Although there had been some relief with adequate doses of antidepressant medication, she continued to fulfil criteria for a major depressive episode at assessment (American Psychiatric Association, 1994). In addition, she fulfilled criteria for both paranoid and avoidant personality disorders by the Personality Diagnostic Questionnaire, Revised version (Hyler et al., 1988). The avoidant traits were (1) she was easily hurt by criticism or disapproval; (2) she had no close friends or confidants other than first degree relatives; (3) she was unwilling to be involved with people unless certain of being liked; (4) she was reticent in social situations because of a fear of saying something inappropriate or foolish or being unable to answer a question; (5) she feared being embarrassed by crying, blushing or showing signs of anxiety in front of other people. The paranoid traits were (1) she expected, without sufficient basis, to be exploited or harmed by others; (2) she questioned without justification, the loyalty or trustworthiness of friends or associates; (3) she was reluctant to confide in others because of unwarranted fear that the information would be used against her; (4) she was easily slighted and quick to react with anger or to counterattack; (5) she questioned, without justification, the fidelity of her husband.

Background Information

She was the third of 4 siblings to working class parents. Her father worked long hours and her mother was the main carer. Her mother was the parent who dealt with chastisement and this was physical, either with hands, slippers, or school shoes. Her mother also threatened to leave home and she remembered frequently going to school or coming home from school in tears, uncertain whether her mother would still be there. Her parents argued and her mother often sulked in silence for up to 3 months at a time. At school she was teased by some children and she bullied others, for which she was frequently reprimanded. Her mother demanded that she leave school at 15 years to work in a factory, as she refused to support her any longer. This was despite average academic performance. She had met her husband at a night club at the age of 25 and married 2 years later.

Early Therapy

Although she identified irritability with her husband as a problem, she prioritized problems with the course work as the most urgent concern. She experienced tiredness and low mood during much of the time that she had available to devote to the course. Her interpretation of this was that, when tired, there was no point in trying to work; she would write "rubbish." Her conclusions were negative automatic thoughts such as "I'm a failure" or "I will fail," depending on the context. In the first six sessions of therapy automatic thoughts related to the course and problem-solving methods to enhance coping were reviewed and evaluated.

Homework assignments focused on reducing the perfectionistic standards she applied to the work. For example, she performed an experiment of working in her normal pattern one evening and then rating the quantity and quality of the work. She normally applied no limit to her work, resulting in her going to bed only when she could no longer tolerate it. The following evening she reduced the amount of time she allocated to 2 hours and found that she got more done and concluded it was of equivalent or only marginally poorer quality. This allowed her to challenge her prediction that she would fail her course, unless she could work very long hours.

Provisional Conceptualization

The provisional formulation was arrived at collaboratively with the patient. She held a core belief of "I am no good" which was activated by her failure to meet perfectionistic standards of mothering after the birth of her son. She further attempted to compensate for it by enrolling in the social work course and applying the same perfectionistic standards. It was a "failure" in both domains that had finally led to her presentation.

Emerging Themes and Difficulties

There were difficulties in the completion of homework assignments particularly in writing down or even identifying automatic thoughts. In session 7 she described an episode of anger at home which she had kept to herself. Her husband had taken the car to play golf, leaving her at home without transport. The next day she experienced depressed mood when alone and relaxing in the garden on a sunny day. Although she thought "I should be feeling happy," she was unable to identify thoughts associated with lowering of mood and the session focused on the metacognitions regarding feeling depressed.

Homework assignments continued not to be completed, with reasons such as, "I just could not find the time." By session 13 she reported that she had been feeling mostly euthymic. There had been an event in a pub garden when friends had left her looking after their child and she had felt depressed. She was feeling alright now, so she did not want to think about it and she had been unable to identify any automatic thoughts. The therapist was experiencing some frustration in attempting to work collaboratively. It seemed that he was trying to force her to perform homework activities. This was shared with the patient and she agreed that that was how she sometimes experienced him. She assented to explore what the processes were which led to this position.

Therapist— What was going through your mind when I asked you about the event in the pub garden?
Patient— I thought that there was no point in talking about it as it was in the past and over with.
Therapist— But I persisted and what happened next for you?
Patient— I thought you were trying to wind me up.
Therapist— How did that make you feel?
Patient— A bit like you were getting at me.
Therapist— What emotion did that make you feel?
Patient— A bit cross, I suppose.
Therapist— I'm wondering, does this happen when you are with your friends?

She reported how she often perceived criticism from others and that when her friends had allowed her to take their child to play, she had interpreted this as them telling her they were relieved for her to go.

Therapist— What do others see when all this is going on?
Patient— Nothing.
Therapist— Is that always the case?

She cried and said that she often attacked others either with implied criticism or else she avoided speaking to them, hence replicating her mother's behavior.

Schema-Focused Work

Over the next three sessions the formulation was expanded. Her core schema, "I'm no good," actually meant "useless at everything" and "unlovable." She did not truly believe that she would be able to make any difference to her emotional state and she thought that the necessary experience and expression of negative emotion would result in rejection. Consequently she avoided writing down her thoughts and experienced the therapist's enquiries as criticism which was a prelude to rejection. She was unable to express her anger about this directly because she perceived herself as unentitled to experience anger.

When this was formulated, she was able spontaneously to relate this to her childhood of criticism and rejection. She considered her anger toward her son to be an echo of her mother's behavior toward herself and of her childhood response to bullying at school. She was also able to identify that she was angry and depressed when she had been left at home to her day of relaxation as this had been experienced as abandonment. Although she sometimes did not do homework because of her desire to avoid negative emotion, at other times she had been angry with the therapist for apparently criticizing her.

The approach to schema change utilized standard cognitive intervention. The components of "lovable" were identified on several continua and she rated herself on these, placing herself just above zero. Previous behavior was reinterpreted as being consequent upon a belief of being unlovable and a natural response to the expectation of rejection. She then engaged in some imagery work where, as an adult, she spoke back to her critical mother on behalf of the child and also asked her father for love. This helped her to believe during highly emotionally charged sessions that her parents had had their own problems, rather than that she was an intrinsically unloveable child.

Discussion

This case illustrates some of the difficulties associated with cognitive therapy of depression when there are underlying personality difficulties. Therapy began with problem-focused interventions, examining automatic thoughts, identifying problematic behaviors and coping strategies. Although helpful to some extent, this approach and examination of her difficulties with homework assignments were processed through an interpersonal schema of perceived criticism, which was reinforced by the therapy itself. Consequently therapy began with some beneficial effects upon the main presenting problems of tiredness and poor motivation concerning her course work. As the relationship developed and exploration examined more schematic material, her avoidant and paranoid traits were activated, particularly in the context of emotional arousal. These impeded further exploration and it was only in the examination of the therapy process that they were made overt. At this point, her main interpersonal schema (criticism, attack, and rejection) was safely identified and its origins and consequences exposed.

As therapy proceeded thereafter, the origin and maintenance of her postnatal depression became understandable in terms of her perceived criticism of her mothering abilities from husband, friends, and son. Her prickliness led to some real rejection and criticism from husband and friends. This, in turn, undermined her authority with her son and led to increasing behavioral disturbance on his part. She consequently experienced increasing helplessness, perceived and real criticism and anger. Whether her husband was overly critical was not established

By the end of therapy, Louise had received 21 sessions and a good understanding of her beliefs, their origins and the way in which they manifested themselves both interpersonally and in the genesis of her depression. She had begun to review and reevaluate these and to put less dichotomous views of herself in place. Her BDI (Beck et al., 1961) score had come down from 34 to 14; her HRSD-17 item (Hamilton, 1960) score had come down from 20 to 8; her Hopelessness scale (Beck et al., 1974) had reduced from 12 to 4.

REFERENCES

Alloy, L. B., & Abramson, L. Y. (1979). Judgement of contingency in depressed and non-depressed students: Sadder but wiser? *Journal of Experimental Psychology, 108,* 441–485.
American Psychiatric Association (1994). *Diagnostic and statistical manual of mental disorders (DSM-IV)* (4th ed.) Washington, DC: APA.
Antonnucio, D. L., Thomas, M. & Danton, W. G. (1997). A cost-effectiveness analysis of
cognitive behavior therapy and fluoxetine (Prozac(r)) in the treatment of depression. *Behavior Therapy, 28,* 187–210.
APA task force on laboratory tests in psychiatry (1987). The dexamethasone suppression test: An overview of its current status in psychiatry. *American Journal of Psychiatry, 144,* 1253–1262.
Arana, G. W., Baldessarini, R. J., & Ornsteen, M. (1985), The dexamethasone supression test for diagnosis and prognosis in psychiatry. *Archives of General Psychiatry, 42,* 1193–1204.
Barber, J. P., & DeRubeis, R. J. (1989). On second thought: Where the action is in cognitive therapy of depression. *Cognitive Therapy and Research, 13,* 441–457.
Baxter, L. R., Schwartz, J. M., Phelps, M. E., Mazziotta, J. C., Guze, B. H., Selin, C. E., Gerner, R. H., & Sumida, R. M. (1989). Reduction of prefrontal cortex glucose metabolism common to three types of depression. *Archives of General Psychiatry, 46,* 243–250.
Beck, A. T. (1963). Thinking and depression. I. Idiosyncratic content and cognitive distortions. *Archives of General Psychiatry, 9,* 324–333
Beck, A. T. (1964). Thinking and Depression. II. Theory and Therapy. *Archives of General Psychiatry, 10,* 561–571.

Beck, A. T. (1967). *Depression: Clinical, experimental and theoretical aspects.* New York: Harper & Row.

Beck, A. T. (1987). Cognitive models of depression. *Journal of Cognitive Psychotherapy, 1*, 5–37.

Beck, A. T., Rush, A. J., Shaw, B. F., & Emery, G. (1979). *Cognitive therapy of depression: A treatment manual.* New York: Guilford Press.

Beck, A. T., Ward, C. H., Mendelson, M., Mock, J. E., & Erbaugh, J. K. (1961). An inventory for measuring depression. *Archives of General Psychiatry, 4*, 561–571

Beck, A. T., Weissman, A., Lester, D., & Trexler, I. (1974). The measurment of pessimism: The Hoplessnesss Scale. *Journal of Consulting and Clinical Psychology, 42*, 861–865.

Beckham, E. E. (1989). Improvement after evaluation in psychotherapy of depression: Evidence of a placebo effect? *Journal of Clinical Psychology Review, 45*, 945–950.

Beckham, E. E. (1990). Psychotherapy of depression. Research at a crossroads: Directions for the 1990s. *Clinical Psychology Review, 10*, 207–228.

Blackburn, I. M., Bishop, S., Glen, A. I. M., Whalley, L. J., & Christie, J. E. (1981). The efficacy of cognitive therapy in depression: A treatment trial using cognitive therapy and pharmacotherapy, each alone and in combination. *British Journal of Psychiatry, 139*, 181–189.

Blackburn, I. M., James, I. A., Milne, D. L., Baker, C., Standard, S., Garland, A., & Reichelt, F. K. (1999). The Revised Cognitive Therapy Scale (CTS-R). II. Psychometric properties. *Behavior Research and Therapy* (Submitted).

Blackburn, I. M., & Moore, R. M. (1997). Controlled acute and follow-up trial of cognitive therapy and pharmacotherapy in out-patients with recurrent depression. *British Journal of Psychiatry, 171*, 328–334.

Blackburn, I. M., Roxborough, H. M., Muir, W. J., Glabus, M., & Blackwood, J. D. R. (1990). Perceptual and physiological dysfunction in depression. *Psychological Medicine, 20*, 95–103.

Blackburn, I. M., Twaddle, V., & Associates (1996). *Cognitive therapy in action.* London: Souvenir Press (E&A) Ltd.

Blaney, P. H. (1986). Affect and memory: A review. *Psychological Bulletin, 99*, 229–246.

Blatt, S. J., Zuroff, D. C., Quinlan, D. M., & Pilkionis, P. A. (1996). Interpersonal factors in brief treatment of depression: Further analysis of the National Institute of Mental Health Treatment of Depression Collaborative Research Program. *Journal of Consulting and Clinical Psychology, 64*, 162–171.

Bower, G. H. (1981). Mood and memory. *American Psychologist, 36*, 129–148.

Bower, G. H. (1987). Commentary on mood and memory. *Behavior Research and Therapy, 25*, 443–455.

Bower, G. H. (1992). How might emotions effect learning? In *S.A. Christianson (Ed.), The handbook of emotion and memory: Research and theory.* Hillsdale, NJ: Erlbaum.

Brewin, C. R. (1996). Theoretical foundations of cognitive behavior therapy for anxiety and depression. *Annual Review of Psychology, 47,* 33–57.

Brewin, C. R., Smith, A. J., Power, M., & Furnham, A. (1992). State and trait differences in depressive self-perceptions. *Behavior Research and Therapy, 30,* 555–557.

Brittlebank, A. D., Scott, J, Williams, J. M. G., & Ferrier, I. N. (1993). Autobiographical memory in depression: State or trait marker? *British Journal of Psychiatry, 162,* 118–121.

Burns, D. D., & Auerbach, A. H. (1992) Does homework compliance enhance recovery from depression? *Psychiatric Annuals, 22,* 464–469.

Burns, D. D., & Nolen-Hoeksema, S. (1992). Therapeutic empathy and recovery from depression in cognitive behavioral therapy: A structural equation model. *Journal of Consulting and Clinical Psychology, 60,* 441–449.

Carney, M. W. P., Roth, M., & Garside, R. F. (1965). The diagnosis of depressive syndromes and the prediction of ECT response. *British Journal of Psychiatry, 111,* 659–674.

Castonguay, L. G., Goldfried, M. R., Wiser, S., Raue, P. J., & Hayes, A. M. (1996). Predicting the effect of cognitive therapy for depression: A study of unique and common factors. *Journal of Consulting and Clinical Psychology, 64,* 497–504.

Clark, D. M., & Teasdale, J. D. (1982). Diurnal variation in clinical depression and accessibility of memories of positive and negative experiences. *Journal of Abnormal Psychology, 91,* 87–95.

Costello, C. G. (1992). Research on symptoms versus research on syndromes: Arguments in favour of allocating more research time to the study of symptoms. *British Journal of Psychiatry, 160,* 304–308.

Coyne, J., & Gotlib, I. (1983). The role of cognition in depression: A critical appraisal. *Psychological Bulletin, 94,* 472–505.

Crews, W. D., & Harrison, D. W. (1995). The neuropsychology of depression and its implications for cognitive therapy. *Neuropsychology Review, 5,* 81–123.

DeRubeis, R. J., Evans, M. D., Hollon, S. D., Garvey, M. J., Grove, W. M., & Tuason, V. B. (1990). How does cognitive therapy work. Cognitive change and symptom change in cognitive therapy and pharmacotherapy for depression. *Journal of Consulting and Clinical Psychology, 58,* 862–869.

DeRubeis, R. J., & Feeley, M. (1990). Determinants of change in cognitive therapy for depression. *Cognitive Therapy and Research, 14,* 469–482.

Dobson, K. (1989). A meta-analysis of the efficacy of cognitive therapy for depression. *Journal of Consulting and Clinical Psychology, 57,* 414–419.

Dobson, K. S., Shaw, B. F., & Vallis, T. M. (1985). Reliability of a measure of the quality of cognitive therapy. *British Journal of Clinical Psychology*, *24*, 295–300.

Elkin, I., Gibbons, R. D., Shea, M. T., & Shaw, B. F. (1996) Science is not a trial (but it can sometimes be a tribulation). *Journal of Consulting and Clinical Psychology*, *64*, 841–847.

Elkin, I., Gibbons, R. D., Shea, M. T., Sotsky, S. M., Watkins, J. T., Pilkonis, P. A., & Hedeker, D. (1995). Initial severity and differential treatment outcome in the National Institute of Mental Health Treatment of Depression Collaborative Research Program. *Journal of Consulting and Clinical Psychology*, *63*, 841–847

Elkin, I., Shea, M. T., Watkins, J., Imber, S. D., Sotsky, S. M., Collins, J. F., Glass, D. R., Pilkonis, D. A., Leber, W. R., Docherty, J. P, Fiester, S. J., & Parloff, M. B. (1989). National Institute of Mental Health Treatment of Depression Collaborative Research Program. *Archives of General Psychiatry*, *46*, 971–982.

Ellis, A. (1962). *Reason and emotion in psychotherapy.* New York: Lyle Stuart.

Ellis, A. (1993). Reflections on rational-emotive therapy. *Journal of Consulting and Clinical Psychology*, *61*, 199–201.

Endicott, J., Spitzer, R. L., Fleiss, J. L., & Cohen, J. (1976). The Global Assessment Scale: A procedure for measuring overall severity of psychiatric disturbance. *Archives of General Psychiatry*, *33*, 766–771.

Evans, D., Hollon, S. D., DeRubeis, R. J., Piasecki, J. M., Grove, W. M., Garvey, M. J., & Tuason, V. B. (1992). Differential relapse following cognitive therapy and pharmacotherapy for depression. *Archives of General Psychiatry*, *49*, 802–808.

Eysenck, M. W. (1991). Theoretical cognitive psychology and mood disorders. In P. R. Martin (Ed). *Handbook of behavior therapy and psychological science: An integrated approach.* (Vol. 164, pp. 103–115). New York: Pergamon Press.

Fava, G. A., Grandi, S., Zielezny, M., Canestrari, R., & Morphy, M. A. (1994). Cognitive behavioral treatment of residual symptoms in primary major depressive disorder. *American Journal of Psychiatry*, *151*, 1295–1299.

Fava, G. A., Rafanelli, C., Grandi, S., Conti, S., & Belluardo, P. (1998). Prevention of recurrent depression with cognitive behavior therapy. *Archives of General Psychiatry*, *55*, 816–820.

Fodor, J. (1983). *The modularity of mind. An essay on faulty psychology.* Bradford, Cambridge, MA: MIT Press.

Gaffan, E. A., Tsaouis, I., & Kemp-Wheeler, S. M. (1995). Researcher allegiance and meta-analysis: The case of cognitive therapy for depression. *Journal of Consulting and Clinical Psychology*, *63*, 966–980.

Garamoni, G. L., Reynolds, C. F., Thase, M. E., Frank, E., & Fasiezka, A. L. (1992). Shifts in affective balance during cognitive therapy of major depression. *Journal of Consulting and Clinical Psychology*, *60*, 260–266.

Garvey, M. J., Hollon, S. D., & Evans, M. D. (1992). Examination of pre-and posttreatment MHPG during cognitive therapy. *Neuropsychobiology, 26,* 182–185.

Gloaguen V., Cottraux, J., Cucherat, M., & Blackburn, I. M. (1998). A meta-analysis of the effects of cognitive therapy in depressed patients. *Journal of Affective Disorders, 49,* 59–72.

Gortner, E. T., Gollan, J. K., Dobson, K. S., & Jacobson, N. S. (1998). Cognitive behavioral treatment for depression. Relapse prevention. *Journal of Consulting and Clinical Psychology, 66,* 377–384.

Guidano, V. F., & Liotti, G. (1983). *Cognitive processes and emotional disorders: A structural approach to psychotherapy.* New York: Guilford Press.

Haaga, D. A., Dyck, M. J., & Ernst, D. (1991). Empirical status of cognitive theory of depression. *Psychological Bulletin, 110,* 215–236.

Hamilton, M. A. (1960). A rating scale for depression. *Journal of Neurological and Neurosurgical Psychiatry, 23,* 59–61.

Hartley, E. (1998, May). The World Health Organization. High depression rate triggers new campaign. *Healthcare Today.*

Henriques, J. B., & Davidson, R. J. (1991). Left frontal hypoactivation in depression. *Journal of Abnormal Psychology, 100,* 535–545.

Hollon, S. D., Evans, M. D., & DeRubeis, R. J. (1990). Cognitive mediation of relapse Prevention following treatment for depression: Implications of differential risk. In R. E. Ingram (Ed.), *Contemporary psychological approaches to depression* (pp. 117–136). New York: Guilford Press.

Hollon, S. D, DeRubeis, R. J., Evans, M. D., Wiemer, M. J., Garvey, M. J., Grove W. M., & Tuason, V. B. (1992). Cognitive therapy and pharma-cotherapy for depression: Singly and in combination. *Archives of General Psychiatry, 49,* 774–781.

Hollon, S. D., & Kendall, P. C. (1980). Cognitive self-statements in depres-sion: Development of all automatic thoughts questionnaire. *Cognitive Therapy and Research, 4,* 383–395.

Hollon, S. D., & Shelton, M. (1991). Contributions of cognitive psychology to assessment and treatment of depression. In P. R. Martin (Ed.), *Handbook of behavior therapy and psychological science: An integrated approach* (vol. 164, pp. 169–195). New York: Pergamon Press.

Hyler, S. E., Rieder, R. O., Williams, J. B. W., Spitzer, R. L., Hendler, J., & Lyons, M. (1988). The personality and diagnostic questionnaire: Development and preliminary results. *Journal of Personality Disorder, 28,* 487–503.

Ingram, R. E. (1984). Toward an information processing analysis of depres-sion. *Cognitive Therapy and Research, 8,* 443–478.

Ingram, R. E. (1990). Depressive cognition: Models, mechanisms and meth-ods. In R. E. Ingram (Ed.), *Contemporary approaches to depression: Theory, research and treatment* (pp. 169–195). New York: Plenum Press.

Jacobson, N. S., Dobson, K. S., Truax, P. A., Addis, M. E., Koerner, K., Gollan, J. K., Gortner, E., & Prince, S. E. (1996). A component analysis of cognitive-behavioral treatment or depression. *Journal of Consulting and Clinical Psychology, 64*, 295–304.

Jacobson, N., & Hollon, S. D. (1996). Cognitive-behavior therapy versus pharmacotherapy: Now that the jury's returned its verdict, it's time to present the rest of the evidence. *Journal of Consulting and Clinical Psychology, 64*, 74–80.

James, I. A., Blackburn, I. M., Milne, D. L., Reichelt, F. K. (1999). Moderators of trainees' competence in cognitive therapy. *British Journal of Clinical Psychology* (Submitted).

Jarrett, R. B., & Nelson, R. D. (1987). Mechanisms of change in cognitive therapy of depression. *Behavior Therapy, 18*, 227–241.

Jarrett, R. B., Eaves, G. G., Granneman, B. D., & Rush, A. J. (1991a). Clinical, cognitive and demographic predictors of response to cognitive therapy for depression: A preliminary report. *Psychiatry Research, 37*, 245–260.

Jarrett, R. B., Giles, D. A., Gullion, C. M., & Rush, A. J. (1991b). Does learned resourcefulness predict response to cognitive therapy in depressed outpatients? *Journal of Affective Disorders, 23*, 223–229.

Jarrett, R. B., Rush, A. J., Khatami, M., & Roffwarg, H. P. (1990). Does the Pretreatment Polysommogram Predict Response to Cognitive Therapy in Depressed Outpatients? A Preliminary Report. *Psychiatric Research, 33*, 285–299.

Kabat-Zinn, J. (1994). *Wherever you go there you are: Mindfulness mediation in everyday life.* New York: Hyperion.

Kahneman, D., Slovic, P., & Tversky, A. (Eds.). (1982). *Judgement under uncertainty: Heuristics and biases.* Cambridge, UK: Cambridge University Press.

Kavanagh, D. J., & Wilson, P. H. (1989). Prediction of outcome with group cognitive therapy for depression. *Behavior Research and Therapy, 27*, 333–343.

Keller, K. E. (1983). Dysfunctional attitudes and the cognitive therapy for depression. *Cognitive Therapy and Research, 7*, 437–444.

Kelly, G. A. (1977). The psychology of the unknown. In D. Bannister (Ed.), *New perspectives in personal construct theories* (pp. 1–19). San Diego, CA: Academic Press.

Kessler, R. C., McGonagle, K. A., Zhao, S., Nelson, C. B., Hughes, M., Eshleman, S., Wittchen, H.-U., & Kendler, K. S. (1994). Lifetime and 12-month prevalence of DSM III R psychiatric disorders in the United States. Results from the National Comorbidity Survey. *Archives of General Psychiatry, 51*, 8–19.

Kind, P., & Sorensen, J. (1993). The cost of depression. *International Journal of Clinical Psychopharmacology, 7*, 191–195.

Klein, D. F. (1974). Endogenomorphic depression. *Archives of General Psychiatry, 31,* 447–454.

Klein, D. F. (1990). NIMH collaborative research on treatment of depression. *Archives of General Psychiatry, 47,* 682–684.

Klein, D. F. (1996). Preventing hung juries about therapy studies. *Journal of Consulting and Clinical Psychology, 64,* 81–87.

Klein, D. F., & Ross, D. C. (1993). Reanalysis of the National Institute of Mental Health Treatment of Depression Collaborative Research Program general effectiveness report. *Neuropsychopharmacology, 8,* 241–251.

Lewinsohn, P. M., Clarke, G. N., Hops, H., & Andrews, J. A. (1990). Cognitive behavioral treatment for depressed adolescents. *Behavior Therapy, 21,* 385–401.

Lloyd, G. G. L., & Lishman, W. A. (1975). Effect of depression on the speed of recall of pleasant and unpleasant experiences. *Psychological Medicine, 5,* 173–180.

Luria, A. R. (1973). *The working brain: An introduction to neuropsychology.* New York: Penguin Books.

Mahoney, M. J. (1993). Introduction to special section: Theoretical development in the cognitive psychotherapies. *Journal of Consulting and Clinical Psychology, 61,* 187–193.

Mahoney, M. J. A., & Lyddon, W. J. (1988). Recent developments in cognitive approaches to counseling and psychotherapy. *The Counseling Psychologist, 16,* 190–234.

McKnight, D. L., Nelson-Grey, R. O., & Barnhill, J. (1992). Dexamethasone suppresion test and response to cognitive therapy and antidepressant medication. *Behavior Therapy, 23,* 99–111.

McLean, P., & Taylor, S. (1992). Severity of unipolar depression and choice of treatment. *Behavior Research and Therapy, 30,* 443–451.

McNamara, K., & Horan, J. J. (1986). Experimental construct validity in the evaluation of cognitive and behavioral treatments for depression. *Journal of Counselling Psychology, 33,* 23–30.

Miranda, J., & Persons, J. B. (1988). Dysfunctional attitudes are mood state dependent. *Journal of Abnormal Psychology, 97,* 76–79.

Moore, R. M., & Blackburn, I. M. (1997). Cognitive therapy in the treatment of non-responders to antidepressant medication: A controlled study. *Behavioral and Cognitive Psychotherapy, 25,* 251–259.

Murphy, G. E., Simons, A. D., Wetzel, R. D., & Lustman, P. J. (1984). Cognitive therapy and pharmacotherapy, singly and together in the treatment of depression. *Archives of General Psychiatry, 41,* 33–41.

Neimeyer, R. A. (1993). An appraisal of constructivist psychotherapies. *Journal of Consulting and Clinical Psychology, 61,* 221–234.

Nofzinger, E. A., Schwartz, R. M., Reynolds, C. F., Thase, M. E., Jennings,

R., Frank, E., Fasinczka, A. L., Garamoni, G. L., & Kupfer, D. J. (1994). Affect intensity and phasic REM sleep in depressed men before and after treatment with cognitive behavioral therapy. *Journal of Consulting and Clinical Psychology, 62*, 83–91.

Nolen-Hoeksema, S. (1991). Responses to depression and their effects on the duration of depressive episodes. *Journal of Abnormal Psychology, 100*, 569–582.

Oei, T. S., & Free, M. L. (1995). Do cognitive behavior therapies validate cognitive models of mood disorders? A review of the empirical evidence. *International Journal of Psychology, 30*, 145–179.

Papageordiou, I., & Wells, A. (1999). Process and metacognitive dimensions of depression and anxious thoughts and relationships with emotional intensity. *Clinical Psychology and Psychotherapy, 6*, 156–162.

Paykel, E. S., & Priest, R. G. (1992). Recognition and management of depression in general practice: Consensus Statement. *British Medical Journal, 305*, 1198–1202.

Persons, J. B. (1993). The process of change in cognitive therapy: Schema change or acquisition of compensatory skills? *Cognitive Therapy and Research, 17*, 123–137.

Persons, J. B., & Burns, D. D. (1985). Mechanisms of action of cognitive therapy: The relative contributions of technical and interpersonal interventions. *Cognitive Therapy and Research, 9*, 539–551.

Peterson, C., & Villanova, P., (1988). An expanded attributional style questionnaire. *Journal of Abnormal Psychiatry, 97*, 87–89.

Power, M., & Dalgleish, T., (1997). *Cognition and emotion. From order to disorder*. Hove: Psychology Press Publishers.

Pyszczynski, T., & Greenberg, J. (1987). Self-regulatory preservation and the depressive self-focusing style: A self-awareness theory of reactive depression. *Psychological Bulletin, 102*, 122–138.

Rachman, S. (1981). The primacy of affect: Some theoretical implications. *Behavior Research and Therapy, 19*, 279–296.

Rachman, S. (1984). A reassessment of the "primacy of affect." *Cognitive Therapy and Research, 8*, 579–584.

Robins, C. J., & Hayes, A. M. (1993). An appraisal of cognitive therapy. *Journal of Consulting and Clinical Psychology, 61*, 205–214.

Robinson, L. A., Berman, J. S., & Neimeyer, R. A. (1990). Psychotherapy for the treatment of depression: A comprehensive review of controlled outcome research. *Psychological Bulletin, 108*, 30–49.

Rosenbaum, M. (1980). A schedule for assessing self-control behaviors: Preliminary findings. *Behavior Therapy, 11*, 109–121.

Roth, A., & Fonagy, P. (1996). *What works for whom? A critical review of psychotherapy research*. New York: Guilford Press.

Rush, A. J., Beck, A. T., Kovacs, M., & Hollon, S. D. (1977). Comparative efficacy of cognitive therapy versus pharmacotherapy in outpatient depression. *Cognitive Therapy and Research, 1,* 17–37.

Rush, A. J., Kovacs, M., Beck, A. T., Weissenburger, J., & Hollon, S. D. (1981). Differential effects of cognitive therapy and pharmacotherapy on depressive symptoms. *Journal of Affective Disorders, 3,* 221–229.

Rush, A. J., Beck, A. T., Kovacs, M., Weissenburger, J., & Hollon, S. D. (1982). Comparison of the effects of cognitive therapy and pharmacotherapy on hopelessness and self-concept. *American Journal of Psychiatry, 139,* 862–866.

Ryff, G. A., & Singer, B. (1996). Psychological well-being. *Psychotherapy and Psychosomatics, 65,* 14–23.

Safran, J. D., & Segal, Z. V. (1990). *Interpersonal processes in cognitive therapy.* New York: Basic Books.

Schwartz, R. M. (1986). The internal dialogue: On asymmetry between positive and negative coping thoughts. *Cognitive Therapy and Research, 6,* 591–605.

Seligman, M. E. P., Castellon, C., Cacciola, J., Schulman, P., Luborsky, L., Ollove, M., & Downing, R. (1988). Explanatory style change during cognitive therapy for unipolar depression. *Journal of Abnormal Psychology, 97,* 13–18.

Shapiro, D. A., Barkham, M., Rees, A. Hardy, G. E., Reynolds, S., & Startup, M. (1994). Effects of treatment duration and severity on depression on the effectiveness of cognitive-behavioral and psychodynamic-interpersonal psychotherapy. *Journal of Consulting and Clinical Psychology, 62,* 522–534.

Shea, M. T., Pilkonis, P. A., Beckham, E., Collins, J. F., Elkin, I., Sotsky, S. M., & Docherty, J. P. (1990). Personality disorders and treatment outcome in the NIMHT Treatment of depression Collaborative Research program. *American Journal of Psychiatry, 147,* 711–718.

Shea, M. T., Elkin, I., Imber, S. D., Sotsky, S. M., Watkins J. T., Collins, J. F., Pilkouis, P. A., Beckham, E., Glass, D. R., Dolan, R. T., & Parloff, M. B. (1992). Course of depressive symptoms over follow-up. Findings from the National Institute of Mental Health Treatment of Depression Collaborative Research Program. *Archives of General Psychiatry, 49,* 782–787.

Simons, A. D., Garfield, S. L., & Murphy, G. E. (1984). The process of change in cognitive therapy and pharmacotherapy for depression: Changes in mood and cognition. *Archives of General Psychiatry, 41,* 45–51.

Simons, A. D., Lustman, P. J., Wetzel, R. D., & Murphy, G. E. (1985). Predicting response to cognitive therapy of depression. *Cognitive Therapy and Research, 9,* 79–89.

Simons, A. D., & Thase, M. E. (1992). Biological Markers Treatment Outcome, and 1-year follow-up of endogenous depression: Electroencephalographic sleep studies and cognitive therapy. *Journal of Consulting and Clinical Psychology, 60,* 392–401.

Sotsky, S. M., Elkin, I., Watkins, J. T., Collins, J. F., Shea, M. T., Leber, W. R., & Glass, D. R. (1990). Mode-specific effects among three treatments for depression. *Journal of Consulting and Clinical Psychology, 58,* 352–359.

Spitzer, R., Endicott, J., & Robins, E. (1978). Research diagnostic criteria: Rationale and reliability. *Archives of General Psychiatry, 35,* 773–782.

Stein, D. J., & Young, J. E. (1992). (Eds). *Cognitive science and clinical disorders.* San Diego: Academic Press.

Stewart, J. W., Mercier, M. A., Agosti, V., Guardino, M., & Quitkin, F. M. (1993). Imipramine is effective after unsuccessful cognitive therapy: Sequential use of cognitive therapy and impramine in depressed outpatients. *Journal of Clinical Pharmacology, 13,* 114–119.

Taylor, S. E., & Brown, J. D. (1988). Illusion and well-being. *Psychological Bulletin, 103,* 193–210.

Teasdale, J. D. (1983). Negative thinking in depression: Cause effect or reciprocal relationship? *Advances in Behavioral Research and Therapy, 5,* 3–25.

Teasdale, J. D. (1993). Emotion and two kinds of meaning: Cognitive therapy and applied cognitive science. *Behavior Research and Therapy, 31,* 339–354.

Teasdale, J. D. (1996). Clinically relevant theory: Integrating clinical insight with cognitive science. In P. M. Salkovskis (Ed.) *Frontiers of cognitive therapy,* (pp. 26–47). New York: Guilford Press.

Teasdale, J. D. (1997). The relationship between cognition and emotion: the mind in place in mood disorders. In D. M. Clark & C. G. Fairburn (Eds.), *Science and practice of cognitive behavior therapy* (pp. 67–93). Oxford: Oxford University Press.

Teasdale, J. D. (1999). Metacognition, mindfulness and the modification of Mood Disorders. *Clinical Psychology and Psychotherapy, 6,* 146–155.

Teasdale, J. D., & Barnard, P. J. (1993). *Affect, cognition and change: Re-modelling depressive thought.* Hove, UK: Erlbaum.

Teasdale, J. D., & Fennell, M. J. V. (1982). Immediate effects on depression of cognitive therapy intervention. *Cognitive Therapy and Research, 6,* 343–351.

Teasdale, J. D., Fennell, M. J. V., Hibbert, G. A., & Amies, P. L. (1984). Cognitive therapy for major depressive disorders in primary care. *British Journal of Psychiatry, 144,* 400–406.

Teasdale, J. D., & Fogarty, S. J. (1979). Differential effects of induced mood on retrieval of pleasant and unpleasant events from episodic memory. *Journal of Abnormal Psychology, 88,* 248–257.

Thase, M. E., & Simons, A. D. (1992). Cognitive behavior therapy and relapse of non-bipolar depression: Parallels with pharmacotherapy. *Psychopharmacology Bulletin, 28,* 117–122.

Thase, M. E., Dubé, S., Bowler, K., Howland, R. H., Myers, J. E., Friedman, E., & Jarrett, D. B. (1996). Hypothalamic-pituatary-adrenocortical activity and response to cognitive behavior therapy in unmedicated, hospitalised depressed patients. *American Journal of Psychiatry, 144*, 1253–1262.

Thase, M. E., Fasiezka, M. A., Berman, S. R., Simons, A. D., & Reynolds, C. F. (1998). Electroencephalographic sleep profiles before and after cognitive behavior therapy of depression. *Archives of General Psychiatry, 55*, 138–144.

Thase, M. E., Reynolds, C. T., Frank, E., Jennings, J. R., Nofzinger, E., Fasioka, A. L., Garamoni, G. L., & Kupper, D. J. (1994). Polysomnographic Studies of unmedicated depressed men before and after treatment with cognitive behavior therapy. *American Journal of Psychiatry, 151*, 1615–1621.

Thase, M. E., Simons, A. D., & Reynolds, C. F. (1996). Abnormal electroencephalographic sleep profiles in major depression. Association with response to cognitive behavior therapy. *Archives of General Psychiatry, 53*, 99–108.

Thase, M. E., Simons, A. D., Cahalance, J., McGreary, J., & Harden, T. (1991). Severity of depression and response to cognitive behavior therapy. *American Journal of Psychiatry, 148*, 784–789.

Ucros, C. G. (1989). Mood state-dependent memory: A meta-analysis. *Cognition and Emotion, 3*, 139–167.

Vallis, T. M., Shaw, B. F., & Dobson, K. S. (1986). The cognitive therapy scale: Psychometric properties. *Journal of Consulting and Clinical Psychology, 54*, 381–385.

Weissman, A., & Beck, A. T. (1978). *Development and validation of the dysfunctional attitude scale: A preliminary investigation.* Paper presented at the 86th Annual Convention of the American Psychological Association, Toronto, Canada.

Wells, A., & Matthews, G. (1996). Modelling cognition in emotional disorder. The S-REF model. *Behavior Research and Therapy, 34*, 881–888.

Whisman, M. A. (1993). Mediators and moderators of change in cognitive therapy of depression. *Psychological Bulletin, 114*, 248–265.

Williams, J. M. G. (1992). *The psychological treatment of depression* (2nd ed.). London: Routledge.

Wilson, P. H. (1992). *Principles and practice of relapse prevention.* New York: Guilford.

World Health Organization (1998). *Well-being measures in primary healthcare / The Depcare project.* Copenhagen: WHO Regional Office for Europe.

World Health Organization (1999). *Press Release. World Health Report 1999 Making a difference.* Geneva: WHO.

Young, J. E., & Beck, A. T. (1980). *Cognitive therapy rating scale.* Unpublished manuscript. Philadelphia, PA: Center for Cognitive Therapy.

Young, J. E., & Beck, A. T. (1988). *Cognitive therapy scale.* Unpublished manuscript, University of Pennsylvania, Philadelphia, PA.

Zajonc, R. B. (1980). Feeling and thinking: Preferences need no inferences. *American Psychologist, 35,* 15–175.

3
Bipolar I Disorder
Monica Ramirez Basco

Bipolar I disorder (BPI) is a chronic and severe mental illness characterized by recurring episodes of major depression and mania. It is life long
once it begins, carries a high risk of suicidality, and often occurs comor-
bidly with substance abuse. Psychiatric medications are the treatment of
choice for controlling episodes of depression and mania, and prophylactic
medications are generally indicated to decrease the risk of recurrence.
Unfortunately, despite the scientific advances in psychopharmacology for
bipolar disorder, medication treatment alone is rarely sufficient to control
or prevent symptoms. This paper provides a conceptual model of bipolar
disorder and makes the case for using cognitive-behavioral therapy (CBT)
to supplement, not replace, pharmacological treatment of this chronic illness by addressing symptoms and difficulties not thoroughly remedied with
medication. A case study example is presented that illustrates the utility of
this treatment approach with individuals who suffer from BPI.

PHENOMENOLOGY OF BIPOLAR DISORDER

The diagnosis of BPI can be made once an individual has experienced his
or her first episode of mania or a mixed episode. Mania is defined by the
Diagnostic and Statistical Manual of Mental Disorders (*DSM-IV*; American
Psychiatric Association, 1994) as a period of expansive, euphoric, or irritable mood lasting one week or less if hospitalization is required. There must
be three additional manic symptoms occurring concurrently with a
euphoric mood or four additional symptoms if the mood is irritable. These
additional symptoms include grandiosity, decreased need for sleep, racing
thoughts, psychomotor agitation, increased goal-directed activity, and behaviors that have a high risk of negative consequences. To be distinguished
from hypomania, mania requires a level of symptom severity that causes

functional impairment or requires hospitalization. BPI can also be diagnosed after a mixed episode. During a mixed episode, symptoms of major
depression and mania exist either concurrently or alternate rapidly. If prior
to the manic or mixed episodes the individual experienced episodes of
major depression, a diagnosis of major depression may have preceded the
diagnosis of BPI. Symptoms can fluctuate with varying intensities.
"Recurrences" of depression, mania, or hypomania are symptomatic
episodes meeting full diagnostic criteria occurring after a period of well-
ness, defined by *DSM-IV* as a period of 2 months or more without symptoms. "Relapses" are a return to a fully symptomatic state after a period of
some improvement in symptoms that lasted less than two months.
"Symptom breakthroughs" are the occurrences of symptoms of depression
or mania that are mild and do not satisfy full *DSM-IV* criteria for a new
episode of illness.

COGNITIVE-BEHAVIORAL FORMULATION OF
BIPOLAR I DISORDER

Figure 3.1 illustrates the cognitive behavioral model of bipolar disorder.
During episodes of depression or mania there are significant changes in
thought and emotion. Emotions vary from euphoria to irritability to dysphoria. As distress increases, emotional shifts can include hopelessness, anxiety, and anger. The cognitive changes include changes in both the thinking
process as well as the content of one's thoughts. Changes in the speed of
thinking (e.g., slower in depression and faster in mania), as well as the
amount, clarity, and organization of thoughts are common. Insight and judgment are commonly impaired as well. The content of thoughts takes on a
negative edge in depression, and a more positive or paranoid edge in mania.
    These changes in thought and emotion have a direct effect on behavior.
Negative thinking and dysphoria can lead to tearfulness and inactivity while
mania can lead to hyperactivity, risk taking, and argumentativeness with
others. These behavioral changes result in poorer psychosocial functioning, such as, less efficiency on the job, conflict with others, and accumula-
tion of problems due to procrastination or disorganization. Although
perhaps not immediately, decreased functioning inevitably leads to psychosocial problems. The decreased activity and efficiency in depression
coupled with a negative cognitive set result in relationship conflicts when
the depressed partner contributes less, isolates from others, and avoids intimacy. The euphoria, hyperactivity, and impaired judgment of mania often
lead to financial difficulties due to overspending, relationship problems
resulting from infidelities, and sometimes legal problems from public
behaviors that are illegal or inappropriate. In many instances, the cycle
builds on itself as the stress and sleeplessness resulting from these psy-

FIGURE 3.1 Cognitive-behavioral model of bipolar I disorder.

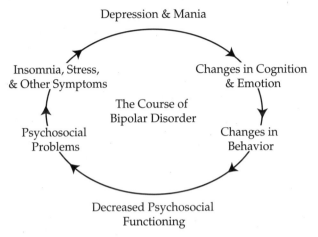

Depression & Mania

Insomnia, Stress, & Other Symptoms

Changes in Cognition & Emotion

The Course of Bipolar Disorder

Psychosocial Problems

Changes in Behavior

Decreased Psychosocial Functioning

Eront Basco, M. R., & Rush, A. J. (1996).
Cognitive-behavioral therapy for bipolar disorder. New York: Guilford Press.

chosocial problems drives the mania further or worsens the depression leaving the individual overwhelmed, hopeless, and suicidal. Stress exacerbates the physical, emotional, cognitive, and behavioral symptoms of the disorder and so the cycle continues.

WHY CBT FOR BIPOLAR DISORDER?

BPI disorder is recognized as a biological illness requiring biological treatment. Since the early 1970s when lithium became available as a mood stabilizer, numerous other medications have been tested and approved for treatment of manic and depressive symptoms in BPI. The new atypical antipsychotic medications are appearing on the scene as effective alternatives for controlling mood swings. The goals of traditional pharmacotherapy for BPI are recovery from an episode of depression or mania and prevention of future episodes. Unfortunately, medication treatments often fail.

The most common reason for failure in pharmacotherapy is patient noncompliance. A meta-analysis (Basco & Rush, 1995) of lithium studies showed a 40% to 60% chance of patient noncompliance at any given point in treatment. While mood stabilizers and other psychiatric medications are undoubtedly effective, getting patients to take these medications regularly is a behavior management problem that can be remedied with CBT. Cochran (1984) demonstrated how a short-term (6 weeks) CBT intervention decreased the frequency of significant noncompliance problems in patients with BPI. Compared to those assigned to receive standard clinical care, those in the CBT group were significantly less likely to have significant adherence problems, including being less likely to terminate lithium against medical advice. During the follow-up periods (3 and 6 months), the CBT group had fewer nonadherence-precipitated episodes and fewer hospitalizations. Unfortunately, even when medication compliance is consistent and medications are used at therapeutic levels, symptom breakthroughs can and do occur. These milder episodes, particularly those of hypomania, are 80% more likely to lead to a full episode of mania (Keller et al., 1991) perhaps because symptoms are not recognized early enough in the course of their development to forestall a relapse. Perry, Tarrier, Morriss, McCarthy, and Limb (1999) at the University of Manchester tested the effectiveness of teaching patients with BPI to identify symptoms early in the course of their development using CBT administered individually over 7 to 12 treatment sessions along with routine medical management. These researchers report significant increases in time to first recurrence of mania (65 versus 17 weeks) as well as a reduction in the number of manic episodes over an 18-month period among those participating in the CBT intervention compared to subjects in the control group. The effect was equivocal for episodes of major depression.

In Perry and colleagues' (1999) study, symptom breakthroughs were treated pharmacologically. Cognitive and behavioral interventions, which have proven effective in controlling symptoms in major depression (e.g., Rush et al., 1977), can also be used to manage symptoms in BPI. For example, there is evidence that sleep disruption caused by emerging hypomania or events such as medical illness, "cramming" for an exam, and travel or schedule changes, can lead to episodes of mania (Wehr, Sack, & Rosenthal, 1987). Cognitive and behavioral strategies have proven effective in both inducing relaxation that facilitates sleep and reducing insomnia (Lichstein & Riedel, 1994; Morin, Colecchi, Ling, & Sood, 1995).

The more informed a person is about his or her illness and its treatment, the more equipped he or she is to actively participate in its management. Numerous studies on the effect of patient education on adjustment to the illness as well as on improvement of treatment compliance show psychoeducation, a basic element of CBT, to improve outcomes (e.g., Altamura & Mauri, 1985; Van Gent & Zwart, 1991; Youssel, 1983).

Despite the effectiveness of medication in controlling an episode of illness, the affective lability, financial extravagance, fluctuations in levels of sociability, sexual indiscretions, and violent behaviors during episodes can leave psychosocial sequelae that add further distress for the patient and his or her family members (Goodwin & Jamison, 1990; Murphy & Beigel, 1974; Spalt, 1975; Winokur, Clayton, & Reich, 1969). Help is often needed to remedy interpersonal conflict, solve problems, find employment, or cope with child behavior problems. CBT provides a framework for coping with these psychosocial issues.

CBT for bipolar I disorder (Basco & Rush, 1996) was developed to enhance medication management by (a) teaching patients and their family members about the illness and treatment options, (b) helping patients improve their adherence to pharmacotherapy, (c) developing personalized methods for identifying subsyndromal symptoms for early intervention, (d) providing methods to combat subsyndromal symptoms of depression and mania, and (e) teaching problem-solving skills to help cope with common psychosocial and interpersonal stressors. Early writings on psychotherapy for bipolar disorder suggested that the nature of the illness precluded those afflicted from participating in the therapy process. Because this intervention goes beyond limited skills training, patients' ability to fully participate in and benefit from a more inclusive approach to therapy must be established.

CBT FOR BPI TREATMENT MANUAL

The CBT for BPI treatment manual (Basco & Rush, 1996) was written to accomplish each of these treatment goals over 20 therapy sessions. The manual provides explicit session-by-session instructions, including a rationale for each intervention and suggested homework assignments. Additional session materials are included if needed as well as information on crisis intervention. A few basic CBT interventions are utilized throughout the model, but additional CBT interventions can be added if deemed necessary to best help the patient. The treatment package is divided into five segments to match each of the five treatment goals. Table 3.1 lists the session topics and corresponding number of sessions involved with each topic.

Patient Education

The educational phase of the treatment protocol is designed to provide information about the symptoms of the illness, course, progression, and treatment options. This is accomplished by having patients watch three brief

TABLE 3.1 CBT for Bipolar I Treatment Sessions

Sessions 1–4:	Educate patients and family members
Sessions 5–6:	Develop an early warning system for symptom recurrence
Session 7:	Improve compliance with pharmacotherapy
Sessions 8–13:	Provide CBT skills for controlling symptoms
Sessions 14–20:	Develop problem-solving skills

videotapes describing the illness and its treatment, providing patients with written materials, and giving them an opportunity to ask questions. Patients usually have some knowledge of the illness and treatment, but just as often have misconceptions or incomplete information. Asking patients what they already know about the illness is the starting place in the education process. This allows the clinician to assess the patient's knowledge and to clear up potential inaccuracies.

Symptom Detection

The symptom detection process begins with gaining a global view of the course of a person's illness using life charts, a historical time line documenting episodes of illness based on Robert Post's work at the National Institute of Mental Health (Post, 1992). At the second level of refinement, within episode signs and symptoms are enumerated using a symptom summary worksheet, a list of physical, cognitive, emotional, and behavioral symptoms that occur during episodes of depression, mania, and mixed episodes. At the closest level of detection, daily mood ratings are used to monitor smaller changes in symptom status.

Life Charts

Post and colleagues (Altshuler et al., 1995; Post, 1992) use life charts to study the interactions between episodes of illness, treatment initiation and discontinuation, and significant life events. A life chart shows graphically the course of a person's illness from onset to present. Across this time line the approximate date of the onset and offset of each depressive, manic, hypomanic, and mixed episode are marked along with the dates of treatments and significant life events. The life chart serves several purposes. For example, it aids diagnosis particuarly if the patient has had concurrent problems with substance abuse or psychotic symptoms have been present. The life chart also helps patients to gain a clearer perspective on their experiences with the illness because they begin to see patterns, times of euthymia, responses to treatment, and times of vulnerability. In essence, patients report that the life chart is highly therapeutic because it helps them to sort out what feels like a lifetime of uninterrupted illness.

Symptom Summary Worksheet

In order to delineate symptoms within episodes, a three-column (depressed, manic, and normal), symptom summary worksheet is used to list the physical, emotional, cognitive, and behavioral symptoms that occur during both manic and depressive episodes. For example, in the "Depressed" column a patient may indicate that he sleeps 10 hours or more, but in the "Manic" column he may indicate that sleep is reduced to 4 to 5 hours per night. In contrast, the usual sleep habits of the individual when not symptomatic (e.g., 7 to 8 hours) may be indicated in the "Normal" column. The symptoms summary worksheet is started in the therapy session and completed as homework. Family members and friends are encouraged to contribute to the list by adding their observations of the patient during symptomatic times. Copies of the symptom summary worksheet are kept in the patient's chart, sent to the treating psychiatrist, and provided to the patient and his or her family members. When the patient or others suspect that symptoms may be reemerging, a review of the list of symptoms may help address this issue. This helps to resolve family conflict in which the patient is "blamed" for family stress because he or she is "sick," or when a patient is uncertain whether a mood swing is "normal" or heralding a recurrence of illness.

Mood Graphs

Mood graphs are used to track daily changes in mood or other cognitive, behavioral, or physical symptoms that signal the onset of a new episode of mania and depression. Although most people can monitor mood changes, some people are more sensitive to changes in attitude or in physical changes such as sleep patterns or energy level. The symptom summary worksheet (Basco & Rush, 1996) can help the clinician and patient decide which symptoms will be most useful to monitor. This is accomplished by selecting the symptom that tends to emerge earliest in the course of the illness.

A simple mood graph is shown in Figure 3.2. The points above the midline, from +1 to +5, represent levels of mania, with +5 indicating a severe manic episode. The points below the midline, from –1 to –5, represent levels of depression, with the lowest points indicating a severe major depressive episode. Patients are instructed to begin to attend to their symptoms more closely when they reach a rating of +2 or –2 and take any protective measures necessary (e.g., normalize sleep, or remember to take medications). A score of –3 or +3 indicates that it is time to intervene to keep the symptoms from worsening with either cognitive-behavioral or pharmacological methods.

Mood graphs can be tailored to the needs of each patient. For example, multiple ratings can be made each day or symptoms other than mood can be monitored. When beginning mood graphing, patients should make notes on the graph regarding the events that may be related to the mood swing. This information can help clinicians design interventions that prevent symptoms.

Methods for Enhancement of Treatment Compliance

The third component of CBT for bipolar disorder is to help patients maximize their compliance with pharmacotherapy. The extensive literature on

FIGURE 3.2 Mood graph.

Name:
Completed By:

		Day 1	Day 2	Day 3	Day 4	Day 5	Day 6	Day 7
	Date							
Manic	Plan							
+5	getting into trouble	Go to hospital	•	•	•	•	•	•	•
+4	manic		•	•	•	•	•	•	•
+3	hypomanic	Call doctor	•	•	•	•	•	•	•
+2	mild hypomania	Take action	•	•	•	•	•	•	•
+1	a little hyper	Monitor closely	•	•	•	•	•	•	•
0	normal		•	•	•	•	•	•	•
−1	feeling a little low	Monitor closely	•	•	•	•	•	•	•
−2	down or sad	Take action	•	•	•	•	•	•	•
−3	moderate depression	Call the doctor	•	•	•	•	•	•	•
−4	very depressed		•	•	•	•	•	•	•
−5	suicidal Depressed	Go to hospital	•	•	•	•	•	•	•

Adapted from Basco, M. R., and Rush, A. J. (1996) *Cognitive-behavioral therapy for bipolar disorder.* New York: Guilford Press.

the difficulties with treatment compliance across disorders (see Meichen-baum & Turk, 1987, for a review) suggests that even under the best cir-cumstances, most people will be unable to comply perfectly with treatment at all times, particularly if treatment is life long. The inevitability of com-pliance problems must be accepted by clinicians rather than denied and normalized for patients. Such validation sets the stage for an open and hon-est discussion of compliance problems and their solution. If the goals and methods of treatment are acceptable to patients, the effort of CBT is to increase the probability that patients can follow treatment as it is prescribed by identification and removal of factors that interfere with compliance.

The intervention for improving compliance consists of three steps. After a rationale for the intervention is provided and the patient is willing to discuss compliance problems, a compliance contract (see Basco & Rush, 1996, for example) is completed, which consists of (a) a summary of treatment plans, (b) a listing of anticipated obstacles to compliance, and (c) problem solving to avoid these obstacles or to remedy them if they occur.

Treatment goals listed in the first segment are written down as specifically as dose schedules (e.g., take 300 mg of lithium in the morning, at noon, and at bedtime), appointment plans (e.g., attend appointment with doctor next Monday, attend Alcoholics Anonymous meetings three times next week), and/or homework assignments (e.g., read pamphlet on bipolar disorder). These are goals that the patient and clinicians have agreed upon, not merely assigned by the clinician.

To identify obstacles to compliance, the clinician simply asks questions such as, "What could keep you from taking your medication?" "What could keep you from making it to your next appointment?" Some patients, eager to please will say that nothing will interfere with their compliance. However, there have generally been factors in the past that have led to noncompliance and these should be explored (e.g., "Have there been times in the past when it was difficult to always take medication that was prescribed for you or when you changed the way you took your medications? What led to that?"). The most common factors interfering with treatment are the medication itself (e.g., medication side effects or complicated dose regimen); poor rapport with clinicians or clinical office staff; outside influences, such as family members discouraging the use of medications; and personal beliefs that medications are unnecessary (Basco & Rush, 1995).

The last section of the compliance contract consists of plans for avoiding or overcoming the obstacles listed in the previous section. For example, if family members are interfering with treatment, a family therapy session is indicated to help others understand the importance of treatment. If the medication regimen is the problem, patients can work with their prescribing physician to reduce bothersome side effects or simply the dose regimen. After completion, the contract is reviewed each visit thereafter to modify the treatment goals if necessary, assess for any problems with compliance, and to modify the plan for addressing treatment obstacles if needed. A therapist should communicate with the treating physician so that they can function as a treatment team. The therapist should know the dose regimen and any modifications the patient is allowed within the regimen. It is helpful for the therapist to know the medication plan when symptoms begin to reemerge, such as when insomnia is a problem. If the patient desires regimen changes, the therapist should encourage the patient to call his or her physician before making any personal regimen changes.

Control of Subsyndromal Symptoms

The fourth component of the intervention is to control subsyndromal symptoms of depression and mania using standard cognitive and behavioral interventions. In this treatment protocol (Basco & Rush, 1996), a small subset of CBT techniques may be utilized during either the depressed or manic phases of the illness. Other CBT techniques can be added that serve the same purpose or better suit the patient's needs and abilities.

CBT for Cognitive Symptoms

Logical analysis of emotionally biased thoughts, whether they be negative automatic thoughts associated with depression, suspicious or angry thoughts accompanying irritability, or overly positive thoughts in mania, can be accomplished with standard cognitive therapy techniques (Beck, Shaw, Rush, & Emery, 1979), such as examining the supporting and refuting evidence for the thoughts or by generating alternative explanations. With angry, irritable, or paranoid thoughts that can herald the onset of mania, it can be particularly helpful to teach patients to gain emotional distance from the stimulus of the thoughts before attempting to evaluate their validity. This emotional distancing can be sufficiently powerful to help the individual gain a less emotional and more accurate perspective on the situation.

With positively biased thoughts, it will not always be the patient, but those around him or her that complain about the overly optimistic and unrealistic thinking, especially when the patient has a "creative" idea for a new activity. If you have established rapport with the patient, he or she can use you to evaluate these ideas. The first step is to consider the "hypothesis" that the overly positive idea is symptomatic of the illness. To determine if this is so, the patient should review the symptom summary worksheet to determine if any other symptoms of hypomnania are present. If other symptoms are present, the necessary precautions should be taken to control the hypomania. If no additional symptoms are present, the patient can be helped to deal with his or her complaining family member. If it is uncertain whether the patient's new idea or positive thinking are indicators that he or she is entering a hypomanic or manic episode, the patient should be encouraged to monitor symptoms closely with a mood graph. In addition to monitoring and controlling symptoms of hypomania, the overly optimistic or positive ideas of the patient can be evaluated in therapy by examining the advantages and disadvantages of pursuing the new activity as well as the advantages and disadvantages of not pursuing the idea. This will help the patient reason through the idea, allow the clinician greater opportunity to observe and determine if grandiosity is present, and increase trust and rapport between patient and clinician because the patient feels that his or her idea is being taken seriously and not merely dismissed as "crazy."

Impaired concentration is another cognitive symptom common in both depression and mania and the intervention can be the same in either episode. The task is to reduce environmental and internal noise (i.e., overstimulation) and focus thinking on one target at a time. In mania, relaxation techniques help many to slow racing thoughts and to limit their thinking to one idea at a time. Symptom monitoring will help patients to detect cognitive changes early in their evolution when they are easier to control.

Control of Behavioral Symptoms

Typically, the goal during the depressed phase of bipolar disorder is to increase activity, particularly those that provide a sense of mastery and pleasure (Beck et al., 1979). This activation leads to cognitive changes such as increased self-confidence and decreased self-criticism. In turn, these cognitive shifts improve mood and increase hopefulness.

A similar behavioral intervention can be used to control the emergence of hypomania; however, the goal is to limit the number of activities attempted each day. In either phase, the treatment plan is to plan and execute a limited number of activities each day. These include an "A list" of two or three activities that must be completed the next day and a "B list" of two or three activities the patient would like to complete if time allows. In hypomania, the added instruction is to complete the "A" list before attempting the "B" list. This helps the patient control the tendency in hypomania to initiate many projects, but complete few of them. It also helps reduce mental overstimulation by focusing on one project at a time. Projects not completed can be added to the next day's list. A new list is made at the end of the each day in preparation for the next day.

One of the most important behavioral interventions for prevention of mania and hypomania is sleep enhancement. One of the symptoms that emerges early in the course of mania is decreased need for sleep. While the urge to sleep less is powerful, it is a behavior that has been shown to drive the episode of mania (Wehr, Sack, & Rosenthal, 1987). Most people with this illness recognize the cycle of having greater energy and less need for sleep. Sleeping less leads to more symptoms and greater insomnia as the mania blossoms. Good sleep hygiene, including normalizing schedules for sleep and rising, limiting caffeine and other stimulants, and regular exercise can be preventive.

Reduction of Psychosocial Stressors

The fifth component of CBT for bipolar disorder is to help patients resolve psychosocial problems that have accumulated over the course of their illness. Financial, job, and relationship problems are common and the consequent emotional upheaval worsens the difficulty by interfering with problem solving. The residual problems can be hurtful to the patient and family members and contribute to a stressful environment that can predispose some to another episode of illness. This last component of CBT for bipolar disorder teaches patients how to resolve existing psychosocial stressors and cope with new problems as they arise, and provides patients with corrective feedback on their interpersonal communication skills so that they can maintain healthy relationships.

The most common reason that people cannot resolve difficulties is that they try to solve too many problems at one time or are unable to define the problem clearly enough to lead to a solution. This is evident when asking the patient and his or her spouse to define a specific family problem. Inevitably in the course of a 10-minute discussion, the couple will run through 5 to 10 different problems that seem to them to constitute one large problem. The "problem" seems unsolvable because it is actually multiple smaller problems they are attempting to fix with a single solution. The clinician can help by teaching methods for problem definition and solution.

Standard problem-solving steps include a clear definition of the problem, generation of solutions, selection and implementation of the solutions, and appraisal of the outcome. Giving patients these instructions slows the process and reduces emotions long enough to solve one problem at a time.

IMPLEMENTATION OF CBT IN A CLINICAL SETTING

In the current business of managing patient care it is not always likely that an insurance company will allow a clinician 20 therapy visits to cover all of the interventions outlined in the bipolar CBT manual (Basco & Rush, 1996). In general practice, it will be necessary to pare down the intervention, providing patients with only the essential elements. If you can only complete a few elements of the intervention, it is important to spend at least one session educating the patient about the illness and its treatment and answering the patient's questions. Second, of the symptom detection methods, the symptom summary worksheet is the most useful to complete because people who have lived with the illness for some time do not often associate the changes they experience with bipolar disorder. For example, they may view their irritability or argumentativeness as being the fault of others, or they may believe that the desire to stay up all night and be creative is merely a break from the depression. The symptom summary worksheet is a useful educational tool because it helps patients to understand their illness and teaches them what to watch for in the future. It is important to emphasize that early detection can lead to a faster intervention and prevention of relapse or recurrence.

The third essential element, treatment compliance, should be discussed during at least at one session and followed if it is a particular problem. Completion of a compliance contract provides a structure for discussing medication compliance. Misconceptions about medication treatment can be clarified ("I just take them when I'm having a bad day" or "When I'm feeling fine I don't need them") and the door to further discussion of compliance can be opened.

Fourth, behavioral management of mania, particularly normalizing sleep and reducing stimulation, is strongly advised. Finally, from the fifth component, learning to better manage a psychosocial stressor that seems to either interfere with sleep or increase conflict, can help to reduce the risk of relapse.

Case Example

Ms. C is a 45-year-old, divorced nurse and mother of two adult daughters. She lives alone, but has friends and regular contact with her extended family. She had been diagnosed with bipolar I disorder approximately 15 years ago, but suffered from mild episodes of depression and flurries of hypomania in her teenage and early adult years. She tried numerous medications, but was inconsistent with treatment, often missing doses or discontinuing treatment altogether without her doctor's consent or knowledge. Her parents did not "believe in psychiatry" or in taking medications. Prior to beginning CBT, she had three psychiatric hospitalizations, had been renounced as "possessed by the devil" by her church, had lost numerous jobs due to aggressive behavior toward other nurses, and had verbal conflict with her mother and brother on a regular basis. Her brother, possibly diagnosable with bipolar disorder as well, had physically beaten the patient during family arguments. She did not drink alcohol or use illicit drugs. She heard the therapist (M.R.B.) give a presentation to a local manic-depressive support group and called to request treatment. At the time of her first visit she had a Hamilton Depression Rating Scale score of 24. She was taking 900 mg of lithium carbonate and 20 mg of Prozac, although not consistently. She reported no suicidal ideation and stated she was committed to her two daughters and did not wish to hurt them any more than had already occurred. Mrs. C was about to be terminated from her job for belligerence with the other nurses and she had had a conflict with her psychiatrist who was unwilling to continue her treatment. She had enough medications to last another month.

From her self-description, Ms. C knew she had bipolar I disorder. She knew her irritability was symptomatic of the illness as was her dysphoria. Given the severity of her depression, no additional education was done at that time. Instead, cognitive restructuring for her constant negative thinking was initiated. She believed that everyone hated her, that she was a terrible mother, that she would never be well, and that she was a total failure. She learned logical analysis of negative automatic thoughts and was able to control most of her negative thinking by the third week of therapy. She remembered that she had supported her two daughters through most of their lives, put herself through nursing school, had some excellent jobs, and was well liked by several friends who "understood her moods." Ms. C liked being a "rational thinker" and continued to use these methods whenever her depressive thinking recurred. The challenge in her treatment was to combat her frequently emerging mania.

The first step in controlling her mania was to define the symptoms using the symptom summary worksheet. This was an enlightening exercise because she had never associated her symptom changes with mania. She learned that her increased interest in men, desire to smoke and drink, argumentativeness, sense of humor, initiation of several new craft activities, and medication noncompliance were all signs of emerging mania. Her losses and hospitalization motivated her to avoid mania in the future; therefore, she was highly motivated to learn to control these symptoms. With some coaching, Ms. C resolved her conflict with the psychiatrist long enough to get a refill of medications and a referral to a local community mental health center. There, she was put on Depakote and slowly withdrawn from the lithium carbonate. Her doctor was experienced with bipolar disorder and was able to find the medication that reduced the frequency and severity of Ms. C's mood swings when she took the medicine regularly. A compliance contract was constructed during one session where the patient volunteered that her reluctance to take medications came from a belief during hypomania that she didn't need it, negative input from her mother regarding medications, and forgetfulness when rushed in the morning to go to work. As she worked through each of these issues, her medication compliance improved, although not to 100%, primarily due to either forgetting to fill her pillbox or leaving for work without it. After two days of not taking her medications, Mrs. C predictably had a recurrence of symptoms and agreed to resume her medication treatment.

The third step in controlling her mania was to reduce overstimulation. This meant limiting late-night television and phone calls to a friend who was also manic. When the urge to "be creative" came upon her, she knew it was likely a symptom, so rather than buying enough art supplies to make a gift for each family member, she limited it to one prototype to start. If the urge was too great, she avoided the craft store altogether. During these periods, increased irritability would emerge and lead to conflict with her mother. A self-imposed limit setting intervention involved avoiding talking with her mother on those days and to only have superficial conversation with her on other days. "Deeper discussions" inevitably led to a conflict of opinions that would make it hard for Ms. C to sleep at night.

These preventive measures seemed to work. Ms. C was able to find stable employment and catch up on her bills. She learned a way to communicate with and enjoy her mother while avoiding conflict. Mrs. C completed 6 months of treatment and was discharged with a Hamilton Depression Rating Scale score of 5 and a Bech-Rafaelson Mania scale score of 3. After 2 years, she was able to avoid additional episodes of depression and mania, although symptom breakthroughs continued to be common. Her medication compliance was generally good. She felt that she had the tools needed to manage her own illness and knew when to call for help.

DISCUSSION

Preliminary feasibility testing for the CBT intervention suggests that patients are able to learn and implement the various treatment strategies to manage their illness and can be highly compliant with the therapeutic interventions and homework. Currently, two treatment outcome studies are underway to test CBT as a method of relapse prevention. Jan Scott and colleagues at the University of Glasgow and the University of Manchester are conducting a five-center study in which the CBT manual is being utilized with some modification to address patients' symptoms in order of severity rather than following the manual in a lock-step fashion. Gary Sachs at Massachusetts General Hospital and Michael Thase and Ellen Frank of the University of Pittsburgh are undertaking a comparative study of CBT, medication treatment, and Frank's social rhythm therapy (Frank et al., 1997) to prevent relapse and improve quality of life. In addition, under the direction of Robert Reiser at the Pacific Graduate School of Psychology, three California–county mental health programs will be testing CBT for bipolar I disorder delivered in a group format compared to treatment as usual.

In clinical use, the CBT methods have been very effective in preventing relapse for patients with bipolar I disorder. The power of the intervention seems to be in identifying symptoms early in the course of their development and intervening quickly. The interventions that seem most helpful are those that maximize medication compliance, reduce stimulation, and improve sleep. At the first signs of mania, patients are instructed to "not make it worse." This translates into making every effort to get a full night's sleep, including taking PRN sleeping medications and reducing stimulation several hours before bedtime. Discontinuing use of caffeine, avoiding overstimulating activities, and controlling the urge to increase activity are standard prescriptions that seem to circumvent episodes of mania.

Perry and colleagues (1999) found that CBT was more effective in controlling mania than in controlling depressive symptoms. Clinically, it seems to be easier to control mania perhaps because the onset of symptoms is easier to detect. Another reason is that the insidious onset of depression is quickly strengthened by the negative schemas that seem to underlie the cognitive distortions in depression. As shown in Figure 3.1, as the episode of depression emerges, it leads to cognitive and emotional changes. The cognitive distortions in depression fall along the lines of existing negative self-schema that are more impervious to change although they can be quieted during asymptomatic times. The emotional and behavioral changes that follow lead to experiences that help to reinforce the negative schemas, thus strengthening the hold of the depression. In contrast, the cognitive distortions in mania do not seem to fall along lines of schemas, but are more stereotypically grandiose or paranoid in nature. While many of the same thinking errors occur, there does not appear to be an emergence of underlying schema that fuel the manic symptoms. A person can recognize changes in her thinking in mania and know that they are familiar, but not necessarily accurate; whereas, with depression the changes in quality of thought seem inherently accurate to the patient because they are consistent with an underlying negative self-view.

The dilemmas facing the assessment of treatment outcome include defining appropriate outcome measures. Unlike acute treatment trials of CBT for depression where a pre- to posttreatment comparison is a good indicator of efficacy, in bipolar disorder depression and mania will continue to recur, and thus a short-term comparison will not be sufficiently informative. A good outcome for this illness is prevention of relapses or recurrences of depression and mania. While prevention is the first goal, the intervention is put to the test when symptom breakthroughs begin to emerge or when they are anticipated with season or stress changes. If the patient can use CBT skills to stop the evolution of symptoms, then the intervention has been a success. This does not mean that CBT skills alone must be used to control symptoms. If the individual uses the symptom-detection methods and recognizes the emergence of mania, he or she might intervene by calling a psychiatrist and asking for sleeping medications to prevent insomnia. This is how psychotherapy and pharmacotherapy complement one another.

To accurately assess the efficacy of the intervention, an adequate posttreatment observation period would be needed that allows time for recurrences of depression and mania. If it were possible to accurately obtain a chronology of pretreatment recurrences of illness, it might be possible to conduct within-person comparisons of treatment and untreated episodes. The events of interest would be those times prior to the CBT intervention when symptom breakthroughs did not lead to full relapses or recurrences of depression or mania. The comparable and fair observation period would occur after the CBT intervention has been completed and the patient returns to treatment as usual.

Another dilemma in assessing treatment outcome is designing an appropriate control condition. It is nearly impossible to provide a structured medication treatment that is suitable for all people with bipolar disorder. The individual variation in the illness and response to treatment will always require individualized medication regimens. As soon as variation in the mediation protocol is introduced, it makes the findings suspect as the comparable efficacy of the medication treatment comes into question even if delivered by the same physician. To account for these variations, protocols can allow variation, but make symptom levels prior to treatment onset comparable, such as requiring a mania–rating scale score at a specified level for a certain number of days or weeks before entering treatment. Another strategy is to use a consensus approach to medication management where a committee of psychiatrists decides if treatment strategies are comparable. In a large enough sample, these issues become less of a concern, particularly if the range of medications can be limited to some degree.

CONCLUSIONS

CBT is a feasible treatment for individuals with bipolar I disorder. It appears to help control symptoms and prevent relapse. Therapists can follow the protocol and patients understand the information and complete homework assignments. Patients find the treatment useful in controlling their symptoms, particularly the methods developed for control of mania. A controlled clinical trial of CBT for bipolar I disorder is needed to determine its efficacy and utility in general clinic settings. Although the protocol described in this paper was developed to include five components delivered over 20 treatment sessions, further study will be needed to determine the usefulness of each of the elements of the protocol. Perhaps individualized treatment is the most practical strategy, relying on clinician judgment to determine the most useful intervention in controlling a given patient's disorder. In general, CBT methods are increasing the available treatment armamentaria for clinicians to use in the treatment of chronic and severe mental disorders. The continued demonstrations of the efficacy of CBT methods strengthen the argument for continued study and use of psychotherapeutic methods as complements to medication treatments in severe and persistent mental illnesses.

REFERENCES

Altamura, A. C., & Mauri, M. (1985). Plasma concentration, information and therapy adherence during long-term treatment with antidepressants. *British Journal of Clinical Pharmacology, 20,* 714–716.

Altshuler, L. L., Post, R. M., Leverich, G. S., Mikalauskas, K., Rosoff, A., & Ackerman, L. (1995). Antidepressant-induced mania and cycle acceleration: A controversy revisited. *American Journal of Psychiatry, 152,* 1130–1138.

American Psychiatric Association. (1994). *Diagnostic and statistical manual of mental disorders* (4th ed.) . Washington, DC: Author.

Basco, M. R., & Rush, A. J. (1995). Compliance with pharmacotherapy in mood disorders. *Psychiatric Annals, 25,* 269–279.

Basco, M. R., & Rush, A. J. (1996). *Cognitive-behavioral therapy for bipolar disorder.* New York: Guilford Press.

Beck, A. T., Shaw, B. F., Rush, A. J., & Emery, G. (1979). *Cognitive therapy of depression.* New York: Guilford Press.

Cochran, S. D. (1984). Preventing medical noncompliance in the outpatient treatment of bipolar affective disorders. *Journal of Consulting and Clinical Psychology, 52,* 873–878.

Frank, E., Hlastala, S., Ritenour, A., Houk, P., Tu, X. M., Monk, T. H., Mallinger, A. G., & Kupfer, D. J. (1997). Inducing lifestyle regularity in recovering bipolar disorder patients: Results from the maintenance therapies in bipolar disorder protocol. *Biological Psychiatry, 41,* 1165–1173.

Goodwin, F. K., & Jamison, K. R. (1990). *Manic-depressive illness.* New York: Oxford University Press. .

Keller, M. B., Lavori, P. W., Kane, J. M., Gelenberg, A. J., Rosenbaum, J. F., Walzer, E. A., & Baker, L. A. (1991). Subsyndromal symptoms in bipolar disorder: A comparison of standard and law serum levels of lithium. Unpublished manuscript.

Lichstein, K. L., & Riedel, B. W. (1994). Behavioral assessment and treatment of insomnia: A review with an emphasis on clinical application. *Behavior Therapy, 25,* 659–688.

Meichenbaum, D., & Turk, D. (1987). *Facilitating treatment adherence: A practitioner's guidebook.* New York: Plenum Press.

Morin, C. M., Colecchi, C. A., Ling, W. D., & Sood, R. K. (1995). Cognitive behavior therapy to facilitate benzodiazepine discontinuation among hypnotic-dependent patients with insomnia. *Behavior Therapy, 26,* 733–745.

Murphy, D. L., & Beigel, A. (1974). Depression, elation, and lithium carbonate responses in manic patient subgroups. *Archives of General Psychiatry, 31,* 643–648.

Perry, A., Tarrier, N., Morriss, R., McCarthy, E., & Limb, K. (1999). A randomized controlled trial of teaching bipolar disorder patients to identify early symptoms of relapse and obtain early treatment. *British Medical Journal, 318*(7177), 149–153.

Post, R. M. (1992). Transduction of psychosocial stress into the neurobiology of recurrent affective disorder. *American Journal of Psychiatry, 149,* 999–1010.

Rush, A. J., Beck, A. T., Kovacs, M., Khatami, M., Fitzgibbons, R., & Wolman, T. (1977). Comparative efficacy of cognitive therapy and imipramine in the treatment of depressed outpatients. *Cognitive Therapy and Research, 1,* 17–27.

Spalt, L. (1975). Sexual behavior and affective disorders. *Diseases of the Nervous System, 36,* 974–977.

Van Gent, E. M., & Zwart, F. M. (1991). Psychoeducation of partners of bipolar manic patients. *Journal of Affective Disorders, 21,* (1), 15–18.

Winokur, G., Clayton, P. J., & Reich, T. (1969). *Manic Depressive Illness.* St. Louis, MO: C. V. Mosby.

Youssel, F. A. (1983). Compliance with therapeutic regimens: A follow-up study for patients with affective disorders. *Journal of Advanced Nursing, 8,* 513–517.

Wehr, T. A., Sack, D. A., & Rosenthal, N. E. (1987). Sleep reduction as a final common pathway in the genesis of mania. *American Journal of Psychiatry, 144,* 201–204.

Part II
Anxiety Disorders

4

Phobias

Deborah R. Fahr and E. Thomas Dowd

There are numerous (albeit overlapping) definitions of "empirically supported" (Kendall, 1998). The term "empirically supported" itself has recently
replaced "empirically validated" because the new term does not suggest that
treatments have been *proven* to be effective but rather that the empirical
evidence to date supports their effectiveness. Research findings do not provide final evidence; rather research is a continuing process that supports but
does not provide final validation (Chambless & Hollon,1998; Kendall, 1998).
  Controversy and disagreement have followed the definitions that are
believed by some to be too restrictive and possibly reduce support of what
might be important findings. Controversy and disagreement, however, can
be seen as the very heart and soul of science. Without controversy and disagreement and ultimately enmeshment of theories, how can we continue
to advance our field? What is important is that we determine which treatments are effective by examining specific factors that lead to successful outcomes in treatment of different disorders (Kazdin & Weisz, 1998).
  American Psychological Association (APA) Task Force on Psychological
Intervention Guidelines (1995) states that research must be conducted in
a controlled environment, and it must be reasonable to conclude that the
cause of the outcome is due to the treatment intervention rather than to
confounding variables. Chambless and Hollon (1998) suggest that the best
way to determine treatment efficacy is through random controlled studies
and single-case experiments. The APA Task Force (1995) argued that the
most important element in determining treatment efficacy is that evidence
indicates the outcome was actually due to the intervention. However, the
Task Force caution also that this alone is not enough. When constructing
treatment guidelines we must also consider whether the treatment will be
equally effective in clinical practice. Chambless and Hollon suggest that,
when reaching this stage of the research, quasi-experimental and nonex-
perimental designs can be employed to determine clinical significance.

Chambless and Hollon (1998) also suggest specific requirements for determining empirically supported therapies. They state that replication by independent investigators is critical. Likewise, it is important, even mandatory, that the methods used ensure dependable data. Furthermore, the population for which the treatment intervention is to be applicable must be clearly defined. Reliability and validity of the instruments used to assess outcomes are also important. Next, although Chambless and Hollon allude to the fact that follow-up may be difficult, the attempt to obtain long-term effects of the treatment is always desirable.

Chambless and Hollon (1998) have divided empirically supported treatments into three groups: (a) possibly efficacious, (b) efficacious, and (c) efficacious and specific. For a treatment outcome to be possibly efficacious, there must be at least one study that shows the intervention to be better than no treatment, a placebo, or an alternate treatment, or be at least equally effective as an alternate treatment for which effectiveness has already been established. The studies must either be randomized, a controlled single-case experiment with a sample size of three or more, or a time-series design. A treatment manual must also have been employed along with valid and reliable outcome measures and a clear definition as to whom the outcome is to be generalized.

To be considered an efficacious treatment, all of the above criteria must have been met with the additional criterion that two independent studies must be included (Chambless & Hollon, 1998). To be efficacious and specific, the intervention must be superior to placebos (medical or psychological), and better than an alternative treatment previously shown to be effective in at least two independent studies.

Although there is extant literature on this topic, the present chapter will follow the basic guidelines previously mentioned when referring to empirically supported evidence for the treatment of phobias. For a more in-depth review of the definitions of empirically supported evidence, we refer you to the authors cited above.

DIAGNOSIS OF PHOBIA

The *DSM IV* (American Psychiatric Association, 1994) lists two types of phobias for diagnosis. The first type is specific phobia, formerly known as simple phobia. The second type is social phobia, also known as social anxiety disorder. To differentiate between specific phobia and social phobia it is necessary to look at the focus of the particular fears. For example, in a given situation such as a trip via air travel, the individual with a specific phobia may fear crashing while the individual with social phobia may fear negative evaluation from the other travelers.

The most common anxiety disorder is specific phobias (Öst, Stridh, & Wolf, 1998). Specific phobia refers to the irrational and persistent fear of, and often attempts to avoid, specific objects and/or situations. The fear is typically narrowed to a specific object or situation, unlike other phobia disorders. A potential list of these objects and situations is endless. The most common specific phobias recognized are particular types of transportation (e.g., flying and driving), public speaking, heights, and darkness. Others may include dogs, cats, birds, and thunderstorms.

Individuals with simple phobias commonly practice avoidance of the feared stimuli. This may be relatively easy when the feared object or situation is not commonly experienced. However, it becomes more difficult when the object or situation is a part of everyday life and is often unwillingly confronted.

Anxiety responses may occur when anticipating an encounter with the feared stimuli or upon exposure to the feared object or situation. Often the fear consists of what may happen when confronted with the feared stimuli, often referred to as the fear of fear. Among other possibilities, individuals may fear losing control, panicking, or fainting when exposed to the feared object or situation. The level of anxiety felt may depend upon the individual's proximity to the stimuli or his or her inability to escape the stimuli.

According to the *DSM IV*, to be diagnosed with specific phobia, the individual must meet seven specific criteria. These seven criteria are (a) marked and persistent fear that is excessive or unreasonable, cued by the presence or anticipation of a specific object or situation; (b) exposure to the phobic stimulus that almost invariably provokes an immediate anxiety response which may take the form of a situationally bound or situationally predisposed panic attack; (c) the individual recognizes that the fear is excessive or unreasonable; (d) the phobic situations(s) is avoided or is endured with intense anxiety or distress; (e) The avoidance, anxious anticipation, or distress in the feared situation(s) seriously interferes with the individual's normal routine, occupational (or academic) functioning, or social activities or relationships, or there is marked distress about the phobia; (f) in individuals under age 18 years, the duration is at least 6 months; and (g) the anxiety, panic attacks, or phobic avoidance are not better accounted for by another mental disorder, such as obsessive-compulsive disorder, posttraumatic stress disorder, separation anxiety disorder, social phobia, panic disorder with agoraphobia, or agoraphobia without history of panic disorder.

As specifiers, the *DSM IV* includes animal type, natural environment type, blood-injection-injury type, situational type, and other type. The subtype of animals includes any phobia that is focused on animals or insects. Natural environment type may include storms, heights, darkness, or water. Both the animal and natural environment type often have a childhood onset. If there is a fear of seeing blood or an injury, or a fear of receiving an injection or other invasive medical procedures, the *DSM IV* suggests that the clinician state blood-injection-injury type as a specifier. Situational type includes any specific situation such as elevators or enclosed places that might elicit an anxiety response. The individual with this subtype may experience a peak in childhood and another peak during their twenties. Other type refers to any other specific fear that is not represented by one of the previous subtypes. These may include situations that are associated with contracting an illness or space phobia.

Individuals with simple phobias are rarely concerned about the most obvious means of threat on which they are focused (S. J. Phillipson, personal communication, 2000). In other words, individuals with a spider phobia tend to focus on the movement of the spider's legs, individuals with a snake phobia fear the slithering of the snake, and likewise, persons with a cat phobia are unsettled by the erratic movement of a cat. Typically, as the phobia develops, associations start to link between the feared object and a feeling of panic and being unsafe. Often an individual with a simple phobia will have an extreme reaction even at the prospect of seeing a picture of the feared item (e.g., in a magazine). These individuals tend not to pursue treatment since it is their general belief that they can get through life by avoiding contact with the feared objects rather than engaging in an exposure-based treatment.

Social phobia is not a subtype of specific phobia but rather is a separate diagnosis. Excessive fear of or anxiety in social situations marks social phobia. This may include meetings, interviews, eating in public, and/or numerous types of interaction with individuals. The phobia may be due to a fear of embarrassment, rejection, making mistakes, or having physiological reactions (e.g., sweating, blushing).

The *DSM IV* lists eight criteria the individual must meet to be diagnosed with social phobia. These criteria include: (a) A marked and persistent fear of one or more social or performance situations in which the individual is exposed to unfamiliar people or to possible scrutiny by others. The individual fears that he or she will act in a way that will be humiliating or embarrassing; (b) exposure to the feared social situation almost invariably provokes anxiety that may take the form of a situationally bound or situationally predisposed panic attack; (c) the person recognizes that the fear is excessive or unreasonable; (d) the feared social or performance situations are avoided or are endured with intense anxiety or distress; (e) the avoidance, anxious anticipation, or distress in the feared social or performance situation(s) seriously interferes with the individual's normal routine, occupational (academic) functioning, or social activities or relationships, or there is marked distress about the phobia; (f) in individuals under age

18 years, the duration is at least 6 months; (g) the fear or avoidance is not due to the direct physiological effects of a substance or a general medical condition and is not better accounted for by another mental disorder; and (h) if a general medical condition or another mental disorder is present, the fear in criterion a is unrelated to it. If the fears include most social situations, a specifier of "generalized" is suggested.

It is important to note that many fears are common, particularly in childhood. It is when these fears seriously interfere with everyday life or cause marked distress that a diagnosis of phobia may be warranted.

As with adults, the difference in definitions need to be carefully examined when using the words anxiety, fear, and phobia as related to children. Anxiety is traditionally defined as an "aversive or unpleasant emotional state involving subjective apprehension and physiological arousal of a diffuse nature" (King, Hamilton, & Ollendick, 1988). Fears are believed to be normal reactions where the individual may experience overt behavioral changes, covert changes of feelings, and physiological changes to real or imagined situations. Many children experience some type of fear during normal childhood development. These fears may typically include darkness, animals, dentists, or imaginary creatures (King et al., 1988). Normal developmental fears are age related and are considered a part of typical childhood development. It is important to have an understanding of developmental stages and the fears that are considered normal within a particular age range (Knell, 2000).

Phobias, however, are a different kind of fear that are not related to age and childhood development. Marks (1969) differentiates phobias from fears by stating that the phobia (a) is out of proportion to the situation, (b) cannot be explained or reasoned, (c) is not within the individual's control, and (d) causes the individual to avoid the feared situation. Miller, Barrett, and Hampe (1974) use Marks's (1969) criteria in establishing a difference between fears and phobias, but add that a phobia (a) persists over a greater length of time, (b) is unable to adapt or habituate, and (c) is not specific to an age or stage.

It is the difficulty in differentiating as to whether the fear is actually a phobia or part of typical developmental fears that occur in normal childhood development that makes diagnosing a phobia in children more confusing than in adults. Basically, phobias and fears are differentiated on the basis of their magnitude, persistence, and maladaptiveness (King et al., 1988). Graziano, DeGiovanni, and Garcia, (1979) suggest that when diagnosing a phobia in a child, it is necessary to examine intensity and duration. They argue that the intensity should be at a level that renders the child dysfunctional in the normal life routine and the duration should be at least 2 years. However, this may be of little use to the clinician presented with a child who is suffering long before 2 years has passed (King et al., 1988). It is also difficult to provide an operational definition to the term "intensity," causing greater confusion in distinguishing the differences between fears and phobias because individuals may differ greatly in their reactions.

OVERVIEW OF EMPIRICALLY SUPPORTED TREATMENTS

In the 1970s, systematic desensitization was developed as a very successful means of treating simple phobia. In systematic desensitization, the principles of reciprocal inhibition (the simultaneous combining of deep relaxation with the anxiety provoking stimuli) were applied in a progressive manner, generally through imagined scenes and scenarios (Phillipson, personal communication, 2000). Another type of intervention used for treatment intervention is exposure/response prevention.

In both therapeutic methods, patients are guided through the development of a stepwise hierarchy in which the progression of feared scenarios are sequentially laid out, agreed upon, and implemented (Phillipson, personal communication, 2000). A major difference between exposure/ response prevention and systematic desensitization is the focus within exposure response prevention on allowing the anxiety response to occur while providing strategies for managing the anxiety. In exposure/response prevention, the anxiety is seen as an experience not to be avoided. The individual is exposed to the anxiety and the avoidance response is prevented. Within systematic desensitization, however, patients are requested not to allow their anxiety level to exceed a previously agreed-upon level.

Exposure therapy has consistently been shown to be the most successful intervention for phobias (Chambless, 1990; Marks, 1987; Öst et al., 1998). Biran and Wilson (1981) randomly assigned 22 subjects with specific phobia to one of two treatment conditions: guided exposure and cognitive restructuring. The significant results suggested that it is better to employ performance-based techniques rather than cognitive therapy alone. These results were found in only five or fewer sessions and were either maintained or improved at 1- and 6-month follow-ups.

Researchers (Beckham, Vrana, May, Gustafson, & Smith, 1990; Denholtz & Mann, 1975; Howard, Murphy, & Clarke, 1983; Öst et al., 1998; Solyom, Shugar, Bryntwick, & Solyom, 1973) have frequently focused on one particular type of specific phobia—flying phobia—and have found CBT to be an effective treatment. Specifically, Öst et al., (1998) hypothesized that one session of CBT would be as effective as five sessions of CBT in causing significant changes in the individual with a flying phobia. Furthermore, they hypothesized that these changes would be maintained or even strengthened at follow-up. The 28 subjects were randomly assigned to one of two conditions: (a) one session, which consisted of 3 consecutive hours of exposure and cognitive restructuring, or (b) five sessions of exposure and cognitive restructuring (four 1-hour sessions and one 2-hour session). The results found both groups to have improved, with 93% of Group 1 and 79% of Group 2 taking an unaccompanied flight.

In another study, Öst and colleagues (1998) looked at 103 individuals with spider phobia to determine if there were variables that could predict treatment success and how much treatment was needed to realize clinically significant improvement. Of course, to determine this, it is necessary to establish that treatment was clinically significant. The four treatment conditions were manualized self-exposure, video treatment, group treatment, and individual treatment. In all groups, treatment components were exposure related. If participants in Groups 1, 2, or 3 did not show clinically significant improvement, they were moved to the next group. Twenty-seven percent of the participants in Group 1 (self-help manual) were clinically improved, 10% in Group 2 (video treatment), 68% in Group 3 (group treatment), and 100% in Group 4 (individual treatment) were found to be significantly clinically improved. While this suggests a variance in results dependent upon method of treatment deliverance, it also supports exposure as an effective treatment for individual with phobias. Likewise, Thorpe and Salkovskis (1997) tested individuals with spider phobia, using a spider-word Stroop test and questionnaires after one session of CBT, and found the treatment to be highly effective.

Like phobias in adults, behavioral and cognitive behavioral treatment interventions with children seem to hold the greatest promise of successful treatment outcome (Ollendick & King, 1998). Weisz, Weiss, Han, Granger, and Morton (1995) concluded in their meta-analytic review of 150 studies that behavioral treatments are more effective than nonbehavioral treatments regardless of the individual's age.

COGNITIVE BEHAVIOR THERAPY AS A TREATMENT

The best way to keep a phobia alive and well is to continue to avoid the situation that is frightening. Therefore, the best way to defeat the phobia is to face it. Although that seems simple and fundamental, for many, perhaps most, phobics this seems an impossible task; otherwise, they would have conquered their fear long ago. But with the correct guidance, it is a task they can complete and a fear they can conquer.

Cognitive-behavior therapy has been found to be the treatment of choice in overcoming a phobia. Although cognitive therapy and behavior therapy have been used alone to treat phobias, the greatest evidence for efficacy is cognitive and behavior therapy used together (Otto, 2000). Nevertheless, it does appear that behavioral interventions may be somewhat more effective than cognitive interventions. CBT is also associated with continued maintenance and even continued gains after the therapy has been discontinued. Cognitive therapy relies on changing behavior by changing patterns of thoughts and beliefs. Although this is an important part of CBT, when used alone to treat phobics, it has been found to be less effective than behavior therapy (Foa & Steketee, 1987). In fact, in some studies the addition of cognitive therapy to behavior therapy did not enhance the outcome (Emmelkamp & Mersch, 1982; Foa & Steketee, 1987). However, cognitive therapy may be part of what may be considered behavior therapy in the treatment intervention with the clinician unaware. This may occur through the discussion of the fears themselves or the patient's beliefs about their fears. Therefore, it is likely that cognitions are being changed as the patient is undergoing exposure procedures, although this is a point of some contention in CBT. Whisman (1993), for example found only tentative evidence that cognitive mediation was responsible for the changes in client outcome due to CBT. Furthermore, clients' engagement and involvement in treatment has been shown to be an important predictor of success in cognitive therapy.

Behavior therapy for phobics is based on exposure treatment that may use different techniques. All of the techniques ultimately expose the clients to their fear. Two types of techniques used are imaginal and in vivo.

Imaginal technique allows for a minimum of anxiety. One imaginal technique is systematic desensitization. A person may become sensitized to a particular stimulus and learn to associate that stimulus to a particular situation (Bourne, 1995). Unfortunately, if that stimulus is anxiety, she or he may learn to strongly associate it to whatever situation she or he was in when it occurred. For fear of experiencing the same level of anxiety the person may avoid the situation in which it occurred. When the situation is avoided and no anxiety occurs, the avoidance is reinforced. Therefore continuous avoidance of that particular situation may occur. This is how phobias may begin.

It is important for phobics to unlearn or break that association. Obviously, as previously mentioned, to continue to avoid the situation only strengthens the association. Confronting the situation to weaken and sever the association becomes necessary. This can be done through a process of desensitization—imaginal or in vivo.

In imaginal desensitization, clients are taught relaxation techniques and then enter, through imagination, the situation they find frightening. As the anxiety increases, they are guided to use the relaxation techniques to begin associating the feeling of peacefulness and relaxation with the feared stimuli, opposing the anxiety that is presently associated with the situation. Anxiety and relaxation are incompatible; therefore, the goal is to become and remain relaxed while imagining the previously feared situation. Bourne

(1995) states that imagery desensitization depends upon the ability of the patient to reach a deep state of relaxation, the establishment of a hierarchy of feared situations, the patient's ability to visualize in detail, and the regular practice of the desensitization techniques.

A hierarchy of aspects of a feared situation should be established, beginning with the lowest anxiety-provoking aspect to the highest anxiety-provoking aspect of the situation. This allows clients to gradually master their fear through the behavioral principle of successive approximations to desired behavior when approaching the feared situation. Once the hierarchy is constructed, the client begins with the situation that will cause the least anxiety and begins to imagine him or herself in that situation, as vividly as possible, while employing the relaxation techniques. It is important to continue this until the level of anxiety decreases. It is also important to begin with an aspect of the situation that arouses only a mild anxiety level so the patient does not become overwhelmed with anxiety and unable to continue.

To being practicing this technique, the client should alternate between visualizing the situation and experiencing deep relaxation (Bourne, 1995). It is important that the client takes time to become completely relaxed using whatever technique is taught or works best. The client places himself or herself in a favorite place where they have felt calm, relaxed, and safe before. Once in a complete state of relaxation, the client is instructed to visualize the first scenario on the hierarchy for only up to a minute, avoiding feelings of anxiety while imagining only confidence and calm. Then the client proceeds to the next step on the hierarchy. If anxiety is felt, the client is instructed to continue visualizing and remain in the scene while focusing on the relaxation technique. The client should then imagine handling the situation in a calm, confident manner. The client then alternates between the favorite site where deep relaxation occurs, and the phobic situation. Once anxiety no longer occurs when at the phobic site, the client is instructed to move another step higher on the hierarchy. If faced with an enormous amount of anxiety at any level of the hierarchy, remove yourself from the scene and go back to the favorite spot until complete relaxation occurs again. Do not move on to a new step in the hierarchy until the previous step no longer holds any anxiety. It is important to practice these steps approximately 15 minutes each day. With a new day's practice, she or he begins at the level on the hierarchy where the anxiety had been replaced with feelings of relaxation.

Another imaginal technique is flooding. In imaginal flooding the client begins at the top of the anxiety hierarchy and is instructed to imagine situations that provide high anxiety for a longer period of time (Foa & Steketee, 1987). It appears that flooding may be more effective for agoraphobics due to the increased arousal, assuming it is physiological arousal that agoraphobics fear.

While it is sometimes suggested that the client begin with imagery desensitization, it is essential to employ real-life desensitization (exposure therapy) to obtain complete recovery (Bourne, 1997). Unlike imaginal techniques, in vivo exposure focuses the client to confront the fear in real life. In vivo exposure has been found to be more effective than imaginal (Foa & Steketee, 1987). Like systematic desensitization, this is ideally done in small, graduated increments. Agoraphobia, social phobias, and many specific phobias are best treated with in vivo desensitization (Bourne, 1997; Foa & Steketee, 1987). Again, it appears that behavior interventions may be more efficacious than cognitive interventions.

The treatment can be very successful and it is likely to be maintained after termination with even further improvement occurring (Bourne, 1997). However, it takes dedication, desire, and commitment on the part of the client. The association of anxiety and the situation may be strong, and attempting to sever the association may cause considerable discomfort. But with sufficient commitment to face the fearful situations and perseverance in practicing repeated exposure, complete recovery can occur.

In vivo desensitization uses the same fundamental rationale and procedure as imagery desensitization, except those modifications necessary to handle the real-life aspects of the problem. Guidelines for the clinician follow:

1. Set clear goals as to what you wish to accomplish, and then break those goals down into manageable steps by creating a hierarchy.
2. Begin the exposure at the first level of the hierarchy. Encourage the client to stay in the situation until the anxiety begins to feel unmanageable, and then leave the situation.
3. Once the anxiety has subsided, the client should return to the situation. This is very different than escaping or avoiding the situation, which might ultimately lead to reinforcing the phobia.
4. Ask the client to do one practice session per day.

Bourne (1997) stated that it is important that clients be willing to take risks. This may be an uncomfortable process; therefore, dedication to mastering the phobia is necessary. Do not attempt to force clients to stay in the situation. Be willing to allow them to step back and let the anxiety decrease before returning to the phobic situation. Teach the clients coping skills to deal with panic or anxiety. Encourage positive thoughts and feedback, go at the clients' own pace, and make sure progress is rewarded. Very importantly, regular practice is needed. Prepare clients for good days and bad days and stress that this is a normal part of the process. Make sure that they expect to have feelings that are uncomfortable; if this was easy, no one would have phobias.

While practicing in vivo desensitization, it is important for clients to remember that there may be some difficult times, uncomfortable feelings, and anxiety. However, it is also important to stress that this treatment is highly successful and with proper guidance and regular practice can conquer phobias.

CASE STUDY

One case, which exemplifies the more recent turn toward exposure response prevention, involves a young woman who came into treatment due to a bird phobia (Phillipson, 2000). Because she lived in a large city, the ever-present pigeons were a daily formidable obstacle, which progressively made her life more challenged and limited. The first sessions were spent in the assessment of her fear and its magnitude to determine the appropriateness of her behavior to the situation. It was concluded that the fear was not within the normal range of overt behavior, covert feelings, or physiological reaction to the situation. Therefore, a hierarchy was developed of feared situations that might be related to the appearance of her feared stimuli, a pigeon. For example, it was easier for her to look at a picture of a bird than to see a live bird in a cage. It was less traumatic for her to see a live bird in a cage than to see a live bird not confined to a cage. In this manner, a hierarchy of her fears was formulated. Within the first two sessions of her treatment program, the development of a hierarchy was established.

As is the case with most phobias, the focal point of her anxiety had nothing to do with what would generally be considered the threatening feature of the animal or situation. Rather, her predominant focus entailed a severe panic reaction to the sight of the eye of the bird. As an individual with a phobia continues to live in fear of the stimuli, avoidance of any contact with the stimuli occurs, and the fear grows. Not only does the fear grow toward the specific stimuli, but it begins to generalize. For example, an individual with a fear of contracting AIDS might avoid blood. The fear of blood may then result in the avoidance of any place he or she might come to contact with blood (e.g., a hospital). Eventually, the fear of blood may generalize to a fear of anything seen that could be blood (e.g., a red spot). In the case of this client with the fear of pigeons, the reaction had generalized to the extent that even the eagle posted on the side of a U.S. Postal Service truck was associated with moderate levels of anxiety.

In developing a hierarchy, it was determined which contact could occur that would cause minimal anxiety. The bottom of the hierarchy (i.e., the item least feared on the hierarchy) began with viewing a basic drawing of a bird. Moving up the hierarchy, contact gradually grew closer such as touching the drawing of the bird, viewing a photograph of a pigeon, touching a photograph of the pigeon, viewing a pigeon through glass, viewing a pigeon in a cage, standing at a distance from pigeons in a park, moving closer to the pigeons in the park, feeding a large group of pigeons, and finally, allowing them to peck at her shoe. Treatment progressed rapidly and steadily as the client in session was willing to participate actively in confronting each of the feared items. It is important that the patient be committed to overcoming the fear. This client confronted each item such that the anxiety would not exceed a level 3 (on a scale of 1 to 10) and remain with the associated distress while cognitively assessing her tolerance and willingness to cope with the unsettling experience. Over the course of 3 months, she participated in regular weekly homework assignments, which entailed having her replicate the exposure in vivo originally introduced in the context of the therapy session. In other words, beginning with the bottom of the hierarchy (e.g., viewing a picture of the pigeon) she was to view this picture several times each day, allowing the anxiety to continue to decrease. When the anxiety had reduced, the next level of the hierarchy had now become less of a threat to her and was introduced as the next assignment. After working through all the levels of the hierarchy, the greatest fear held a lower degree of fear. Upon completion of treatment, the client was willing to feed a large group of pigeons and have them come into contact with her shoe and not experience more than a level 1 visceral reaction. She demonstrated no avoidant behavior or escape responses after the termination of treatment. At 6-month and 1-year follow-ups, she described no relapse and indicated that she would engage in self-directed exposure exercises as a means of maintaining her progress. The self-directed exposure exercises were a replication of the exercises that had been conducted during the course of treatment.

CONCLUSION

"What treatment, by whom, is most effective for this individual with that specific problem, under which set of circumstances, and how does it come about?" (Paul, 1969, p. 44). Menzies (1996) reminds us that traditional research has often failed to answer this question to the satisfaction of clinicians. Equally disturbing, Menzies also points to a claim about treatment for phobias by Barlow, Hayes, and Nelson (1984), which states: "Despite the well-advanced conclusions of this progression of research, and despite numerous examples of successful clinical innovation, it is probably safe to say that the majority of fears and phobias are still treated by nonexposurebased methods around the world" (p. 45). This brings us back to the out-lived and ongoing separation between researcher and clinician. Research overwhelmingly shows CBT, especially exposure-based methods, to be the most efficacious form of treatment for all phobias. Therefore, it seems that where we go from here is not necessarily more research to offer more sup-port for "What treatment, by whom, is most effective for this individual with that specific problem, under which set of circumstances, and how does it come about?" (Paul, 1969, p. 44), but how to get researchers and clinicians to join forces. Our ultimate goal, as always, should be to find and practice what is supported to be the most effective treatment course and therefore the most likely beneficial outcome for our patients.

Cognitive-behavioral therapy is the treatment of choice when dealing with any type of phobia, yet some clinicians appear to be unaware of this. Therefore, we need to focus on how to get this information to those it would most benefit. With this information in the hands of competent cli-nicians, individuals who suffer from phobias can find relief.

REFERENCES

American Psychiatric Association. (1994). *Diagnostic and statistical manual of mental disorders.* Washington, DC: Author.

American Psychological Association Task Force on Psychological Inter-vention Guidelines. (1995). *Template for developing guidelines: Interventions for mental disorders and psychological aspects of physical disorders.* Washington, DC: American Psychological Association.

Barlow, D. H., Hayes, S. C., & Nelson, R. D. (1984). *The Scientist Practitioner: Research and Accountability in Clinical and Educational Settings.* New York: Pergamon.

Beckham, J. C., Vrana, S. R., May, J. G., Gustafson, D. J., & Smith, G. R. (1990). Emotional processing and fear measurement synchrony as indicators of treatment outcome in fear of flying. *Journal of Behavior Therapy and Experimental Psychiatry, 21,* 153–162.

Biran, M., & Wilson, G. T. (1981). Treatment of phobic disorders using cog-nitive and exposure methods: A self-efficacy analysis. *Journal of Consulting and Clinical Psychology, 49,* 886–899.

Bourne, E. L. (1995). *The anxiety and phobia workbook.* Oakland, CA: New Harbinger.

Chambless, D. L. (1990). Spacing of exposure sessions in treatment of ago-raphobia and simple phobia. *Behavior Therapy, 21,* 217–229.

Chambless, D. L., & Hollon, S. D. (1998). Defining empirically supported therapies. *Journal of Consulting and Clinical Psychology, 66,* 7–18.

Denholtz, M. S., & Mann, E. T. (1975). An automated audiovisual treatment of phobias administered by non-professionals. *Journal of Behavior Therapy and Experimental Psychiatry, 6,* 111–115.

Emmelkamp, P. M. G., & Mersch, P. P. (1982). Cognition and exposure in vivo in the treatment of agoraphobia: Short-term and delayed effects. *Cognitive Research and Therapy, 18,* 77–90.

Foa, E. B., & Steketee, G. (1987). Behavioral treatment of phobics and obsessive-compulsives. In N. S. Jacobsen (Ed.), *Psychotherapists in clinical practice* (pp. 89–134). New York: Guilford Press.

Graziano, A. M., DeGiovani, I. S., & Garcia, K. A. (1979). Behavioral treatment of children's fears: A review. *Psychological Bulletin, 86,* 804–830.

Howard, W. A., Murphy, S. M., & Clarke, J. C. (1983). The nature and treatment of fear of flying: A controlled investigation. *Behavior Therapy, 14,* 557–567.

Kazdin, A. E., & Weisz, J. R. (1998). Identifying and developing empirically supported child and adolescent treatments. *Journal of Consulting and Clinical Psychology, 66,* 19–36.

Kendall, P. C. (1998). Empirically supported psychological therapies. *Journal of Consulting and Clinical Psychology, 66,* 3–6.

King, N. J., Hamilton, D. I., & Ollendick, T. H. (1988). *Children's phobias: A behavioral perspective.* New York: Wiley.

Knell, S. M. (2000). Cognitive-behavioral play therapy for childhood fears and phobias. In H. G. Kaduson & C. E. Schaefer (Eds.), *Short term play therapy for children* (pp. 3–27). New York: Guilford Press.

Marks, I. M. (1969). *Fears and phobias.* New York: Academic Press.

Marks, I. M. (1987). *Fears, phobias and rituals.* Oxford: Oxford University Press.

Menzies, R. G. (1996). Individual response patterns and treatment matching in the phobic disorders: A review. *British Journal of Clinical Psychology, 35,* 1–10.

Miller, L. C., Barrett, C. L., & Hampe, E. (1974). Phobias of childhood in a prescientific era. In A. Davids (Ed.), *Child personality and psychopathology: Current topics: Vol. 1* (pp. 89–134). New York: Wiley.

Ollendick, T. H., & King, N. J. (1998). Empirically supported treatments for children with phobic and anxiety disorders: Current status. *Journal of Clinical Child Psychology, 27,* 156–167.

Öst, L. G., Stridh, B. M., & Wolf, M. (1998). A clinical study of spider phobia: prediction of outcome after self-help and therapist-directed treatments. *Behaviour Research and Therapy, 36,* 17–35.

Otto, M. W. (2000). *Cognitive behavior therapy for social phobia: Theory, outcome, and future directions.* Unpublished manuscript, Massachusetts General Hospital and Harvard Medical School, Boston.

Paul, G. (1969). Behavior modification research: Design and tactics. In C.

M. Franks (Ed.), *Behavior therapy: Appraisal and status* (pp. 29–62). New York: McGraw-Hill.

Solyom, L., Shugar, R., Bryntwick, S., & Solyom, C. (1973). Treatment of fear of flying. *American Journal of Psychiatry, 130,* 423–427.

Thorpe, S. J., & Salkovskis, P. M. (1997). The effect of one-session treatment for spider phobia on attentional bias and beliefs. *British Journal of Clinical Psychology, 36,* 225–241.

Weisz, J. R., Weiss, B., Han, S. S., Granger, D. A., & Morton, T. (1995). Effects of psychotherapy with children and adolescents revisited: A meta-analysis of treatment outcome studies. *Psychological Bulletin, 117,* 450–468.

5

Panic Disorder

William C. Sanderson and Simon A. Rego

Panic disorder (PD) (with and without agoraphobia) is a debilitating condition with an estimated lifetime prevalence of 1.5% (American Psychiatric Association, 1994). Approximately twice as many women as men suffer from PD. Although PD typically first appears between late adolescence and early adulthood, it can also begin in childhood or in later life. While data on the course of PD are lacking, retrospective patient accounts indicate that PD appears to be a chronic condition that waxes and wanes in severity. Unfortunately, the chronicity of the disorder may be due, in part, to a lack of appropriate treatment.

As defined in the *Diagnostic and Statistical Manual of Mental Disorders* (*DSM-IV*; American Psychiatric Association, 1994), the essential feature of PD is the experience of recurrent, unexpected panic attacks. A panic attack is defined as a discrete period of intense fear or discomfort that develops abruptly and reaches a peak within ten minutes and is accompanied by at least *four* of the following thirteen somatic and cognitive symptoms: shortness of breath, dizziness, palpitations, trembling, sweating, feeling of choking, nausea/abdominal distress, depersonalization, paresthesias (numbness/tingling), flushes/chills, chest pain, fear of dying, fear of going crazy, or doing something uncontrolled. To warrant the diagnosis of PD in accordance with the *DSM-IV*, the individual must experience at least two unexpected panic attacks followed by at least one month of concern about having another panic attack. The frequency of attacks in individuals with PD varies widely, ranging from several attacks each day to only a handful of attacks per year.

Although community estimates suggest that approximately one-half of individuals who experience PD also develop agoraphobia, the prevalence of agoraphobia is much higher in clinical samples. In fact, the vast majority of PD patients seeking treatment present with agoraphobia. The *DSM-*

IV defines agoraphobia as the experience of anxiety in situations in which escape might be difficult or where help may not be immediately available in the event of the occurrence of a panic attack. Common agoraphobic situations include airplanes, buses, trains, elevators, being alone, being in a crowd of people, and so on. As a result of the anxiety experienced in these situations, individuals often develop phobic avoidance resulting in a constricted lifestyle. The severity of agoraphobia may range from relatively mild (e.g., travels unaccompanied when necessary but typically avoids traveling alone) to quite severe (e.g., unable to leave home alone).

THE COGNITIVE MODEL OF PANIC DISORDER

The cognitive model of PD is based on the proposition that panic attacks occur when individuals perceive certain somatic sensations as considerably more dangerous than they truly are and, as a result, interpret them to mean that they are about to experience sudden, imminent disaster (Clark, 1986). For example, individuals may develop a panic attack if they misinterpret heart palpitations as signaling an impending heart attack or misinterpret jittery, shaky feelings as indicating that they will lose control or go crazy.

Clark (1986) suggests that these "catastrophic misinterpretations" may arise not only from fear but also from a variety of other emotions (e.g., anger) or from other stimuli (e.g., caffeine, exercise). The vicious cycle culminating into a panic attack develops when a stimulus perceived as threatening creates feelings of apprehension. If the somatic sensations that accompany this state of apprehension are catastrophically misinterpreted, the individual experiences a further increase in apprehension, elevated somatic sensations, and so on, until a "full-blown" panic attack occurs.

The fact that PD patients report having thoughts of imminent danger during their panic attacks (e.g., heart attacks or insanity) and report that these thoughts typically occur after they notice specific bodily sensations, provides corroborative support for the cognitive model of panic. Other evidence in support of Clark's (1986) hypothesis is the finding that laboratory-provoked attacks may lead to similar physiological sensations in PD patients and normal controls, but only PD patients who catastrophically misinterpret these sensations will go on to develop panic attacks (cf. Sanderson & Wetzler, 1990). Furthermore, only patients who develop panic attacks in the laboratory following the administration of a panicogenic substance report fears of going crazy or losing self-control. Additional support for Clark's cognitive model comes from studies demonstrating that panic attacks can be alleviated with cognitive techniques, such as cognitive restructuring, which attempts to challenge and substitute catastrophic misinterpretations with more rational thoughts.

EMPIRICALLY SUPPORTED TREATMENT COMPONENTS

The following psychological interventions have been shown to be effective, either alone or in a "package" of treatment strategies, for PD in controlled research studies (for a detailed review of empirically supported psychological treatments, see Woody & Sanderson, 1998).

Psychoeducation

By the time PD patients consult with a mental health professional, they typically have been to many different doctors without receiving a clear diagnosis and explanation of PD. In the absence of such information, these patients often imagine that they are going to die, go crazy, or lose control. In almost all cases, they suspect that the doctor has overlooked some life-threatening physical condition that would account for their symptomatology. Therefore, the psychoeducation phase consists of a didactic presentation about PD, within the framework of the cognitive behavioral model of panic (cf. Barlow & Craske, 1989).

During the initial session(s), anxiety, panic, and agoraphobia are defined. Each symptom is identified as a feature of PD, and shown to be harmless. Common myths about the danger of panic attacks (e.g., panic attacks are a sign of an undetected brain tumor, palpitations cause heart attacks, hyperventilation leads to fainting, etc.) are debunked. The development of the disorder is understood as a psychological response to stress, and avoidance behavior and anticipatory anxiety are viewed as ways to ward off a recurrence of the panic attacks.

Written materials, such as pamphlets and books, are valuable educational tools because they may be reread whenever the patient desires. We recommend several excellent "self-help" books or websites that offer simple, supportive information about PD (e.g., Barlow & Craske, 1989; Burns, 1989; Wilson, 1987; National Institute of Mental Health, Panic Disorder: www.nimh.nih.gov/anxiety/panicmenu.cfm). In addition, we encourage patients to join the Anxiety Disorders Association of America (6000 Executive Blvd., Rockville, MD 20852; www.adaa.org). For a nominal fee, patients receive a bimonthly newsletter providing self-help tips and educational information (e.g., latest research findings), and have access to many other valuable resources. In this way, psychoeducation becomes an ongoing venture for the patient and not just one component of the therapy.

Cognitive Restructuring

The cognitive restructuring component of CBT derives from Beck's seminal work on how faulty information processing may underlie anxiety and related dysfunctional behaviors (Beck & Emery, 1985). Therapeutic change is achieved as these faulty cognitions (i.e., thoughts, beliefs, and assumptions) are identified, and then subjected to rigorous reality testing. The first step is to help the patient identify how certain cognitions accentuate or provoke panic. This is done by retrospectively examining the thoughts, beliefs, and assumptions elicited during a typical panic or anxiety episode. The first and most recent panic attacks are vividly remembered, and a detailed discussion of those two experiences is a useful place to begin this examination. Through a series of questions, the therapist tries to determine the patient's idiosyncratic panic sequence and to uncover unrealistic catastrophic thoughts. Under such questioning, the validity of these cognitions are implicitly and explicitly challenged.

A typical panic sequence follows:

1. I was sitting in a meeting at work.
2. I noticed my heart began to beat faster (physical symptom).
3. I assumed these palpitations were the early signs of a panic attack, and that I would lose control and start to yell. Everyone would think I was crazy! (Catastrophic thought).
4. I became even more anxious, worried about losing control, and started to perspire profusely (escalation of physical symptom).
5. I excused myself from the meeting (escape and avoidance).
6. I felt depressed and discouraged because I couldn't even handle an innocuous work meeting (hopelessness).

The above description of a typical panic sequence reveals the PD patient's interior monologue. In therapy, it is necessary to make these private thoughts explicit since most patients are unaware of their own thinking. For the most part, people process information automatically, and stimuli are interpreted rapidly. There is also a tendency to deny catastrophic ways of thinking because these beliefs seem so incredible once the panic attack has subsided. The therapeutic setting should promote the patient's sense of comfort and acceptance in order to facilitate disclosure. But in addition, we recommend that patients self-monitor their cognitions during episodes of panic. A written numbered format may be used, as in the example above. After several sessions of reviewing these panic-related cognitions, a clear panic sequence emerges, and patients begin to appreciate the role cognitions play.

Once the patient becomes aware of the importance of their cognitions in eliciting and fueling their panic attacks, then they are in a position to reevaluate the validity of these cognitions, and ultimately to challenge them. In particular, catastrophic misinterpretations of panic-related somatic cues are targeted (Clark, 1986). But other common misinterpretations include the overestimation of the consequences of panic (e.g., public humiliation, losing one's job, or interpersonal rejection).

We use a "thought record" to quickly identify the patient's thoughts, examine their validity, and challenge the patient to respond with more rational thoughts (cf. Sanderson & McGinn, 1997). The patient is provided with a list of 10 cognition distortions, misinterpretations, or types of illogic as defined by Burns (1989). By identifying distortions, the patient is able to correct the illogical conclusion by substituting a more rational response. It is important to note that cognitive restructuring is not "positive thinking," but instead, is a focus on teaching people to think realistically (i.e., weighing out evidence).

The final phase of cognitive restructuring is to decatastrophize the situation with the patient, especially when dealing with agoraphobic avoidance. This is easily accomplished through a series of questions such as: What if your worst fears came true? Would they really be as bad as you imagine? Consider a patient who believes they will have a panic attack on a plane, causing them to scream wildly and try to escape. In fact, if their worst fears were realized and they did have a panic attack, the most likely outcome would be a feeling of great discomfort, not screaming, attempts to escape, and embarrassment. Decatastrophizing greatly reduces the patient's need to avoid panic-related situations.

Respiratory Control

Respiratory control helps the patient regain a sense of control over the somatic features of panic and anxiety. Patients are taught a method of breathing that increases relaxation and prevents hyperventilation (Clark, Salkovskis, & Chalkley, 1985). Hyperventilation initiates a cascade of somatic symptoms such as dizziness, chest pain, breathlessness, and parasthesias that culminate in panic. These symptoms instill a frightening sense that one's body is out of control.

Under stress and anxiety, respiration rate often increases, characterized by the use of chest muscles and short, shallow breaths. To combat this tendency, the patient is taught diaphragmatic breathing (i.e., breathing that involves in and out movement of the abdomen, not chest) at a regular rate (i.e., approximately 12 breaths per minute). This exercise is then practiced outside of the session in many different situations. The patients learn to quickly control their breathing, and come to recognize that this is an effective strategy that they can rely on in panic-provoking situations.

Relaxation Training

Relaxation training is a progressive muscle exercise also intended to help a patient gain a greater sense of control over his or her body. It is practiced daily as a way to identify and decrease tension that might otherwise escalate into a panic attack. The basic technique involves tensing and relaxing muscles to achieve a more serene state. Specific step-by-step details regarding this exercise may be found in an excellent text by Barlow and Cerny (1988).

Visualization

In therapy, discussion of anxiety-provoking situations and experiences is all too often devoid of the vivid images, associations, and emotion necessary to foster real change. Visualization is meant to enhance this dialogue. When the patient closes his or her eyes and imagines such situations, he or she is often flooded with anxiety. By confronting such anxiety-provoking situations in their mind's eye, patients learn how to cope before they have to confront them for real.

The therapist helps the patient to visualize the situation in as much detail as possible. As the patient describes the image, the therapist asks relevant questions about the associated thoughts and feelings. This is meant to elaborate the image, but it is also a useful assessment (reporting on cognitions and emotions in an imagined situation in the present is usually more accurate than recalling cognitions and emotions in a real situation from the past). In time, the patient is asked to visualize effective coping techniques and responses. In this way, visualization serves as an inoculation—if the patient can handle small amounts of manufactured anxiety, he or she will be better prepared to handle anxiety in a naturalistic setting.

Exposure

Exposure is the final component of CBT in which patients confronts anxiety- and panic-provoking stimuli. These phobic stimuli may be external situations or internal sensations (i.e., interoceptive desensitization). By repeatedly facing their anxiety in a structured situation, patients learn to develop appropriate coping mechanisms and becomes further inoculated.

Based on the patient's individualized hierarchy of feared situations, he or she is exposed to each of these situations in a progressive, systematic fashion, where the therapist guides the patient to use coping skills when confronting anxiety-provoking situations. Similarly, interoceptive exposure is based on the patient's individualized hierarchy of feared internal sensations (e.g., dizziness or palpitations). Exposure to these sensations may be achieved using idiosyncratic methods, such as overbreathing, spinning, and physical exertion (e.g., ride on an exercise bicycle for 2 minutes).

The use of a hierarchy of least-feared to most-feared stimuli allows the therapy to progress and build on past accomplishments. The patient first learns to cope with mildly anxiety-provoking situations, and later faces the more difficult situations. Facing anxiety within a supportive therapeutic setting helps the patient to utilize his or her newly developed coping skills.

The patient learns to tolerate anxiety without the need to escape. This lesson is passed on from one anxiety-provoking situation to the next.

As always, practice between sessions is expected and essential for rapid progress. We encourage patients to confront phobic stimuli at least three times during the week between sessions. First, the patient completes the exposure exercise with the assistance of the therapist, such as inducing heart palpitations by walking up and down stairs for three minutes, and later they practice this exercise at home. The patient's self-confidence soars as they realize that the therapist has confidence that they can handle this formerly anxiety-provoking experience on their own.

REVIEW OF EMPIRICAL SUPPORT OF CBT FOR PD

The treatment of PD has been studied extensively, with many "Type 1" (i.e., most methodologically stringent) studies supporting the efficacy of cognitive-behavioral interventions. These interventions typically included a combination of several of the treatment components described in the previous section, including a psychoeducation component, cognitive restructuring, respiratory control, relaxation training, visualization, and exposure (to external situations and/or interoceptive cues). As evidence for the cognitive-behavioral treatment (CBT) for PD accumulated, researchers shifted their focus to the comparison of cognitive-behavioral treatments with (a) nonspecific psychological interventions and (b) several of the medications that are typically used to treat PD. Next, the research focused on comparing traditional cognitive-behavioral treatments with (a) new, briefer forms of cognitive-behavioral therapy, (b) other psychological treatments, and (c) several of the core "components" of cognitive-behavioral therapy, delivered in isolation. Most recently, as the efficacy of several of the core components delivered in isolation were established, studies have begun to compare the core components with medications. Several major studies highlighting each of these areas are described below. A summary of these appears in Table 5.1.

CBT versus Nonspecific Treatments

Shear, Pilkonis, Cloitre, and Leon (1994) compared CBT with a manualized nonprescriptive treatment (NPT) for PD. Subjects were divided into two groups, with each group receiving three sessions of panic-related information followed by 12 sessions of either NPT or a CBT package. The results indicated that 66% of the CBT group and 78% of the NPT group were free of panic for two weeks at posttreatment. Ten percent of the CBT subjects (versus 0% of the NPT subjects), however, had experienced four or more panic attacks in the 2 weeks posttreatment. At 6-month follow-up, 75% of

TABLE 5.1 Review of Empirical Support of CBT for PD

Study	CBT Components	Efficacy of CT	Comments
Beck, Sokol, Clark, Berchick, and Wright (1992)	"Cognitive strategies."	At 8 weeks, 71% of the CT subjects were panic-free. At 1-year follow-up, 87% of the CBT subjects were panic-free.	The focused CT group achieved significantly greater reductions in panic symptoms and general anxiety after 8 weeks of treatment than did a group receiving brief, supportive psychotherapy.
Black, Wesner, Bowers, and Gabel (1993)	Reproducing symptoms using various procedures, correcting misattributions, breathing exercises, positive affirmation statements, refocusing techniques, application of techniques in vivo.	At 4 weeks, 40% of the CT subjects were rated moderately improved or better, and 25% of the CT subjects were free of panic. At 8 weeks, the frequency of spontaneous and situational panic attacks decreased in 93% of subjects given CT, with 53% of the CT subjects being panic-free.	Fluvoxamine was found to be superior to CT on many variables and produced improvement earlier than CT. The CT group showed improvement, but this did not differ significantly from a placebo group for most comparisons.

TABLE 5.1 *(continued)*

Study	CBT Components	Efficacy of CT	Comments
Clark Salkovskis, Hackmann et al. (1994)	Cognitive procedures: identifying and challenging misinterpretations, substituting more realistic interpretations, restructuring images. Behavioral procedures: Inducing feared sensations, stopping safety behaviors.	At 3 months 90% of the CT subjects were panic-free and 80% reached high end-state functioning. At 6 months, 75% of the CT subjects were panic-free, and 65% reached high end-state functioning. At 15 months, 85% of the CT subjects were panic-free, and 70% reached high end-state functioning.	At 3 months, CT was superior to AR and imipramine; AR and imipramine were not significantly different from each other; CT produced a significantly greater number of subjects who were panic-free and had reached high end-state functioning than AR or imipramine; and there were no significant differences among any of the groups on the Beck Depression Inventory (BDI). At 6 months, there were no significant differences between CT and imipramine, and both were superior to AR; CT and imipramine did not differ in number of subjects who were panic-free or had reached high end-state functioning; and CT and imipramine were both superior to AR on the BDI.

TABLE 5.1 (continued)

Study	CBT Components	Efficacy of CT	Comments
			At 15 months, CT was again superior to AR and imipramine, with AR and imipramine not differing from each other; and CT was superior to AR on number of subjects who were panic-free and had reached high end-state functioning, but was not significantly different from imipramine.
Côté, Gauthier, Laberge, Cormier, and Plamondon (1994)	(a) Presentation of treatment rationale and information about PD. (b) Training in anxiety-management techniques, progressive muscle relaxation, distraction strategies, and coping self-statements. (c) "Cognitive therapy." (d) Exposure to internal anxiety cues and panic symptoms. (e) Exposure to external anxiety cues.	At posttreatment, 82% in the reduced-therapist group and 90% in the therapist-directed group were panic-free. At 6 months, 91% in the reduced therapist group and 90% in the therapist directed group were panic-free. At 12 months, 91% in the reduced therapist and 100% in the therapist directed group were panic-free.	This study lends support to the assertion that PD can be successfully treated with CBT, using either reduced therapist contact or a therapist-directed approach. Both procedures can have long-lasting effects.

TABLE 5.1 (continued)

Study	CBT Components	Efficacy of CT	Comments
Craske, Brown, and Barlow (1991)	The AR condition involved training in progressive muscle relaxation, followed by its application to items from an individualized hierarchy of anxiety-producing situations. The IE+C condition consisted of identification and challenging of anxiety-provoking thoughts, breathing retraining, and the application of cognitive and breathing skills to a hierarchy of anxiety-provoking items.	At 6 months (excluding drop-outs), 22% of the AR, 71% of the IE+C, and 83% of the combination groups achieved panic free status and high end-state functioning. At 6 months (including drop-outs), 14% of the AR, 62.5% of the IE+C, and 50% of the combination groups achieved panic-free and high end-state functioning At 24 months (excluding drop-outs), 56% of the AR, 87% of the IE+C, and 60% of the combination groups were panic-free and 44%, 53%, and 50% of the AR, IE+C, and combination groups, respectively, reached high end-state functioning.	Panic attacks were more effectively controlled by interoceptive exposure and cognitive restructuring treatments than by relaxation training.

TABLE 5.1 (*continued*)

Study	CBT Components	Efficacy of CT	Comments
		At 24 months (including drop-outs), 36% of the AR, 81% of the IE+C, and 43% of the combination groups were panic-free, and 29%, 50% and 36% of the AR, IE+C, and combination groups, respectively, reached high end-state functioning.	
Craske, Maidenberg, and Bystritsky (1995)	Four sessions of CBT: 1. Education about the nature of anxiety and panic, the physiology underlying panic attack symptoms, and the principles of cognitive restructuring. 2. Continuation of cognitive restructuring and the introduction of breathing retraining.	At posttreatment, 53% of the CBT subjects reported no panic attacks, and 38% of the CBT subjects achieved clinically significant change.	CBT led to significant reductions in worry about the recurrence of panic, and in the overall rating of phobic distress. Nondirective supportive therapy did not produce any significant effects.

TABLE 5.1 (continued)

Study	CBT Components	Efficacy of CT	Comments
	3. Continuation of cognitive restructuring and the introduction of interoceptive exposure. 4. Review of the concepts and skills learned in the first three sessions.		
Klosko, Barlow, Tassinari, and Cerny (1990)	Rationale and education about panic disorder, with an emphasis on exposure to interoceptive cues; cognitive approaches; progressive muscle relaxation training; and respiration training.	At posttreatment (for completers), 87% of the CBT subjects were free of panic attacks.	CBT was significantly more effective than both placebo and wait-list conditions on most measures. Alprazolam did not differ significantly from either the CBT or placebo conditions. Alprazolam may work more quickly than CBT, but may also interfere with the effects of CBT treatment.

TABLE 5.1 *(continued)*

Study	CBT Components	Efficacy of CT	Comments
Öst, Westling, and Hellström (1993)	AR: description and analysis, various forms of relaxation training, and a review. Exposure: gradual training in phobic situations (including an introduction and analysis, instructions for coping with panic during exposure, and a summary session). CT: rationale and analysis, developing positive self-instructions and cognitive coping procedures, attribution training, cognitive restructuring of images and attitudes, and a summary.	Clinically significant improvement was fulfilled by 87% of the AR, 80% of the E, and 60% of the CT subjects at the end of treatment; and by 85% of the AR, 69% of the E, and 67% of the CT subjects at follow-up.	All three treatments yielded significant improvements that were maintained at follow-up. Between group differences were observed on only two measures, with both favoring AR over CT.

TABLE 5.1 *(continued)*

Study	CBT Components	Efficacy of CT	Comments
Shear, Pilkonis, Cloitre, and Leon (1994)	Explanation of an ethological model of panic. Breathing retraining, progressive muscle relaxation, identification of cognitive errors, exposure to interceptive cues, exposure to agoraphobic situations.	At posttreatment, 66% of the CBT subjects were free of panic for 2 weeks, but 10% of the CBT subjects had experienced four or more panic episodes. At 6 months 75% of the CBT subjects were panic-free.	posttreatment and 6-month follow-up assessments revealed a good response to both treatments. A high rate of panic remission and significant improvement in associated symptoms was observed for subjects in each treatment group. The results raise questions about the specificity of CBT.

TABLE 5.1 (continued)

Study	CBT Components	Efficacy of CT	Comments
Telch, et al. (1993)	1. Education and corrective information about panic. 2. Cognitive therapy techniques aimed at helping to identify, monitor, and alter faulty appraisals of threat that contribute to panic occurrence. 3. Training in slow diaphragmatic breathing. 4. Interoceptive exposure exercises designed to reduce the fear of somatic sensations.	At posttreatment, the mean recovery rate was 81% for the CBT subjects versus 30.5% for untreated controls. Using a more stringent "composite" criteria, 64% of the treated group and 9% of the untreated group evidenced recovery at posttreatment. At 6 months, there was a 79% "mean" recovery rate and a 63% "composite" recovery rate in the treated group.	CBT is a viable alternative to pharmacotherapy in the treatment of PD. This study used a more stringent, normative approach that conceptualized recovery as the extent to which subjects attained normal functioning on three clinically relevant dimensions (panic attacks, anxiety, and agoraphobic avoidance). The authors argued that while the more stringent criteria would provide a more conservative estimate of recovery, it would be a more ecologically valid index of recovery.

subjects in the CBT group and 68% of subjects in the NPT group were free of panic. Both treatments had significant pre–post and pre–follow-up differences on each measure of PD symptoms. No significant differences were found between the groups before treatment, after treatment, or at 6-month follow-up.

Therefore, the researchers concluded that CBT and NPT were equivalent in almost every way, and that both treatments were powerful in achieving relief of panic symptoms. It is important to note, however, that while the treatment gains were maintained at 6 months for both groups, the CBT subjects continued to show further improvement in their panic symptoms, while the NPT subjects showed a slight decline. The NPT subjects, however, showed further improvement on several secondary symptoms in which CBT subjects showed either no or minimal improvement.

As a result, the authors suggested that CBT is not necessary to achieve relief of panic disorder symptoms. It is also important to note that they did not find support for the hypothesis that breaking the link between bodily sensations and fear is necessary for panic remission (as predicted by the cognitive model). Recall, however, that in order to ensure the credibility of the control treatment (which was necessary in order for meaningful comparisons to be made), each group received three sessions of panic-related information. As this is a typical, if not central, component of CBT, it may have confounded the results. In addition, despite the fact that a manual was used for each condition, it should be noted that when treatment adherence was checked, the CBT group only received a rating of 4.5 out of a maximum score of 8.

CBT versus Medications

Black, Wesner, Bowers, and Gabel (1993) used a double-blind design to compare fluvoxamine, an abbreviated, manualized cognitive therapy (CT), and a placebo in the treatment of PD. Using both completer and endpoint analyses, the fluvoxamine group showed significantly greater improvement than both the CT and placebo groups on the Clinical Anxiety Scale (CAS) and Clinical Global Impression (CGI) ratings by Week 8. When using an endpoint analysis, both the fluvoxamine and CT groups showed a greater reduction than the placebo group in the mean panic attack severity score at Weeks 4 and 8. When using a completer analysis, however, only the fluvoxamine group was superior to the placebo group. In addition, significantly more subjects in the fluvoxamine group achieved panic-free status—a finding that became apparent after only 4 weeks of treatment. While the CT subjects also showed some improvement (see below), they were not statistically better off than the placebo subjects.

Support for the use of CT for panic disorder includes the fact that the frequency of spontaneous and situational panic attacks decreased in 93%

of subjects treated with CT, with 53% of subjects achieving panic-free status by Week 8. Subjects treated with CT also showed significant improvement on several other measures (e.g., CGI, and mean weekly panic attack severity score) at Weeks 4 and 8 when compared with the placebo group. The major outcome of this study, however, was that CT was not found to be superior to fluvoxamine on *any* measures, while fluvoxamine was found to be superior to CT on several measures. With regard to the poor efficacy of CT, Black and colleagues (1993) do note that their findings are in contrast to those of Sokol and associates (1989), as well as Klosko, Barlow, Tassinari, and Cerny (1990). Black et al. also acknowledge that their study did not examine relapse, did not assess for symptoms occurring at the discontinuation of fluvoxamine, and failed to measure long-term effects. Finally, the authors note that the CT was only provided for 8 weeks (instead of the more typical 12 weeks), which may have had an impact on the efficacy of the treatment.

Klosko et al. (1990) compared alprazolam with CBT in the treatment of PD. The CBT group received 15 sessions using a detailed cognitive-behavioral therapy manual, which included a rationale and education component, an emphasis on exposure to interoceptive cues, cognitive approaches, progressive relaxation training, and respiration training. At posttreatment, the alprazolam and CBT treatment groups were significantly more improved than a wait-list group on measures of panic frequency and intensity. Also of note was the fact that approximately half of the study completers achieved high end-state functioning (achieving a rating of less than 4 [nonclinical severity] on the Anxiety Disorders Interview Schedule—Revised [ADIS-R]). In addition, the CBT group was significantly more improved than the wait-list group (both with and without dropouts) on measures of panic and general anxiety. For the alprazolam group, 63% of subjects were panic-free before the taper withdrawal, meaning that slightly fewer alprazolam subjects were experiencing panic attacks in comparison with posttreatment. Of those who still were experiencing panic, however, the attacks were more frequent and more severe in comparison with posttreatment. Therefore, the authors concluded that CBT was an effective treatment for PD. Over 85% of subjects receiving CBT achieved panic-free status for 2 weeks at the end of treatment, which was significantly better than the wait-list and placebo groups. While this result was not significantly better than the alprazolam group, the alprazolam group itself did not differ from the CBT or the placebo groups.

Briefer Forms of CBT

Beck, Sokol, Clark, Berchick, and Wright (1992) examined the short- and long-term effects of a focused (12-week) course of cognitive therapy (CT) for PD. The authors also used an 8-week brief supportive psychotherapy

(BST) group (based on Carl Rogers' "nondirective" therapy) as a comparison group. Using both clinician ratings and patient self-ratings, they found that the focused CT accomplished significantly greater reductions in both panic symptoms and general anxiety after only 8 weeks of treatment. At the 8-week point, 71% of the CT group were panic-free, compared with 25% of the BST group. After 12 weeks, 94% of the CT group were panic-free. At a 1-year follow-up, 87% of the CT group remained panic-free and continued to have significantly lower scores (compared to their pretreatment scores) on *all* of the assessment measures used in the study (e.g., Beck Depression Inventory, Beck Anxiety Inventory, and Specific Fear Inventory). Based on these results, the authors concluded that (a) panic attacks are particularly sensitive to cognitive interventions, and (b) because of the relatively low rate of relapse and absence of side effects, CT offers a promising, nonpharmacological alternative for the treatment of PD.

Côté, Gauthier, Laberge, Cormier, and Plamondon (1994) examined reduced therapist contact in the cognitive behavioral treatment of PD. The participants in this study were assigned to either 17 weeks of therapist-directed or reduced-contact treatment. In the reduced contact group, treatment was self-administered over 17 weeks with a manual and limited therapist contact (seven irregularly scheduled meetings at the clinic and eight brief, irregularly scheduled telephone consultations). Interestingly, the authors found that both methods of administration produced significant and comparable improvements on all of the outcome measures.

For frequency of panic attacks, there was a significant reduction from pre- to posttreatment, with no significant changes beyond the posttreatment period. For apprehension of panic attacks there was a significant improvement from pre- to posttreatment, from posttreatment to 6-month follow-up, and from posttreatment to 12-month follow-up. At posttreatment, 90% of subjects in the therapist-directed group and 82% of subjects in the reduced therapist-contact group were panic-free. At 6-month follow-up, 90% of subjects in the therapist-directed group and 91% of subjects in the reduced therapist-contact group were panic-free. At 12-month follow-up, 100% of subjects in the therapist-directed group and 91% of subjects in the reduced therapist-contact group were panic-free.

Significant improvements were also found for both groups on a measure of mobility and agoraphobic cognitions, on a measure of fear of bodily sensations, and on three measures of perceived self-efficacy. Treatment credibility and expectancies were high in both conditions, and no significant differences were found between the groups. While there were no significant therapist effects found, the reduced therapist contact was determined to be significantly more efficient (i.e., percentage of improvement on each panic attack variable divided by the total therapist contact time) than therapist-directed treatment in reducing the frequency of panic attacks (from pre- to posttreatment, from pretreatment to 6-month follow-up, and from pretreatment to 12-month follow-up).

Therefore, Côté, et al. (1994) concluded that their findings support the notion that panic disorder can be successfully treated with CBT, using either the traditional therapist-directed or reduced therapist-contact approach, and that both procedures can have long-lasting effects. In this case, the therapeutic effects for both treatments were clinically as well as statistically significant. At posttreatment follow-ups, the percentage of panic-free subjects ranged from 82% to 100%, and half of the subjects who were not entirely "panic-free" after the treatment had only one panic attack during the entire follow-up assessment period (which was longer than normal in this study).

Craske, Maidenberg, and Bystritsky (1995) compared a brief form of CBT with a nondirective supportive treatment (NST) for PD. The participants received four 60- to 90-minute sessions of a manualized CBT or NST. The authors found that CBT subjects reported less worry at posttreatment than pretreatment, while the worry ratings did not change over time for the NST subjects. The number of agoraphobic situations avoided (as rated by the interviewer), however, did not change over time or differ between the groups. In addition, neither anxiety sensitivity nor depression scores were reduced significantly over time and did not differ between the groups.

At posttreatment, 53% of CBT subjects reported they did not experience panic attacks, compared with 23% of NST subjects, a nonsignificant difference. Of the subjects treated with CBT, 38% had clinically significant results, compared with 8% of those treated with NST, which the authors state "approached" significance. The authors also note that while 4 weeks of CBT was somewhat effective, it was considerably less effective than what is typically achieved in 12 to 16 weeks of treatment. They also point out that NST did not produce any significant effects in this study.

Telch, Lucas, Schmidt, Hanna, Jaimez, and Lucas (1993) examined cognitive-behavioral group treatment (CBGT) for PD. Participants were matched for panic severity and then randomly assigned to either a treatment or delay group. The treatment took place in small groups of four to six subjects. The subjects received twelve 90-minute sessions, delivered over an 8-week period. The delay group was measured at Weeks 0 and 9, and then offered the experimental treatment. The CBGT included four major treatment components: education, cognitive therapy techniques, training in methods of slow diaphragmatic breathing, and interoceptive exposure.

The results at posttreatment indicated that subjects receiving CGBT displayed marked improvement on all major indices of treatment outcome. In addition, these subjects scored significantly less pathological than untreated controls on all measures, even after controlling for between group differences at baseline. The authors also note that while the treated subjects achieved highly significant improvement on all measures, the untreated subjects failed to show significant improvement on any measure. For example, using clinical significance of treatment gains, Telch and colleagues (1993) found that the mean recovery at posttreatment was 81% for the CBT group, compared with 31% for the untreated controls. In addition, when using a more stringent "composite" recovery criterion, 64% of the treated group (versus 9% of the untreated group) evidenced recovery on the three selected measures at posttreatment. While recovery estimates at 6-month follow-up were essentially identical to those at posttreatment (suggesting a general trend for maintenance of improvement), two subjects did appear to have relapsed. Therefore, Telch and associates (1993) concluded that this study demonstrated the efficacy of CBGT for PD. A complete resolution of panic attacks was observed in over 85% of the treated cases, compared with only 30% for the delayed-treatment controls. Using a more stringent, normative conceptualization of recovery (which would be more conservative but also more ecologically valid), between 63% and 80% of the treatment group displayed full recovery—which the authors point out is comparable to results achieved in well-controlled drug trials. Yet, in contrast to the substantial relapse observed in drug treatment trials, the recovery estimates at 6-month posttreatment using CBGT were essentially identical to those observed at the 8-week posttreatment assessment.

Components of CBT

Craske, Brown, and Barlow (1991) conducted a 2-year follow-up study on the components of CBT for PD. Subjects were assigned to either 15 weekly sessions of applied progressive muscle relaxation (AR), interoceptive exposure plus cognitive restructuring (IE+C), the combination of AR and IE+C, or a wait list. Treatment manuals were used for each of the treatment conditions.

While subjects in the AR condition showed deterioration at 6-month follow-up, the IE+C and combined-treatment subjects maintained their treatment gains. In addition, a significantly greater percentage of subjects treated in the IE+C (71%) and combined-treatment (83%) conditions were panic-free at 6-month follow-up, versus 22% of AR subjects. This same pattern was also observed when examining the distribution of subjects achieving high end-state functioning (achieving a rating of clinical severity less than or equal to two [mild] and zero panic attacks in the past month). All of the treatment groups maintained their gains at 24-month follow-up. In addition, the proportion of subjects reporting zero panic attacks was equally distributed across the three treatment conditions (56% of AR, 87% of IE+C, and 60% of the combined-treatment subjects). Similarly, the percentage of subjects reaching high end-state functioning was 44%, 53%, and 50% for the AR, IE+C, and combined-treatment groups respectively, which were nonsignificant differences.

Craske, et al. (1991) note, however, that a different pattern emerged when dropouts were included (assuming that these subjects were continuing to panic). With dropouts included, 36% of the AR subjects, 81% of the IE+C subjects, and 43% of the combined-treatment subjects reported zero panic attacks (which was significant). However, no significant differences emerged when dropouts were included in the calculation of the proportion of subjects reaching high end-state functioning. Therefore, based on these results, the investigators concluded that panic attacks are controlled more effectively by interoceptive exposure plus cognitive restructuring than by relaxation training. They also found that the therapeutic effects of short-term CBT were maintained for up to 2 years following treatment completion, particularly for subjects receiving IE+C treatment. In addition, the investigators noted that while IE+C subjects tended to maintain their post-treatment status, AR subjects tended to deteriorate (and also had high attrition rates). Finally, they suggest that adding AR to interoceptive exposure plus cognitive restructuring procedures does not enhance the effects of the treatment, and may even weaken the long-term effects of treatment.

Öst, Westling, and Hellström (1993) compared applied relaxation (AR), exposure in vivo (E), and CBT in the treatment of PD. The study's design allowed the researchers to compare the effects of three different behavioral methods, each of which was focused on a different anxiety component (in vivo exposure focuses on avoidance behaviors; applied relaxation focuses on physiological reactions; and cognitive treatment focuses on negative cognitions), and delivered within the context of self-exposure instructions. The treatment was comprised of twelve 1-hour sessions that were delivered weekly. A telephone maintenance program that ran for 6 months post-treatment (with the therapist having a total of 90 to 120 minutes of phone contact with each patient) followed each treatment program.

On agoraphobic self-report measures, all three groups improved to approximately the same extent, and all maintained their improvements up to the follow-up assessment. On psychopathology self-report measures, all three groups showed improvement on other phobias, as well as state and trait anxiety and depression, and all three groups maintained their improvements up to the follow-up assessment. On behavioral test measures conducted at posttreatment, the AR group completed a significantly higher mean number of situations on the individualized behavior test (Behavioral Avoidance Test) than the CBT group, while the E group did not differ significantly from either of these groups on this measure. At follow-up, the AR group maintained its improvement, while the E and CBT groups showed further improvement. The results on the self-rating of anxiety showed that, on average, subjects managed Situation 3 (mildly anxiety provoking) at pretreatment, Situation 11 (highly anxiety provoking) at post-treatment, and Situation 12 (highly anxiety provoking) at follow-up.

On cognitive measures conducted at posttreatment, subjects in all three groups reduced their frequency of negative, self-defeating statements to a large extent, but made only minor changes to their positive and neutral self-statements. Using a ratio of positive self-statements / (positive + negative self-statements), the researchers found that at pretreatment both the AR and E groups had a state of mind (SOM) characterized by negative dialogue, while the CBT group had an SOM in the negative monologue range. At posttreatment, the AR group had changed to an SOM of positive monologue, while the E and CBT groups were in the positive dialogue range. Finally, at follow-up, the E group remained in the positive dialogue range, the AR group changed to positive dialogue range, and the CBT group changed to an internal dialogue of conflict.

Öst et al. (1993) also assessed the degree of clinically significant improvement achieved by the patients. Using the percentage of situations completed in the Behavioral Avoidance Test, this criterion was fulfilled by 87% of the AR subjects, 80% of the E subjects, and 60% of the CBT subjects at posttreatment, and by 85%, 79%, and 67% of the AR, E, and CBT subjects, respectively, at follow-up. It should be noted that the differences at post-treatment and follow-up were nonsignificant, and there were also no relapses at follow-up. Using a score on the Agoraphobia Scale, the criterion was fulfilled by 53% of the AR subjects, 47% of the E subjects, and 60% of CBT subjects at posttreatment. At follow-up the percentages were 46%, 50%, and 47% for the AR, E, and CBT groups, respectively. These differences were nonsignificant.

Therefore, the researchers concluded that all three treatments yielded significant improvements on all types of measures (i.e., not just self-report, but also on behavioral and cognitive measures, as well as measures of general anxiety and depression). In addition, these effects were maintained at 1-year follow-up. As only a few significant differences were found between the groups, the researchers concluded that the three different methods perform about equally well in the treatment of agoraphobic subjects.

In addition to the above experiment, Öst and Westling (1995) later directly compared cognitive therapy and applied relaxation. Once again, the results indicated that cognitive therapy and applied relaxation were both associated with substantial improvements in panic frequency, panic-related distress and/or disability, and generalized anxiety (as cited in Clark, 1997). And once again, no significant differences were found between the treatments. It was later discovered, however, that Öst included each of the four therapists' initial training cases in cognitive therapy in this study (Clark, 1997). The inclusion of the initial cases had a major impact on the results, as only 25% of the training cases became panic-free, while 87% of the subsequent cognitive therapy cases became panic-free and achieved high end-state functioning by the end of treatment (as cited in Clark, 1997). Most importantly, Clark points out that when the data were reanalyzed without including the four cognitive therapy training cases, a significant difference emerged between cognitive therapy and applied relaxation (in terms of the percentage of patients reaching high end-state functioning at posttreatment), with 87% of cognitive therapy patients reaching high end-state functioning (versus 47% of applied relaxation).

Components versus Medications

Clark, Salkovskis, Hackmann, Middleton, Anastasiades, and Gelder (1994) compared cognitive therapy (CT), applied relaxation (AR), and imipramine in the treatment of PD. The subjects in the CT or AR groups received up to 12 sessions in the first 3 months, followed by up to three "booster" sessions in the next 3 months. The subjects in the imipramine group received a similar number of sessions (but of briefer duration) during the first 3 months, after which time they were maintained at maximum dose for the next 3 months, and then gradually withdrawn from their medication. The researchers also included a wait-list control group in their study.

While all three treatments were effective when compared with the wait list, several differences emerged among them. For example, at 3 months CT was superior to AR and imipramine on most measures, while AR and imipramine did not differ significantly from each other. In addition, the proportion of subjects who were panic-free and had achieved high end-state functioning was significantly greater in the CT group than in the AR and imipramine groups. At 6 months the CT and imipramine treatments produced equivalent results on a number of measures (e.g., the number of subjects reaching panic-free status and high end-state functioning), and both were superior to AR on several measures (e.g., Agoraphobic Cognitions Questionnaire and Beck Depression Inventory). Between the 6- and 15-month assessments, however, a number of imipramine subjects deteriorated and relapsed and, as a result, by 15 months CT was again superior to both AR and imipramine (but on fewer measures than at 3 months). At this point, the imipramine and AR groups again did not differ significantly from each other. While CT was superior to AR based on the proportion of subjects achieving panic-free status and high end-state functioning, it was not significantly different from imipramine. It should be noted, however, that imipramine subjects were more likely to relapse (and therefore receive additional treatment).

It is interesting to note that Clark and associates (1994) found preliminary evidence for the notion that sustained improvement at the end of treatment is dependent on cognitive change having occurred during the course of treatment. According to the authors, this finding suggests that clinicians should aim not only for panic-free status, but also for a marked cognitive change in the patient. Related to this was the finding that cognitive measures (e.g., Body Sensations Questionnaire) and Agoraphobic Cognitions Questionnaire taken at the end of treatment were significant predictors of outcome at follow-up.

APPLICATION OF CBT FOR PANIC DISORDER: CASE ILLUSTRATION

RL is a 40-year-old white male who presented with a primary complaint of panic attacks and agoraphobia. He was never married and lives alone in New York City, where he was born. RL reported a relatively unremarkable childhood, although he recalled being an "anxious kid" as far back as he could remember. RL was employed by a bank.

RL experienced his first panic attack 17 years ago while traveling following his graduation from college. While he was vacationing in Miami, he experienced several panic attacks and continuous anxiety. He began to fear that he would "go crazy and end up in a psychiatric hospital" from the anxiety, and quickly returned home. The attacks began to occur more frequently, and RL developed moderate agoraphobia (e.g., avoided trains, elevators, crowded places, traveling outside of a 20-mile radius, and social situations). RL had a received two prior unsuccessful treatments for PD: a 2-year course of traditional psychotherapy 10 years ago, and more recently, a brief 6-week trial of Paxil. He terminated both treatments because he believed they were not helping. RL decided he had to accept and live with PD because the treatments he tried were unsuccessful. However, approximately 2 months prior to seeking out the current treatment, RL watched a television show on PD that discussed new medications and cognitive behavioral treatment. Because this seemed like something different than what he had in the past, RL decided to initiate treatment, and received a referral to one of us from the Anxiety Disorders Association of America.

Assessment

Following a clinical interview, RL was assigned the diagnosis of PD with moderate agoraphobia in accordance with *DSM-IV* criteria. The anxiety symptoms were systematically assessed using the following measures to assess the full range of symptoms (panic, generalized anxiety, depression, phobia, and functional impairment): Panic Attack Diary (Barlow & Cerny, 1988), Individualized Fear and Avoidance Hierarchy (Barlow, 1988), Beck Anxiety Inventory (BAI; Beck, Epstein & Brown, 1988), Beck

Depression Inventory (BDI; Beck, Steer, & Garbin, 1988), and Sheehan Disability Scales (Leon, Shear, Portera, & Klerman, 1992).

Treatment Implementation

During the second session, the therapist (W.C.S.) discussed the diagnostic formulation with RL, and reviewed relevant problems. The therapist discussed the treatment components (as described above) that would be used and provided a rationale for each. Cognitive behavioral treatment was initiated and during the next session RL was provided with an education about anxiety, PD, and agoraphobia. Surprisingly, despite his substantial history of treatment, he was never formally diagnosed with PD nor provided with any information about it, and therefore, often feared that he had something worse (e.g., schizophrenia or heart disease). In addition, because of the stigma attached to emotional disorders, he felt it necessary to hide the fact that he had PD, which ultimately led to his living a somewhat isolated lifestyle, which in turn prevented him from developing intimate relationships. Thus, giving RL the message that PD is a relatively common, well-researched condition that is treatable, and not a precursor to schizophrenia or heart disease, was quite reassuring. To bolster the psychoeducation phase, the therapist recommended he read *Don't Panic* (1987) by Reid Wilson and *The Feeling Good Handbook* (1989) by David Burns. Both are cognitive-behaviorally oriented self-help books that contain a significant amount of information about panic, phobia, and anxiety. While we are not proponents of self-help books as alternatives to treatment, we do believe they can be effective adjuncts to therapy in that (a) they reinforce the information covered within the session assisting in compliance with exercises outside of sessions; and (b) they provide more extensive information than may be allowed within the therapy session (e.g., a detailed explanation of the physiology of anxiety and the biological basis of symptoms may be easier to understand when reading versus heard via oral explanation in session). RL obtained both books early in treatment and found them to be useful adjuncts to the psychotherapy sessions, especially when the therapist would point out relevant chapters corresponding to information covered within the therapy session.

In the next several sessions, RL learned strategies to help him reduce his physical arousal (e.g., muscle tension, palpitations, and insomnia), including progressive muscle relaxation and deep breathing exercises. He was instructed to begin using these procedures when he noticed an increase in anxiety as a way to calm his system. To facilitate his utilizing the progressive muscle relaxation at home, the relaxation exercise was taped in session so that he would have the therapist's instructions. Deep breathing exercises are intended to facilitate slow (10 to 12 breaths/minute), diaphragmatic breathing, and decrease the likelihood of hyperventilation that frequently occurs in panic patients during anxiety episodes, which may be responsible for many of the most uncomfortable sensations (e.g., suffocation). Once RL was able to master the techniques to reduce arousal, we focused on cognitive restructuring. With the assistance of the therapist, RL learned to identify his catastrophic thoughts. In RL's case, most of these involved ideas and images that he would go crazy and end up in a psychiatric hospital or have a heart attack during a panic attack. As a result, RL often avoided situations where escape was difficult, as he believed that if he was stuck in a situation and experienced a panic attack, it would lead to one of these consequences. We began challenging his catastrophic thoughts in session, and generated more realistic thoughts to replace the anxiety-provoking ones. In addition to this, RL started using the information he had received about PD to challenge these catastrophic thoughts. In fact, RL was able to recall several situations where he was unable to escape, and realized that the anxiety always passed (e.g., a time he was stuck on a subway train). RL noticed that in conjunction with his relaxation exercises, challenging his catastrophic thoughts with more realistic thoughts resulted in decreasing his anxiety and circumventing the panic attacks that were occurring at home.

Although RL did not intend to address his agoraphobic avoidance when he entered treatment because he believed his "life was over," the fact that he was able remediate the panic attacks while at home led him to reconsider his initial posture. The therapist explained the rationale of exposure therapy, used in conjunction with relaxation exercises and cognitive restructuring, and attempted to motivate RL in this direction by pointing out that there were many things he wanted to do, such as traveling to Florida. The therapist consulted with RL's physician at this point to explain the process of exposure therapy and determine if there were any medical contraindications. The physician attested that RL was extremely healthy, he had no medical problems, and was able to exercise. As a result of RL's long-standing health concerns related to panic (i.e., fear of heart disease), he adopted a lifestyle that resulted in behaviors that actually resulted in being healthy (eating low-fat foods, keeping his weight down, and regular exercise). Thus, the next several sessions involved systematic exposure to feared agoraphobic situations (e.g., using express subway trains and buses, going into elevators, going on trips of increasing "difficulty" and distance—Atlantic City, Philadelphia, Boston with the ultimate goal being Miami). For the most part, exposure was patient generated. However, on a few occasions, especially early on in the exposure phase, the therapist accompanied RL into an elevator, with his agreement, to facilitate his coping responses "in vivo." As is typical, the therapist included and started with low items on the hierarchy so that the patient could not "fail" (e.g., items that the patient reported avoiding when possible, but able to do if necessary), in order to strengthen coping skills for when the anxiety is more overwhelming, as well as to demonstrate the effectiveness of repeatedly facing a situation within a short period of time. This strategy, as is usual, was effective, and repeated exposure to low- and then high-level anxiety-provoking situations resulted in habituation. As a result, there was a significant decrease of agoraphobia and elimination of panic attacks.

Following approximately 20 sessions during which the therapist implemented the psychological interventions spelled out in Barlow and Cerny (1988), RL had made substantial progress, as confirmed by the re-administration of the assessment battery described above. By this point, RL was no longer experiencing panic attacks, he was able to travel (e.g., trips to Atlantic City) and attend social functions (e.g., parties and sporting events). Clearly, there was a substantial increase in the quality of RL's life as a result of the treatment of his PD. Treatment was maintained for 7 additional months on a once-per-month basis following the acute phase of treatment to facilitate his movement through the entire fear and avoidance hierarchy and continue to address residual generalized anxiety. Once he reached the endpoint, treatment was terminated.

SUMMARY AND CONCLUSION

Panic disorder is a debilitating condition affecting approximately 1.5% of the population. In addition to panic attacks, patients frequently suffer from agoraphobia, depression, and chronic anxiety. Several pharmacological treatments have shown to be effective for this condition. However, CBT is the only empirically supported psychological intervention for panic disorder. Thus, as set forth in clinical practice guidelines, CBT should be the first-line psychosocial intervention utilized by clinicians. A typical course of CBT for panic disorder includes several interventions: psychoeducation, cognitive restructuring, relaxation training, respiratory control, and interoceptive and situational exposure therapy. Numerous controlled research trials have demonstrated that almost all patients receiving CBT improve, and perhaps as many as 90% of patients are panic-free at the end of relatively brief therapy (i.e., 12 to 15 weekly sessions). Several effectiveness studies that examined the efficacy of CBT in "true" clinical populations support its transportability outside of research clinics.

REFERENCES

American Psychiatric Association. (1994). *Diagnostic and statistical manual of mental disorders* (4th ed.). Washington, DC: Author.

Barlow, D. H. (1988). *Anxiety and its disorders*. New York: Guilford Press.

Barlow, D. H., & Craske, M. G. (1989). *Mastery of your anxiety and panic*. Albany, NY: Graywind Publications.

Barlow, D. H., & Cerny, J. (1988). *Psychological treatment of panic*. New York: Guilford Press.

Beck, A. T., & Emery, G. (1985). *Anxiety disorders and phobias: A cognitive perspective*. New York: Basic Books.

Beck, A. T., Epstein, N., & Brown, G. (1988). An inventory for measuring clinical anxiety. *Journal of Consulting and Clinical Psychology, 56*, 893–897.

Beck, A. T., Sokol, L., Clark, D. A., Berchick, R., & Wright, F. (1992). A crossover study of focused cognitive therapy for panic disorder. *American Journal of Psychiatry, 149*(6), 778–783.

Beck, A. T., Steer, R. A., & Garbin, M. G. (1988). Psychometric properties of the Beck depression inventory: Twenty-five years later. *Clinical Psychology Review, 8*, 77–100.

Black, D. W., Wesner, R., Bowers, W., & Gabel, J. (1993). A comparison of fluvoxamine, cognitive therapy, and placebo in the treatment of panic disorder. *Archives of General Psychiatry, 50*, 44–50.

Burns, D. D. (1989). *The feeling good handbook: Using the new mood therapy in everyday life*. New York: Morrow.

Clark, D. M. (1997). Panic disorder and social phobia. In D. M. Clark & G. Fairburn (Eds.), *Science and practice of cognitive behaviour therapy* (pp. 12–153). New York: Oxford University Press.

Clark, D. M. (1986). A cognitive approach to panic. *Behaviour Research and Therapy, 24*, 461–471.

Clark, D. M., Salkovskis, P. M., & Chalkley, A. J. (1985). Respiratory control as a treatment for panic attacks. *Journal of Behavior Therapy and Experimental Psychiatry, 16*, 23–30.

Clark, D. M., Salkovskis, P. M., Hackmann, A., Middleton, H., Anastasiades, P., & Gelder, M. (1994). A comparison of cognitive therapy, applied relaxation, and imipramine in the treatment of panic disorder. *British Journal of Psychiatry, 164*, 759–769.

Côté, G., Gauthier, J. G., Laberge, B., Cormier, H. J., & Plamondon, J. (1994). Reduced therapist contact in the cognitive behavioral treatment of panic disorder. *Behavior Therapy, 25*, 123–145.

Craske, M. G., Brown, T. A., & Barlow, D. H. (1991). Behavioral treatment of panic disorder: A two-year follow-up. *Behavior Therapy, 22*, 289–304.

Craske, M. G., Maidenberg, E., & Bystritsky, A. (1995). Brief cognitive-behavioral versus nondirective therapy for panic disorder. *Journal of Behavior Therapy and Experimental Psychiatry, 26*(2), 113–120.

Klosko, J. S., Barlow, D. H., Tassinari, R., & Cerny, J. A. (1990). A comparison of alprazolam and behavior therapy in treatment of panic disorder. *Journal of Consulting and Clinical Psychology, 58*(1), 77–84.

Leon, A. C., Shear, M. K., Portera, L., & Klerman, G. L. (1992). Assessing impairment in patients with panic disorder: The Sheehan Disability Scale. *Social Psychiatry and Psychiatric Epidemiology, 27*, 78–82.

Öst, L. G., Westling, B. E., & Hellström, K. (1993). Applied relaxation, exposure in vivo and cognitive methods in the treatment of panic disorder with agoraphobia. *Behavior Research and Therapy, 31*(4), 383–394.

Sanderson, W. C., & McGinn, L. K. (1997). Psychological treatment of anxiety disorder patients with comorbidity. In S. Wetzler & W. C. Sanderson (Eds.), *Treatment strategies for patients with psychiatric comorbidity* (pp. 75–104). New York: Wiley.

Sanderson, W. C., & Wetzler, S. (1990). Five percent carbon dioxide challenge: Valid analogue and marker of panic disorder? *Biological Psychiatry, 27*, 689–701.

Shear, M. K., Pilkonis, P. A., Cloitre, M., & Leon, A. C. (1994). Cognitive behavioral treatment compared with nonprescriptive treatment of panic disorder. *Archives of General Psychiatry, 51*, 395–401.

Sokol, L., Beck, A. T., Greenberg, R. L., Wright, F. D., & Berchick, R. J. (1989). Cognitive therapy of panic disorder: A non-pharmacologic alternative. *Journal of Nervous and Mental Disease, 177*, 711–716.

Telch, M. J., Lucas, J. A., Schmidt, N. B., Hanna, H. H., Jaimez, T. L., & Lucas, R. A. (1993). Group cognitive behavioral treatment of panic disorder. *Behavior Research and Therapy, 31*(3), 279–287.

Wilson, R. R. (1987). *Don't panic: Taking control of anxiety attacks.* New York: Harper & Row.

Woody, S. R., & Sanderson, W. C. (1998). Manuals for empirically supported treatments: 1998 update from the task force on psychological interventions. *The Clinical Psychologist, 51*(1), 17–21.

6

Obsessive Compulsive Disorder

Sabine Wilhelm

DIAGNOSIS OF OCD

Obsessive compulsive disorder (OCD) is a severe psychiatric disorder that affects up to 3% of the population (e.g., Bland, Orn, & Newman, 1988; Robins et al., 1984), making it one of the most prevalent anxiety disorders. OCD is classified as an anxiety disorder because obsessions increase anxiety or discomfort, whereas compulsions decrease anxiety or discomfort. Obsessions are intrusive and distressing thoughts, impulses, or images. Individuals with OCD usually try to suppress those thoughts or to neutralize them with other thoughts or actions (*DSM-IV*; American Psychiatric Association, 1994). Typical themes for obsessions refer to sexuality, harming, contamination, concerns with disease, religion, superstition, or otherwise neutral thoughts ("What if I cannot stop thinking about my eye blinking?"). Ordinarily the thoughts are egodystonic, but not all patients are convinced that the thoughts are senseless (Kozak & Foa, 1994).

Compulsions are overt or mental acts, and frequent compulsions include checking, cleaning, ordering, repeating, and counting (Rasmussen & Eisen, 1988). A less prevalent OCD symptom is obsessional or compulsive slowness in which the patient takes several hours to perform a routine activity. OCD patients often have more than one type of symptom and they generally know that their obsessions or compulsions are excessive or unreasonable.

OCD has an equal sex distribution, and it typically begins in adolescence or early adulthood (Rasmussen & Eisen, 1990). Most individuals have a fluctuating and often chronic course. Obsessions and compulsions often replace functional behaviors, and avoidance of situations involving obsessions and compulsions often leads to marital, social, and occupational difficulty (Steketee, 1997). In its most severe forms, OCD incapacitates its sufferers, keeping some housebound for many years. Given the high prevalence and personal cost, the development and investigation of treatments for this disorder is an important goal.

OVERVIEW OF EMPIRICALLY SUPPORTED TREATMENTS FOR OCD

OCD is currently treated with pharmacological and psychological approaches. Pharmacotherapy for OCD predominantly involves the use of serotonin reuptake inhibitors that have been shown to be successful in reducing OC symptoms (Jenike, Baer, & Greist, 1990). In a large controlled trial by Marks, et al. (1988), nearly one-third of the patients who refused to participate (22 of 64) declined pharmacotherapy (clomipramine). OCD patients often refuse pharmacological interventions due to the fear of their short- and long-term side effects (Rasmussen, Eisen, & Pato, 1993). Psychosocial treatments do not have any known side effects. Behavior therapy, particularly exposure with response prevention (ERP; i.e., extended exposure to the situations that trigger OCD symptoms combined with prevention of compulsions during the exposure exercises and afterward) has been considered the psychological intervention of choice. In more than 30 studies of behavior therapy for OCD (for reviews, see Abramowitz, 1996; Baer & Minichiello, 1998) about 63% of OCD patients had a positive response to ERP (Stanley & Turner, 1995). Many sufferers refuse ERP treatment because they are unwilling or unable to undergo the difficult exposure exercises and approximately 20% to 30% are resistant to this intervention. Moreover, the dropout rate is 20% (Rachman & Hodgson, 1980).

A review of the literature suggests that cognitive interventions for OCD may be as effective as ERP (see Abramowitz, 1997), but to date only few investigations of cognitive treatments for OCD have been reported. Cognitive treatments are intended to assist individuals make changes with respect to their thinking and beliefs, with the aim to also generate emotional and behavioral changes. The first cognitive therapy studies for OCD examined rational emotive therapy (RET; Ellis, 1962) with favorable outcomes, and more recently, a promising Beckian treatment has been developed. A detailed review of studies and case reports of Beckian cognitive therapy for OCD is provided elsewhere (Steketee, Frost, Rhéaume, & Wilhelm, 1998). Recently the first large controlled trial was conducted (van Oppen et al., 1995). Twenty-eight OCD sufferers were randomly assigned to cognitive therapy and 29 to self-exposure. In the cognitive therapy group, 57% of the patients were rated as recovered and 75% were reliably changed. In the exposure group, however, only 31% were rated as recovered and 57% were reliably changed. Thus, the results of this study suggested that cognitive therapy was at least as and perhaps even more effective for OCD than ERP.

Freeston and colleagues (1997) compared 29 patients who had mental rituals and avoidance but no overt compulsions treated with exposure and CT to a wait-list control group. Cognitive interventions focused on patients' (a) overestimation of the importance of thoughts, (b) overestimation of the probability and severity of feared consequences, and (c) beliefs of personal responsibility and (d) perfectionism. This combined treatment produced a high (84%) success rate. Cottraux and associates (1998) recently presented preliminary data of a comparison of cognitive therapy to ERP. Seventy-four percent of the patients responded to treatment, and CT and ERP were equally effective in reducing OCD symptoms. Moreover, CT was more effective than ERP in reducing depression symptoms.

To illustrate the application of cognitive therapy, a single case example is used throughout this article. The patient described herein was treated with a new manual developed for a study examining Beckian cognitive therapy for OCD (Wilhelm, Steketee, & Reilly-Harrington, 1999).

CASE EXAMPLE

History of the Problem

Gary, a 29-year-old carpenter, sought treatment because he had "terrible thoughts" that he "could not shake off." This problem began 10 months prior when he moved from a small town in Mississippi to the northeast United States. During the first session he was too embarrassed to discuss his symptoms in detail but he explained that frequently "perverse" sexual images came to his mind. He had thoughts and images about incest with family members, in particular his mother. Gary realized that his intrusive thoughts were excessive and senseless. The thoughts were usually followed by extreme guilt or anxiety. In a struggle to control his thoughts, he tried to suppress or neutralize them with numerous rituals such as tensing all his muscles or walking in a certain way. His worst fear was that he might get aroused by the sexual thoughts about his mother or sister, and he therefore developed extensive avoidance behaviors. Initially, he avoided only his mother, but finally he avoided most women and any activity that might be pleasurable and thus arousing. He could not go shopping, only ate when his wife was around, and he rarely socialized. Gary also reported that if he had an intrusive thought while he was doing something pleasurable, whatever he was doing would be ruined. Therefore, he avoided all activities during which he once had an intrusive thought. At the time of the intake assessment, he indicated that the obsessive thoughts occurred nearly constantly throughout the day. The thoughts were very distressing and interfered with concentrating at work and at home. Moreover, Gary described contamination fears and cleaning rituals. He was disgusted with bodily waste and insects, spent over 90 minutes per day washing his hands, and avoided public bathrooms. Nevertheless, Gary stated that the contamination fears were not nearly as bothersome as the sexual obsessions and resulting compulsions.

A structured clinical interview (SCID; First, Spitzer, Gibbon, & Williams, 1995) conducted as part of Gary's pretreatment assessment revealed that he also met diagnostic criteria for social phobia (fear of public speaking) and specific phobia (fear of flying), in addition to OCD. The patient had never been in psychiatric treatment before and was reluctant to take medication. He had two brothers and a sister who did not have any known psychiatric problems. He described his father as having very high moral standards, and reported that his mother was the person he loved and respected the most. Gary also reported that discussions about sexual topics were taboo in his family. Influenced by his religious upbringing, Gary held that he should not have bizarre sexual thoughts and felt very guilty and ashamed about thinking in such a way about his mother. He believed that if he could only exercise enough will power he should be able to gain control over his thoughts, and he became very anxious when his attempts to try to stop the intrusive thoughts failed.

Gary also thought that having sexual thoughts meant that he was a bad person, and that if he did not control his thoughts, something catastrophic would happen. He was convinced that he could not have peace of mind as long as he had intrusive thoughts. These beliefs made him susceptible to interpreting his recurrent thoughts in an anxiety- or guilt-provoking way. He thought that it was dangerous to let his thoughts come and go naturally. Gary's interpretation of his thoughts and his behavior in response to them certainly facilitated the expression of OCD symptoms.

Cognitive Model for OCD

Current cognitive models and treatments for OCD are rooted in theories that explain intrusive thoughts as occurrences that everybody experiences (e.g., Freeston, Rhéaume, & Ladouceur, 1996; Guidano & Liotti, 1983; Salkovskis, 1985, 1989). According to those theories, individuals who suffer from OCD do not differ from those without OCD with respect to the content of their thoughts, but only in the way they react to and interpret these thoughts. Healthy individuals ignore intrusive thoughts and judge them as being unimportant, while people with OCD pay attention to them and may interpret them as being significant (Rachman & deSilva, 1978). The extent of the attention is assumed to be determined by beliefs that were acquired through religious or cultural training or in a family context. If individuals underestimate their coping strategies for dealing with intrusions, they might try to suppress intrusive thoughts, develop mental compulsions, or engage in avoidance behaviors. Thought suppression as a strategy to rid oneself of intrusions is likely to be a fruitless endeavor because studies suggest that when individuals try to suppress specific thoughts, those thoughts occur more, and not less frequently (Wegner, 1989). Distorted interpretations of intrusions have been categorized in several cognitive domains by an international working group (Obsessive Compulsive Cognition Working Group [OCCWG], 1997; for a detailed review see also Steketee et al., 1998) that are described bellow:

Overimportance of Thoughts and the Need to Control Thoughts

Many OCD sufferers impute too much importance to their thoughts and erroneously believe that other people do not have intrusive thoughts. They may conclude that just because a thought occurs, it is meaningful, or just because they may be thinking about something it will take place. Mistaken beliefs about the importance of thoughts can lead to beliefs about having to exert control over them. In fact, OCD sufferers often overemphasize the importance of having complete control over intrusions.

Overestimation of Danger

OCD sufferers often overestimate the likelihood and the severity of danger, negative consequences, and of making errors. They might appraise situations as threatening until guaranteed safe, whereas most people assume that a situation is safe unless it is established as dangerous (Foa & Kozak, 1986).

Intolerance of Uncertainty

Perhaps because OCD sufferers tend to overestimate the likelihood of danger, they often have problems with uncertain and ambiguous situations, and with making decisions. In fact, people who scored high on measures of OCD symptoms have been shown to have greater qualms about the accuracy of their decisions (Frost & Shows, 1993). Rhéaume, Freeston, and Dugas (1995) found significant correlations among concern over mistakes, doubts about actions, and OCD symptoms. Moreover, they found that perfectionism accounted for a significant portion of the variance in obsessive compulsive symptom severity. However, perfectionism does not seem to be specific to OCD and may be associated with a wide variety of disorders (for a review, see Steketee et al., 1998).

Nevertheless, it may be an important factor in determining the course of OCD.

Perfectionism

Several theories of OCD have linked intolerance of uncertainty to perfectionism. For instance, OCD sufferers may have doubts about the quality of their attempts to reduce danger when a perfect solution cannot be discerned, or they might consider perfect performance necessary to avoid risk or criticism (Guidano & Liotti, 1983).

Excessive Responsibility

Excessive responsibility pertains to the belief that one has the primary power to generate or avert unwanted outcomes (e.g., Salkovskis, 1985). Excessive responsibility can lead to guilt, which is then relieved by compulsions.

On the basis of discussions with Gary about the importance he attributed to particular themes and of questionnaires measuring beliefs and attitudes characteristic of individuals with OCD (Obsessional Beliefs Questionnaire and Interpretation of Intrusions Inventory in OCCWG, 1997), it was evident that Gary had some problems with most cognitive domains listed above. However, he had the most severe difficulties with overimportance assigned to thoughts, beliefs about the need to control thoughts, and overestimation of danger.

Treatment

Treatment Outline

Gary's treatment consisted of 8 weekly, 1-hour sessions. The treatment was relatively short, because he was planning to go on an extended trip soon after the start of treatment. The structure of the sessions followed the format suggested by Beck (1995). The therapist initiated the session with a brief OCD symptom and mood check. Then the therapist (and later in treatment both Gary and the therapist) determined the agenda for each treatment session. The agenda was influenced by the phase of treatment (e.g., explanation of the cognitive model early in treatment, and focus on relapse prevention in the last treatment session) and the cognitive domains Gary had difficulties with (e.g., learning specific techniques to address the need to control thoughts). Next, Gary and the therapist reviewed the homework assignments that Gary had completed since the last treatment session. Problems occurring while completing those assignments were also discussed. Thereafter, Gary and the therapist worked on the agenda items and decided on new homework. At the

end of the session, it was summarized by Gary and then he was encouraged to comment on the session.

As noted already, initially Gary was too embarrassed to talk about his
intrusive thoughts openly. To help the patient feel more comfortable,
the therapist's attitude toward the patient was encouraging, warm, and
nonjudgmental. The therapist expressed confidence in the cognitive
treatment and stressed the importance of a collaboration between the
patient and therapist.

In the first treatment session, Gary was educated about OCD and the
cognitive model for this disorder. He was given an alternative interpretation of his intrusive thoughts by characterizing them as common occurrences that most people have (see Rachman & deSilva, 1978). The
therapist helped Gary to increase his awareness of circumstances that
influenced his negative interpretations of intrusions (past family experience, mood state, recent stressors, etc.) and educated him about the
role of avoidance and mental rituals in the maintenance of obsessions.

In subsequent treatment sessions Gary acquired skills to recognize
maladaptive appraisals and reactions to intrusive thoughts and learned
to develop alternative interpretations of intrusions, assisted by the
Socratic questioning technique. Examples included "Is your appraisal of
the intrusion helpful right now? Is your appraisal realistic? What would
you tell another OCD patient about this?" Gary was instructed in filling
out thought records (see Wilhelm et al., 1999), a technique that helps
patients to identify irrational or negative appraisals of intrusions and to
develop rational alternatives. Thought records were completed during
treatment sessions and as homework assignments.

After Gary had been trained in these central cognitive therapy tools,
he and the therapist determined which cognitive domains were most relevant on the basis of recurrent themes on thought records and during
sessions. Then they decided in what order these domains should be
addressed in therapy. The therapist first addressed Gary's need to control thoughts and his overestimation of their importance, because these
were the domains in which Gary had the most severe problems. In later
treatment sessions, they worked on Gary's tendency to overestimate the
probability and severity of danger.

Over the course of treatment the therapist showed Gary a number of
cognitive techniques. Some were pertinent for several cognitive domains,
such as making a list of advantages and disadvantages of believing in a
certain interpretation. Other techniques were only relevant for specific
cognitive domains, such as the thought suppression test to illustrate the
paradoxical effects of trying to control thoughts (see Wilhelm et al.,
1999, for a detailed description of these techniques). Behavioral experiments pertinent to the material discussed in sessions were introduced

for most cognitive domains to test the empirical basis of dysfunctional thoughts and beliefs.

The final session focused on terminating treatment and relapse prevention. The cognitive model and techniques that Gary had used successfully over the course of treatment were reviewed. Gary and therapist also discussed that it was likely that OCD symptoms would occasionally flare up, but that Gary would know how to cope with them. He was advised to keep working on OCD symptoms after the end of treatment. Finally, techniques to handle setbacks and relapses were discussed.

Specific Techniques

The most important interventions that were employed in Gary's treatment are described in detail below.

Thought suppression experiment. According to the cognitive model underlying the treatment, Gary's sexual thoughts became a problem because of the way he reacted to them. Gary held that the intrusions were important and unacceptable. He was bothered by them; therefore he tried to suppress and get rid of them. But it is nearly impossible to suppress thoughts. This was explained to Gary with the help of a thought suppression experiment (see also Freeston & Ladouceur, 1997). First, Gary was asked to think about and imagine a giraffe for a minute. He was instructed to lift his finger every time the giraffe disappeared from his mind. As the therapist anticipated, it was difficult to concentrate on the giraffe ceaselessly, and Gary had to lift his finger over and over again. Subsequently, the therapist reversed instructions and asked Gary to *not* think about the giraffe for a minute, and to lift his finger every time a thought about the giraffe appeared. Gary once again had to lift his finger over and over again, this time indicating problems suppressing the thought. Thus, Gary's attempt to suppress thoughts resulted in an increase rather than a decrease of those thoughts, and conversely, trying to retain the thought proved difficult. Gary and the therapist discussed the relationship between the thought suppression experiment and Gary's efforts to suppress and stop intrusive sexual thoughts. Gary came to the conclusion that thought suppression is not a good approach to cope with obsessions because it makes them occur more frequently.

Psychoeducation. Gary's obsessions were normalized by educating him about sexual thoughts, fantasies, and arousal. He was informed that one may be thinking about or may be aroused by a wide range of stimuli including those unrelated to sexual behavior. He was encouraged to read sex education books to learn more about sexual fantasies and arousal. Although he was initially too embarrassed to read about those topics, he eventually did read some books that somewhat improved his catastrophic interpretations of sexual fantasies.

Downward arrow technique. The downward-arrow technique (Burns, 1980) was especially beneficial for Gary's treatment. After Gary and the therapist identified an intrusive thought, the therapist kept inquiring about the meaning of the intrusion. That is, the therapist kept asking, "And if that thought were true, what would it mean?" until one or more fundamental beliefs were disclosed. An example of Gary's thoughts and underlying beliefs identified with the downward arrow technique is shown here:

Images and thoughts about sex with mother
⇓
These thoughts are disgusting
⇓
I need to get rid of these thoughts
⇓
If I cannot control these thoughts, I might act on them
⇓
I am evil

Advantages and disadvantages. The need to suppress the intrusions discovered by means of the downward-arrow technique was disputed with a discussion of the thought suppression experiment (described above) and by discussing the usefulness of this kind of thinking. The therapist asked Gary what the advantages and disadvantages of believing that he could control his thoughts were. Gary listed under each heading all advantages and disadvantages that came to mind. After the advantages and disadvantages were identified, the validity of the advantages was examined with Socratic dialogue. This technique helped Gary to reduce his attempts to control his thoughts, which led to a substantial improvement in OCD symptoms.

Examining the evidence and behavioral experiments. The downward-arrow technique also revealed ideas that Gary was afraid that he would act on the thoughts if he was not able to control them. The therapist started challenging this assumption by illustrating that thinking about something does not make it more likely to happen from the patient's own experience. The therapist suggested similar types of situations to the patient and asked whether he believed that thinking about those would make them more likely to happen. Examples were riding the subway and thinking about sticking his tongue out, sitting in the waiting room and thinking about throwing all the magazines in the garbage can, and so on. In addition, behavioral experiments were used to illustrate that thinking about something does not make it more likely to happen. One experiment Gary conducted to test whether thoughts cause outcomes was thinking about dancing naked in the waiting room. Prior to conducting the exercises, the patient was instructed to see them as experiments in which he was a scientist trying to collect evidence to prove or disprove his hypothesis. Gary noted his prediction (e.g., if I think of something sexual, immoral or embarrassing, I will not be able to resist doing it) and rated the strength of his belief in it. After the experiment, the therapist and Gary reviewed Gary's initial prediction that he will act on his thoughts if he does not control them. Gary began to understand that his feared predictions never occurred and that thinking about something does not automatically make it happen.

Challenging core beliefs. During the downward-arrow procedure, the belief "I am evil" emerged. The therapist assisted Gary to become aware of this strongly held belief and then carefully introduced the idea that a more a accurate belief may be "I am extremely worried about acting immorally and hurting my mother." One strategy to accomplish this was that the therapist and Gary examined whether there was any evidence, apart from the intrusive thoughts, that Gary was evil. Next, they investigated whether there was any evidence that Gary was not "evil." This strategy helped Gary to see himself in a more realistic way and he concluded that the belief that he was evil was not accurate.

Cognitive continuum technique. Another effective technique to challenge the belief that Gary was evil was the cognitive continuum technique (Beck, 1995). On a visual analogue scale from 0 (most moral person ever) to 100 (most immoral/evil person ever) Gary rated how evil he was for thinking about sex with his mother. Then the therapist asked him to rate how bad/immoral a mass murderer is, a rapist, and so on. The therapist encouraged Gary to keep making these ratings and writing them on the scale. After each new example Gary re-rated his own badness for having thoughts about sex with his mother. Eventually Gary realized that having an intrusive thought about his mother was relatively harmless and not nearly as "evil" as he had appraised it initially.

Examining the evidence and behavioral experiments. Gary avoided pleasurable experiences such as eating or buying new clothes because he was concerned that his intrusive thoughts would spoil the event. The therapist and Gary discussed whether this was always true or whether he ever had enjoyed activities in spite of the intrusions. Thereafter, the validity of the belief that he could not derive pleasure from events if he had intrusions was investigated with a behavioral experiment. Gary and the therapist agreed that Gary would engage in an activity he used to enjoy (buying new clothes). He rated the level of pleasure he anticipated to experience, which was fairly low (see also Freeston et al., 1996). When he went to buy the clothes he had a few intrusions, but he enjoyed it more than he had initially expected.

Calculate the probability of harm. As described earlier, although less severe than the sexual obsessions, Gary had contamination and illness fears, and related cleaning rituals. The techniques described above include examination of the evidence and behavioral experiments that were also used to treat contamination and illness fears. However, one method illustrated by van Oppen and Arntz (1994) and Steketee (1999) was especially useful in challenging Gary's overestimates of danger related to the contamination fears. The therapist taught Gary to contrast his original probability estimation of harm to the multiplied estimations of the entire sequence of events that would be necessary to result in the feared outcome. Gary and the therapist used the following steps:

1. Gary estimated the probability of negative outcomes.
2. In collaboration with the therapist, he established each of the individual steps that would have to take place to result in the dangerous outcome.
3. Gary was asked to estimate the chance of each of these individual events occurring separately.
4. With the help of a calculator, Gary calculated the final cumulative probability by multiplying all of the probabilities of each individual event.
5. Gary and the therapist compared this probability estimate to Gary's initial estimate.

In the following example, Gary's original estimate of the probability of developing AIDS by shaking his dentist's hand was 30%. Gary and the therapist then discussed that the following sequence of steps would have to occur for Gary to develop AIDS:

Step	Chance	Cumulative chance
1. The dentist must have HIV-positive blood on his hands	1/1000	1/1000
2. I came in touch with the virus while shaking his hands	1/10	1/10,000
3. My skin was broken at the point of contact	1/10	1/100,000
4. The virus generates HIV	1/10	1/1,000,000
5. HIV develops into AIDS	1/10	1/10,000,000

Gary was quite surprised when he realized how low those probabilities calculated from his own estimates were, compared with his original estimate (30%).

Outcome of Therapy

Measures

Gary completed the 10-item *Yale-Brown Obsessive Compulsive Scale* (Y-BOCS; Goodman et al., 1989) at the beginning and end of treatment. The Y-BOCS assesses the severity of obsessions and compulsions and has well-established reliability and validity (see Woody, Steketee, & Chambless, 1995). Moreover, he completed the Disability Inventory at the beginning and end of treatment (see Leon, Shear, Portera, & Klerman, 1992). This scale assesses work, social, and family disability on 10-point scales and overall disability on a 5-point scale. It has been used in a variety of pharmacological studies and has demonstrated acceptable reliability (via alpha and factor analyses), and satisfactory construct- and criterion-related validity (Leon et al., 1992). Furthermore, Gary completed the Clinical Global Improvement Scale (CGI; Guy, 1976) after treatment to rate improvement from 1 (very much improved) to 7 (very much worse).

Results

Gary's pretreatment score on the self-rated Y-BOCS was 35, indicating that his OCD was very severe. However, at the posttreatment assessment his Y-BOCS score had dropped to 18, thus showing considerable improvement in OCD symptoms. With a symptom reduction of about 49%, he was considered a treatment responder. Gary's pretreatment score on the disability scale for impairment in work, social life/leisure activities, and family life was 9, indicating that his impairment was marked to very severe in all of those areas of functioning. He also indicated that symptoms radically changed or prevented work life on the overall 5-point disability scale. At the end of treatment, Gary's ratings for work, social, and family disability had dropped to 2 (mildly impaired) on the 10-point scales, and to 3 (minor interference of symptoms with normal work and social activities) on the overall 5-point disability scale. On the CGI, Gary rated himself as "much improved" at the end of treatment. The therapist agreed with this rating. Gary's treatment was unusually brief because he had to move to another city soon after he started. His symptoms were reassessed 2 months after the end of treatment and he described that he used the skills he learned during treatment on a regular basis. His Y-BOCS score had dropped to 8, indicating only mild OCD symptoms. Gary's ratings for work, social, and family disability had dropped to 1 (not at all to mildly impaired) on the 10-point scales, and to 2 (mild interference of symptoms with normal work and social activities) on the overall 5-point disability scale. On the CGI, Gary now rated himself as "very much improved," a rating that was consistent with that of the therapist. Thus, a considerable drop in symptom severity as well as functional improvement were achieved in just a few sessions and Gary improved even further after treatment ended.

CONCLUSION

Gary's treatment outcome data indicate that cognitive therapy may be an effective intervention for patients suffering from OCD. Gary's compulsive and avoidance behavior changed substantially after he evaluated and modified his dysfunctional thinking and he started feeling better after just a few sessions. However, his treatment was very brief and it is likely that a longer treatment would have reduced his OCD symptoms even further. In addition, it might have been helpful to gradually taper treatment sessions toward the end of treatment to give Gary the opportunity to strengthen skills between sessions while at the same time preparing for termination.

The most important elements in Gary's treatment were to help him understand the cognitive model, and to educate him about identifying, evaluating, and responding to maladaptive appraisals of intrusions. Although the treatment included a large number of different techniques, the therapist was careful not to jump from technique to technique but rather stayed focused on working on Gary's central beliefs. Therapist and patient always tried to relate any new maladaptive interpretations to the overall conceptualization. Gary's treatment also included behavioral experiments that can be similar to exposure exercises. But Gary was never directly instructed to engage in an exposure exercise or in response prevention. In behavioral experiments, unlike in exposure exercises, the focus was on testing a hypothesis, rather than confronting a situation Gary feared. Thus, it was not necessary for Gary to stay in feared situations for extended periods of time, or until habituation occurred. He only remained for as long as it took to test the hypothesis.

Gary was treated with a manual that is currently being further developed and revised (Wilhelm et al., 1999). The manual focuses on domains of beliefs relevant to OCD as identified by the OCCWG (1997). Techniques described in the manual are informed by the work of several other researchers who have utilized cognitive techniques for the treatment of OCD, such as van Oppen and Arntz (1994), Salkovskis (1985), and Freeston, et al. (1996).

Gary's favorable treatment response is consistent with the outcomes of several recent studies suggesting that cognitive therapy may be helpful for individuals suffering from OCD. In a preliminary investigation, we recently found that cognitive therapy was more acceptable than and as efficacious as comparable studies investigating ERP (Wilhelm, Steketee, Reilly-Harrington, & Baer, 1998). Thus, cognitive therapy may be of value for the substantial number of refusers and potential dropouts of behavioral treatment. In summary, these preliminary results of cognitive treatment are very encouraging, but more studies are needed before firm conclusions about its efficacy can be made.

REFERENCES

Abramowitz, J. S. (1996). Variants of exposure and response prevention in the treatment of obsessive-compulsive disorder: A meta-analysis. *Behavior Therapy, 27*, 583–600.

Abramowitz, J. S. (1997). Effectiveness of psychological and pharmacological treatments for obsessive-compulsive disorder: A quantitative review. *Journal of Consulting and Clinical Psychology, 65*, 44–52.

American Psychiatric Association. (1994). *Diagnostic and statistical manual of mental disorders* (4th ed.). Washington, DC: Author.

Baer, L., Minichiello, W. E. (1998). Behavior therapy for obsessive-compulsive disorder. In M. A. Jenike, L. Baer, & W. E, Minichiello (Eds.), *Obsessive-compulsive disorder: Theory and management* (3rd ed., pp. 368–399). Chicago: Mosby.

Beck, J. S. (1995). *Cognitive therapy: Basics and beyond.* New York: Guilford Press.

Bland, R. C., Orn, H., Newman, S. C. (1988). Lifetime prevalence of psychiatric disorders in Edmonton. *Acta Psychiatrica Scandinavica, 77* (Suppl 338), 24–32.

Burns, D. D. (1980). *Feeling good: The new mood therapy.* New York: Signet.

Cottraux, J., Note, I., Dartigues, J. F., Yao, S. N., Note, B., Saurteraud, A., Mollard, E., Dubroca, B., Bourvard, M., & Bourgeois, M. (1998, September). *A multicenter controlled trial of cognitive therapy versus intensive behaviour therapy.* Paper presented at the 3rd International Obsessive Compulsive Disorder Conference, Madeira, Portugal.

Ellis, A. (1962). *Reason and emotion in psychotherapy.* New York: Lyle Stuart.

First, M. B., Spitzer, R. L., Gibbon, M., & Williams, J. B. W. (1995). *Structured clinical interview for DSM-IV axis I disorders: Patient edition (SCID-I/P, version 2.0).* New York: New York State Psychiatric Institute, Biometrics Research Department.

Foa, E. B., & Kozak, M. J. (1986). Emotional processing of fear: Exposure to corrective information. *Psychological Bulletin, 99*, 29–35.

Freeston, M. H., Ladouceur, R., Gagnon, F., Thibodeau, N., Rhéaume, J., Letarte, H., & Bujold, A. (1997). Cognitive-behavioral treatment of obsessive thoughts: A controlled study. *Journal of Consulting and Clinical Psychology, 65*, 405–413.

Freeston, M. H., & Ladouceur, R. (1997). The cognitive behavioral treatment of obsessions: A treatment manual. Unpublished treatment manuscript.

Freeston, M. H., Rhéaume, J., & Ladouceur, R. (1996). Correcting faulty appraisals of obsessional thoughts. *Behaviour Research and Therapy, 34,* 433–446.

Frost, R. O., & Shows, D. (1993). The nature and measurement of compulsive indecisiveness. *Behavior Research and Therapy, 26,* 275–277.

Goodman, W. K., Price, L. H., Rasmussen, S. A., Mazure, C., Fleischman, R. L., Hill, C. L., Heninger, G. R., & Charney, D. S. (1989). The Yale-Brown Obsessive-Compulsive Scale: Development, use, and reliability. *Archives of General Psychiatry, 46,* 1006–1011.

Guidano, V. F., & Liotti, G. (1983). *Cognitive processes and emotional disorders.* New York: Guilford Press.

Guy, W. (Ed.). (1976). *ECDEU assessment manual for psychopharmacology.* (Rev. ed.) (DHEW Pub. No. [ADM] 76–338). Rockville, MD: National Institute of Mental Health.

Kozak, M. J., & Foa, E. B. (1994). Obsessions, overvalued ideas, and delusions in obsessive-compulsive disorder. *Behaviour Research and Therapy, 21,* 57–62.

Jenike, M. A., Baer, L., & Greist, J. H. (1990). Clomipramine versus fluoxetine in obsessive-compulsive disorder: A retrospective comparison of side-effects and efficacy. *Journal of Clinical Psychopharmacology, 10,* 122–124.

Leon, A. C., Shear, M. K., Portera, L., & Klerman, G. L. (1992). Assessing impairment in patients with panic disorder: The Sheehan Disability Scale. *Social Psychiatry and Psychiatric Epidemiology, 27,* 78–82.

Marks, I. M., Lelliott, P., Basoglu, M., Noshirvani, H., Monteiro, W., Cohen, D., & Kasvikis, Y. (1988). Clomipramine, self-exposure and therapist-aided exposure for obsessive-compulsive rituals. *British Journal of Psychiatry, 152,* 522–534.

Obsessive Compulsive Cognition Working Group. (1997). Cognitive assessment of obsessive-compulsive disorder. *Behaviour Research and Therapy, 35,* 667–681.

Rachman, S., & deSilva, P. (1978). Abnormal and normal obsessions. *Behavior Research and Therapy, 16,* 233–248.

Rachman, S., & Hodgson, R. (1980). *Obsessions and compulsions.* Englewood Cliffs, NJ: Prentice Hall.

Rasmussen, S. A., & Eisen, J. L. (1988). Clinical and epidemiologic findings of significance to neuropharmacologic trials in OCD. *Psychopharmacological Bulletin, 24,* 466–470.

Rasmussen, S. A., & Eisen, J. L. (1990). Epidemiology and clinical features of obsessive-compulsive disorder. In M. A. Jenike, L. Baer, & W. E. Minichiello (Eds.), *Obsessive-compulsive disorders: Theory and management* (2nd ed., pp. 10–29). Chicago: Year Book Medical Publishers.

Rasmussen, S. A., Eisen, J. L., & Pato, M. T. (1993). Current issues in the pharmacologic management of obsessive-compulsive disorder. *Journal of Clinical Psychiatry, 54* (Suppl. 6), 4–9.

Rhéaume, J., Freeston, M. H., & Dugas, M. L. (1995). Perfectionism, responsibility, and obsessive-compulsive symptoms. *Behavior Research and Therapy, 33,* 785–794.

Robins, L. N., Helzer, J. E., Weissman, M. M., Orvaschel, H., Gruenberg, E., Burke, J. D., & Regier, D. A. (1984). Lifetime prevalence of specific psychiatric disorders in three sites. *Archives of General Psychiatry, 41,* 958–967.

Salkovskis, P. M. (1985). Obsessional-compulsive problems: A cognitive-behavioral analysis. *Behaviour Research and Therapy, 23,* 571–584.

Salkovskis, P. M. (1989). Cognitive-behavioural factors and the persistence of intrusive thoughts in obsessional problems. *Behaviour Research and Therapy, 27,* 677–682.

Stanley, M. A., & Turner, S. M. (1995). Current status of pharmacological and behavioral treatment of obsessive-compulsive disorder. *Behavior Therapy, 26,* 163–186.

Steketee, G. (1997). Disability and family burden in obsessive compulsive disorder. *Canadian Journal of Psychiatry, 42,* 919–928.

Steketee, G. (1999). *Overcoming obsessive-compulsive disorder: A behavioral and cognitive protocol for the treatment of OCD.* Oakland, CA: New Harbinger

Steketee, G., Frost, R. O., Rhéaume, J., Wilhelm, S. (1998). Cognitive theory and treatment of obsessive-compulsive disorder. In M. A. Jenike, L. Baer, & W. E. Minichiello (Eds.), *Obsessive-compulsive disorder: Theory and management* (3rd ed., pp. 368–399). Chicago: Mosby.

van Oppen, P., & Arntz, A. (1994). Cognitive therapy for obsessive-compulsive disorder. *Behaviour Research and Therapy, 32,* 79–87.

van Oppen, P., de Haan, E., van Balkom, A. J. L. M., Spinhoven, P., Hoogduin, K., & van Dick, R. (1995). Cognitive therapy and exposure in vivo in the treatment of obsessive-compulsive disorder. *Behaviour Research and Therapy, 33,* 379–390.

Wegner, D. M. (1989). *White bears and other unwanted thoughts.* New York: Viking, Penguin.

Wilhelm, S., Steketee, G., & Reilly-Harrington, N. (1999). Cognitive therapy for obsessive-compulsive disorder. Unpublished treatment manuscript.

Wilhelm, S., Steketee, G., Reilly-Harrington, N. A., & Baer, L. (1998, November). *Cognitive therapy for obsessive-compulsive disorder: A work in progress.* Paper presented at the 32nd Annual Convention of the Association for Advancement of Behavior Therapy, Washington, DC.

Woody, S. R., Steketee, G., & Chambless, D. L. (1995). Reliability and validity of the Yale-Brown Obsessive Compulsive scale. *Behaviour Research and Therapy, 33,* 597–605.

7

Posttraumatic Stress Disorder

Sherry A. Falsetti and Heidi S. Resnick

There are now several cognitive and cognitive behavioral therapies available for the treatment of posttraumatic stress disorder (PTSD). These treatments have undergone or are currently undergoing trials for efficacy
and/or comparison to each other. Before discussing treatment, however,
we will review the diagnostic criteria for PTSD, provide a review of cognitive behavioral theories as they apply to the development and treatment of
PTSD, and discuss relevant assessment issues.

DIAGNOSIS OF PTSD

The diagnosis of PTSD is unique in that it requires the presence of a traumatic event. Specifically, the *Diagnostic and Statistical Manual of Mental
Disorders* (*DSM-IV*; American Psychiatric Association, 1994) requires that the
person be exposed to a traumatic event in which both of the following were
present: (a) The person experienced, witnessed, or was confronted with an
event that involved actual or threatened death or serious injury, or a threat
to the physical integrity of self or others, and (b) the person's response
involved intense fear, helplessness, or horror. Examples of such events are
rape, physical assault, a serious car accident, the murder of a family member or close friend, a natural disaster, or military combat.

There are three main sets of symptom criteria pertaining to the diagnosis of PTSD: reexperiencing, numbing and avoidance, and arousal symptoms. Reexperiencing symptoms include having thoughts about the event
even when the individual is not trying to think about it, distressing dreams
about the event, acting or feeling as though the traumatic event was occur-

ring again, feeling very distressed when confronted with reminders of the traumatic event, and experiencing physical symptoms that were experienced at the time of the traumatic event (i.e., heart racing or sweating) when reminded of the event.

Avoidance and numbing symptoms include trying to avoid thoughts, feelings, or conversations that are reminders of the traumatic event; avoidance of activities, places, or people that are reminders of the traumatic event; not being able to remember important parts of the traumatic event; and not feeling very interested in participating in activities that used to be of interest. Another avoidance and numbing symptom that may be experienced includes a sense of foreshortened future, such as thinking he or she will never get married or have children or a career, or not expecting to have a normal life span. Finally, numbing of emotions may occur. An example of this would be difficulty experiencing loving feelings.

The final set of PTSD symptoms are arousal symptoms. These include difficulty falling or staying asleep, irritability or outbursts of anger, difficulty concentrating, feeling on guard even when there is no reason to be, and being more easily startled by unexpected or sudden noises. In order to diagnose this disorder the following criteria must be met: one reexperiencing symptom, three avoidance and numbing symptoms, and two arousal symptoms for a least 1 month after the trauma. As can be seen, there are really two components to diagnosing PTSD: determining the traumatic event history and assessing for the symptoms of PTSD.

THEORIES OF VICTIM REACTIONS

Several cognitive-behavioral and cognitive theories have been applied to victim reactions, including learning theories, information processing theories, and more recently cognitive constructivist theories. These theories will be reviewed briefly to provide an overview and framework for understanding assessment and treatment of victims of crime.

Learning Theory

Learning theory has been proposed to explain victim reactions by several researchers (Becker, Skinner, Abel, Axelrod, & Cichon, 1984; Holmes & St. Lawrence, 1983; Kilpatrick, Veronen, & Best, 1985; Kilpatrick, Veronen & Resick, 1982). In general, learning theory proposes that the fear and anxiety reactions of victims are acquired through classical conditioning, stimulus generalization, and second-order conditioning. Classical conditioning accounts for how previously neutral cues can become fear cues. When a victim is in a high state of arousal, previously neutral stimuli become conditioned stimuli that acquire the capacity to evoke fear and anxiety. Furthermore, avoidance responses are negatively reinforced by anxiety reduction following avoidance behavior. Fear and anxiety responses can also generalize to stimuli that are similar to the conditioned stimuli. Second-order conditioning can take place at any time the conditioned response is present with new stimuli. These stimuli then also become paired with the fear and anxiety response.

Learning theory accounts for many of the symptoms of PTSD. Specifically, the intense psychological distress and the physiologic reactivity at exposure to events that symbolize or resemble an aspect of the traumatic event, and the avoidance symptoms of PTSD are accounted for by learning theory. However, learning theory is unable to account for other symptoms. For instance, persistent reexperiencing of the event and other intrusive symptoms, such as nightmares and flashbacks, cannot be fully accounted for by learning theory. This is evident in cases of individuals who were not direct victims, but who lost a family member by murder. Oftentimes surviving family members suffer from reexperiencing symptoms of what they imagine their loved one's death to have been, even if they were not present at the time of the death. In addition, numbing symptoms are not adequately accounted for within a learning theory framework. Clearly, more is involved than conditioning, or many of the preassault, assault, and postassault variables that have been found to be relevant to the development of symptoms would not play a role. For example, conditioning models cannot adequately account for why rape causes more disturbances than many other crimes, such as robbery. Nor can it account for why certain cognitive factors, such as causal attributions and self-blame, are strong predictors of PTSD.

Information Processing Theory

Out of this need for a better understanding of victim reactions and variables that influence recovery, information processing theories have been applied within the victim reaction research. For example, Chemtob, Roitblat, Hamada, Carlson, and Twentyman (1988) have developed a "cognitive action" theory of PTSD based on their work with Vietnam veterans. They propose that people suffering from PTSD develop fear structures that hold images and memories of threatening events as well as information regarding emotions and plans for action. These fear structures comprise threat schema that Chemtob, et al. propose are weakly activated at all times in people with PTSD. Thus, for someone with PTSD, the activated threat schema can cause many events to be interpreted as potentially dangerous, and can also bring forth memories, emotions, and physiologic reactions associated with traumatic events.

Foa, Steketee, and Olasov-Rothbaum (1989) have also proposed an information processing theory to explain PTSD. Similar to Chemtob and colleagues (1988), Foa and associates conceptualize PTSD as primarily an anxiety disorder that results from the development of a fear network. Their theory is based on the work of Lang (1977) and is based on the notion that an internal fear structure is developed that is a program for escape and avoidance behavior. Thus, stimuli that access the fear schema can cause the victim to avoid. Any stimuli that were associated with the crime can become part of the fear schema; thus, not only do certain places or objects become fear producing, but sounds, smells, and physical sensations can also become part of the fear schema.

Cognitive Constructivist Theory

More recently, constructivist theory has been applied to understand reactions to victimization. Constructivist theorists propose that individuals actively construct their own mental representations of the world (Meichenbaum, 1993). These representations, sometimes referred to as schema, have personal meaning and are based on each individual's unique life experiences.

McCann and Pearlman (1990) proposed that there are specific schema that may be disrupted by victimization. These include safety, trust, independence, power, esteem, and intimacy schema. According to McCann and Pearlman, individuals have such schema about themselves and about other people. Depending upon the individual's previous life experiences, victimization may either serve to disrupt or confirm prior beliefs. For example, for someone who has a previous victimization history, another victimization may serve to confirm negative beliefs about being able to trust others. Conversely, for someone who has never experienced any prior victimization and is perhaps very trusting of others, being victimized would disrupt positive beliefs about trusting others.

Resick and Schnicke (1993) have taken a broader approach in their investigations of rape victims by combining principles from learning, information processing, and constructivist theories. They suggest that victims suffer from many more negative affective reactions than simply fear. In their conceptualization of PTSD, they have proposed that rape is such a traumatic experience that victims are often unable to integrate the event successfully with prior beliefs and experiences. Instead, the event is either changed to fit prior beliefs (assimilation) or prior beliefs are altered (accommodation). They further hypothesize that symptoms of intrusion and avoidance occur because the event has not been either assimilated or accommodated successfully. In addition, their treatment approach, cognitive processing therapy, directly addresses disruptions in the schema proposed by McCann and Pearlman (1990). Although information processing and cognitive theories of victim reactions appear to explain victim reactions better than either crisis theory or learning theories alone, there is still much needed research to test these theories with victims of crimes other than rape to determine if such theories adequately account for both the symptoms and other variables identified as important to the understanding of victim reactions.

ASSESSMENT OF PTSD AND OTHER TRAUMA-RELATED PROBLEMS

A thorough trauma history assessment instrument can assist in determining traumatic event history as well as event characteristics such as type of event, fear of injury, and actual injury that are important in determining risk for the development of PTSD. Identification of trauma history is important in settings where patients may present with problems that are not obviously trauma related as well as in settings where patients are clearly seeking treatment for trauma-related symptomatology. Between 40% and 70% of individuals within general population samples have been exposed to crime or other traumatic events included in the PTSD diagnostic criteria (Breslau, Davis, Andreski, & Peterson, 1991; Norris, 1992; Resnick, Kilpatrick, et al., 1993) and many individuals have been exposed to more than one traumatic stressor (Breslau et al., 1991; Resnick, Kilpatrick, et al., 1993). Rates of trauma in patient populations may be even higher, and some patients may not disclose trauma-related symptomatology as their presenting problem. Thus, even in settings where the treatment of trauma victims is not the focus, screening for trauma history is important.

One option for trauma screening is to use a measure such as the Trauma Assessment for Adults Self-Report (Resnick, Best, Kilpatrick, Freedy, & Falsetti, 1993). This is a self-report measure that patients can fill out along with other self-report measures as a part of the initial evaluation. It assesses a wide range of traumatic events including military combat, serious accidents, natural disasters, serious illness, sexual assault, physical assault, other events that involve serious injury, witnessing someone else seriously injured or violently killed, and homicide of a family member or close friend using behaviorally specific terms. This measure has been used successfully in settings for the treatment of anxiety disorders other than PTSD and is a more sensitive instrument than the SCID in assessing traumatic events (Falsetti et al., 1996). The Trauma Assessment for Adults Self-Report takes only 10 minutes for the patient to complete and also provides information about age(s) at the time of event(s), fear of death or serious injury during event(s), presence of physical injury during event(s), and relationship of perpetrator.

A broad trauma screening combined with a thorough clinical interview that includes assessment of previous psychiatric history and perception of vulnerability to traumatic events can lay the groundwork for problem identification and provide information about factors that are associated with trauma reactions. During the interview, more information can be gathered about traumatic events identified in the screening and the clinician can explain the relevance of this information to treatment planning.

In a setting that specializes in treatment of trauma victims, a trauma interview may be routinely conducted. If an interview format is used, it is important to use sensitive behaviorally specific questions rather than legal terminology, particularly in the assessment of sexual assault (Kilpatrick & Veronen, 1983; Koss, 1985). Following is a specific example of the questions from the National Women's Study PTSD Module about unwanted sexual advances:

"Has a man or boy ever made you have sex by using force or threatening to harm you or someone close to you? Just so there is no mistake, by sex we mean putting a penis in your vagina."

"Has anyone ever made you have oral sex by force or threat of harm? Just so there is no mistake, by oral sex we mean that a man or a boy put his penis in your mouth or someone penetrated your vagina or anus with their mouth or tongue."

"Has anyone ever made you have anal sex by force or threat of harm?"

"Has anyone ever put fingers or objects in your vagina or anus against your will by using force or threats?"

The assessment of traumatic events is an area under development, and research is needed to further develop standardized instruments that can be used across clinical populations. For a more in-depth review of these issues as well as other published and unpublished instruments, see Resnick and Falsetti (1996) or Resnick, Kilpatrick, and Lipovsky (1991).

After establishing the presence of a traumatic event history the symptom criteria of PTSD should be assessed. There are currently several interview and self-report measures available for the assessment of PTSD. The most frequently used interviews include the Structured Clinical Interview for DSM-IV (SCID; Spitzer, Williams, Gibbon, & First, 1990) and the Diagnostic Interview Schedule (Robins, Helzer, Cottler, & Goldring, 1988). The Clinician Administered PTSD Scale (CAPS) includes assessment of symptom frequency and intensity, and is described in Blake, et al. (1990). Cutoff scores for the CAPS have been developed and there is high agreement between this measure and the SCID (.89) in diagnosing PTSD.

With regard to self-report instruments, Rothbaum, Foa, Riggs, Murdock, and Walsh (1992) report data on predictive utility of cutoff scores obtained within the first few weeks posttrauma on the Impact of Events test(Horowitz, Wilner, & Alvarez, 1979) and Rape Aftermath Symptom Test (RAST; Kilpatrick, 1988) in predicting chronic PTSD among rape victims. The

RAST contains items from the Symptom Checklist 90-Revised (Derogatis, 1983) and the Modified Fear Survey (Seidner & Kilpatrick, 1988), and is relevant for administration to individuals who have experienced a wide variety of stressor events, not just rape.

Finally, there are now some promising self-report measures that cover more comprehensively all the PTSD criteria symptoms within a single instrument. These instruments include the PTSD Symptom Scale (PSS; Foa, Riggs, Dancu, & Rothbaum, 1993) and the Modified PTSD Symptom Scale–Self-Report (MPSS-SR; Resick, Falsetti, Resnick, & Kilpatrick, 1991), which is a modification of the PSS that includes changes in several individual items and an assessment of severity of symptoms as well as frequency of symptoms. Both instruments consist of 17 items that correspond to the *DSM-IV* symptom criteria for PTSD. Like the PSS, the MPSS-SR is designed to assess PTSD symptoms for the 2-week period prior to the time of administration. Furthermore, in recognition of the high prevalence of multiple stressor events that may be experienced, the respondent is instructed to report symptom frequency and severity within the past 2 weeks that may relate to any of the Criterion A stressor events that have been evaluated as part of the thorough stressor event assessment. Both the PSS and the MPSS-SR can be scored as dichotomous (yes/no for each symptom) or continuous (a range of scores) measures of symptom distress. The MPSS-SR has high internal consistency (.96) as well as good concurrent validity with the Structured Clinical Interview for *DSM-IV*. Further data related to reliability and validity of the MPSS-SR are presented in Falsetti, Resnick, Resick, and Kilpatrick (1993).

Saunders, Mandoki, and Kilpatrick (1990) reported results of a PTSD scale derived from the Symptom Checklist 90-Revised instrument that discriminated between current PTSD positive and negative cases identified using structured diagnostic interviews within a large community sample. This scale as well as the PSS Self-Report and the MPSS-SR are brief self-report instruments that can be given following the trauma screening for a quick and efficient assessment of PTSD symptomatology at initial assessment. If many of the PTSD symptoms are endorsed, then a more thorough trauma assessment, such as the CAPS, can be completed. Self-report measures are also useful for assessing PTSD symptomatology during the course of treatment. For a more in-depth review of PTSD symptom assessment issues and instruments, see Resnick and associates (1991) and Resnick and Falsetti (1996).

Depression is often found to be comorbid with PTSD, with rates of 40% to 80% reported (Ellis, Atkeson, & Calhoun, 1981; Frank & Stewart, 1984; Hough, 1985; Resick, 1989). The most common instruments used to assess depression in this population include the Structured Diagnostic Interview for DSM-IV (Spitzer et al., 1990) and the Beck Depression Inventory (BDI;

Beck, Ward, Mendelson, Mock, & Erbaugh, 1961). Atkeson, Calhoun, Resick, and Ellis (1982) found the BDI to discriminate between rape victims and nonvictims 2 months after the assault. Beck, et al. reported a split-half reliability of .93. Although it should not be used alone to diagnose clinical depression, the BDI is a helpful screening instrument and can also be given periodically throughout treatment to assess progress.

Panic attacks are also commonly associated with PTSD in trauma victims (Falsetti & Resnick, 1997a). The *DSM-IV* includes a revision in which panic attacks are listed prior to the criteria for anxiety disorders, therefore allowing the specification of the absence or presence of panic attacks with other anxiety disorders. This allows for the diagnosis of PTSD with panic attacks, thus providing a more accurate clinical description for many patients who have suffered trauma. Falsetti and Resnick (1997a) found that 69% of 62 clients seeking treatment for trauma-related symptomatology suffered from panic attacks.

Because panic disorder (PD) has traditionally not been assessed in relation to victimization there are no instruments specifically designed for use with trauma victims to assess PD. However, there are several instruments designed to assess PD that have been used in general clinic and anxiety treatment settings, including the SCID Panic Disorder Module (Spitzer et al., 1990) and the Anxiety Disorder Interview Schedule-Revised Panic Disorder Module (Di Nardo et al., 1985). Both modules are interview formats that include instructions and require some clinical judgment for proper diagnosis. These modules are typically brief enough to allow for routine use within clinical settings.

In addition, the Physical Reactions Scale (Falsetti & Resnick, 1992), a brief self-report measure that assesses panic symptoms, can be used to assess panic attacks in relation to traumatic events. This scale assesses frequency and severity of panic attack symptoms in the 2-week period prior to assessment. After determining the presence or absence of panic attacks, patients are asked whether they had panic attacks when reminded of the traumatic stressor.

The assessment of individual panic attacks throughout treatment can be an important indicator of improvement. The *Mastery of Your Anxiety and Panic Manual* (Barlow & Craske, 1988) provides panic attack records for this purpose. The number of panic attacks each week can then be charted in a graph over the course of treatment.

Substance abuse is often another common problem for victims of civilian trauma. Kilpatrick, Edmunds, and Seymour (1992) found higher rates of substance use reported by crime victims compared to individuals who did not report a victimization history in a large national probability sample of 4,008 adult women. Fifty-two percent of rape victims reported using marijuana compared to only 16% of nonvictims; almost 16% of victims reported cocaine use compared to 2.5% of nonvictims; and 12% of victims reported using other hard drugs compared to only 1% of nonvictims. Furthermore, victims who also had PTSD were five times more likely to have two or more major alcohol-related problems compared to victims who did not have PTSD. Finally, victims with PTSD were four times more likely to have two or more serious drug-related problems compared to victims without PTSD. These findings indicate a strong need to assess for substance abuse in victims of crime, particularly in victims who have been diagnosed with PTSD.

Many clinicians have not formally assessed for substance abuse with victims of crime until recently. At the National Crime Victims Research and Treatment Center, we use a brief alcohol and drug screening interview based on the CAGE (Ewing, 1984; Ewing & Rouse, 1970) that provides enough information to determine if a more thorough assessment of substance abuse is warranted. For a more thorough assessment, the Structured Clinical Interview for *DSM-IV* (SCID) includes assessment of psychoactive substance use disorders that can be used to diagnose substance abuse disorders, as does the Diagnostic Interview Schedule (Robins et al., 1988).

The assessment of social support, cognitions, and causal attributions are also important for the planning of treatment. The Social Adjustment Scale (Weissman & Paykel, 1974) assesses functioning in major role areas in the 2 weeks prior to assessment. In addition to an overall adjustment score, subscale scores can be derived from the sections of work, social and leisure, extended family, marital, parental, family unit, and economic. Test-retest reliability after one month was computed at $r = .74$ (Resick, Calhoun, Atkeson, & Ellis, 1981), and results of the same study indicated that this scale is useful in detecting victimization-related problems in role functioning.

Several researchers have noted the importance of changes in cognitions and cognitions about the trauma in relation to PTSD (Dunmore, Clark, & Ehlers, 1997; Ehlers & Steil, 1995; Falsetti & Resick, 1995; Frazier & Schauben, 1994). The cognitive effects of victimization and causal attributions about the trauma can be assessed using the World Assumption Scale (WAS; Janoff-Bulman, 1989) and/or the Personal Beliefs and Reactions Scale (PBRS; Mechanic & Resick, 1993). The WAS is a 32-item scale that assesses basic assumptions about the world on a 6-point Likert scale. Three main subscales can be derived that are labeled benevolence of the world, meaningfulness of the world, and self-worth. Reliability coefficients for these subscales range from .76 to .87. Eight smaller subscales can also be computed: benevolence of the world, benevolence of people, luck, justice, randomness, control, self-worth, and self-control. Reliability coefficients for these subscales range from .66 to .76. The PBRS is composed of 55 statements that make up 10 subscales: beliefs, undoing, self-blame, safety, trust, competency/power, esteem, intimacy, self, and others. This scale has been used extensively with rape victims to assess cognitions (Mechanic & Resick, 1993).

After completing the assessment of factors that may contribute to symptomatology and the symptomatology itself, possible factors that might get in the way of goal attainment (i.e., reducing trauma-related symptomatology) should be assessed. With trauma victims, behavioral avoidance of trauma-related, conditioned cues and lack of coping skills are common impediments. The level of behavioral avoidance can be assessed by reviewing results of the PTSD assessment measures, which include diagnostic questions about avoidance. Coping skills can be assessed in clinical interview by asking the patient what she or he is currently doing to cope with the trauma, and how she or he has coped in the past with stressful events. Sometimes coping skills are dysfunctional and self-destructive (e.g., substance abuse or overeating), but other times are very helpful (e.g., exercise or meditation) and can be built upon in the course of treatment.

In summary, the assessment process should be broad in the range of traumatic event assessment and then focused on specific disorders that are known to result from exposure to traumatic events. The assessment process can be streamlined by using screening instruments to assist in determining areas of further assessment. Finally, in addition to the assessment of trauma and trauma-related symptomatology, the assessment of pretrauma functioning, cognitions, coping skills, social support, and behavioral avoidance are also important.

TREATMENT ALTERNATIVES FOR PTSD

Cognitive behavioral therapy is widely used and highly effective in the treatment of PTSD. Cognitive processing therapy (CPI; Resick & Schnicke, 1993), developed for the treatment of PTSD in rape victims, employs mainly a cognitive approach. This treatment focuses on changes in cognition that result from trauma. Components of stress inoculation training (SIT; Kilpatrick, Veronen, & Resick, 1982) and multiple channel exposure therapy (MCET; Falsetti & Resnick, 1997b) also employ cognitive techniques. Prolonged exposure therapy (PET), although primarily a behavioral treatment, is based on an information processing theory, which is cognitively focused and may change faulty cognitions. We will review the components of each of these treatments and then present the research on efficacy. For full descriptions of SIT, PET, CPT, and MCET, readers are referred to the following resources:

SIT—   Kilpatrick, Veronen, and Resick (1982); Foa, Rothbaum, and Steketee (1993); Resnick and Newton (1992); Resick and Jordan (1988); Veronen and Kilpatrick (1983).

PE—   Foa, Rothbaum, Riggs, and Murdock (1991); Foa, Rothbaum, and Steketee (1993); Foa and Rothbaum (1998).

CPT—   Resick (1992); Resick and Schnicke (1990); Resick and
        Schnicke (1992); Resick and Schnicke (1993); Calhoun and
        Resick (1993).
MCET—   Falsetti (1997).

Stress Inoculation Training

Based on learning theory, SIT was originally developed from Meichenbaum's
(1974) stress inoculation and was adapted by Kilpatrick, Veronen, and
Resick (1982) and Veronen and Kilpatrick (1983) to treat the fear and anxiety experienced by rape victims. SIT consists of three treatment phases:
education, skill building, and application (Resick & Jordan, 1988).
Generally, treatment requires 8 to 14 sessions depending upon individual
needs of the client and the specific approach.

Educational Phase

The first session or two of treatment includes an overview of treatment, a
presentation about how the fear response develops based on learning theory, information about sympathetic nervous system arousal, and instruction in progressive muscle relaxation. Clients are asked to practice
progressive relaxation and to identify cues that trigger fear reactions. In
the following session(s) the information previously given is reviewed, and
the fear response is described in further detail as occurring in three
response channels: the body (physiologic reactions), the mind (thoughts),
and behavior (actions). Practice of relaxation training, identification of
fear cues, and identification of safety factors are practiced outside of sessions as homework.

Skill Building Phase

This phase of treatment emphasizes the development of coping skills for
the three channels described above. Most descriptions of SIT include teaching diaphragmatic breathing, thought stopping, covert rehearsal, guided
self-dialogue, and role playing (Kilpatrick et al., 1982; Resick & Jordan,
1988; Resnick & Newton, 1992). In addition, Resick and Jordan include the
"quieting reflex," a brief relaxation technique developed by Stroebel
(1983), and problem-solving techniques as skill building components.
These techniques are described in the references provided above, and thus
will not be described again here.

Application Phase

In the application phase of treatment, the goal is to have clients integrate
and apply the skills they have learned and to use the following steps of stress
inoculation: (a) assess the probability of feared event, (b) manage escape

and avoidance behavior with thought stopping and the quieting reflex, (c) control self-criticism with guided self-dialogue, (d) engage in the feared behavior, and, (e) self-reinforcement for using skills. Clients are asked to develop fear hierarchies to continue exposure work after therapy has ended. The final session consists of a review of the training program.

Prolonged Exposure Therapy

Also referred to as flooding, PET has proven to be an effective treatment for many Vietnam veterans with PTSD (Fairbank & Keane, 1982; Keane, Fairbank, Caddell, & Zimering, 1989; Keane & Kaloupek, 1982), and more recently has been investigated as a treatment option for rape victims with PTSD (Foa et al., 1991; Foa et al., 1999). This treatment approach is based on principles of learning and information processing theories. One of the primary goals of exposure therapy is to confront the feared stimuli in imagination so that fear and anxiety decrease. This is similar to watching a frightening movie over and over. At first it may be very frightening, but by the 20th viewing it would not be as frightening. Analogously, replaying a frightening memory becomes less frightening as it is recounted numerous times in an objectively safe environment. Clients are also asked to confront fear cues that are not dangerous, but that may have been paired with danger at the time of the traumatic event. In vivo exposure to fear cues is used to extinguish the fear associated with these stimuli. This involves exposure to objects or situations in real life.

Foa and colleagues (1991) described PET for rape victims with PTSD within nine biweekly 90-minute sessions. The first two sessions of treatment were used for the initial interview, to explain the rationale of treatment, and to plan treatment. The remaining seven sessions consisted of imaginal exposure to the rape. Clients were asked to describe their rape in great detail in the present tense; as though it is really happening. They were instructed to repeat the account over and over for about an hour. Typically, during the first two imaginal exposure sessions, clients were allowed to choose the level of detail that was tolerable to them. In the remaining exposure sessions, clients were asked to describe the assault in as much detail as possible. Subjective units of distress ratings were assessed within and across sessions to monitor fear and anxiety levels. Exposure sessions were recorded and given to clients to take home and listen to at least once a day to provide further exposure trials. In addition, clients were encouraged to practice exposing themselves to situations that are not dangerous, but that they fear because of the rape. Examples of such situations for rape victims often include dating, going out with friends, watching the news or reading the newspaper (often avoided because of stories about similar crimes), and other situations that were specific to their experience.

Cognitive Processing Therapy

CPT was developed by Resick and Schnicke (1990, 1992, 1993) for rape victims suffering from PTSD and depression. Resick and Schnicke proposed that PTSD consists of more than a fear network. Victims may also suffer from other strong feelings such as disgust, shame, and anger. As a framework for understanding how other intense emotions might develop they have highlighted the work of Hollon and Garber (1988), who have suggested that when a person is exposed to information that is schema discrepant, assimilation or accommodation takes place. Put simply, this means that when something unusual happens that we either do not really have a category (schema) for, or that does not happen in the way our schema indicates it should (e.g., rapes only happen to bad people who walk in dark alleys at night), then we either must alter the information (assimilation) or alter our schemas (accommodation). Examples of assimilation include self-blaming statements ("It must be my fault because I was wearing a short skirt," or "Maybe it wasn't really rape, but I really wanted it like he said"), whereas accommodation often results in extreme cognitive distortions, such as, "I never feel safe," "I trust no one," and "I have to be in control at all times."

The goal of CPT is to assist in integrating the event, with complete processing of emotions and accommodation of schema while helping the client to maintain or achieve a healthy outlook and balanced perception of the world. Furthermore, the following issues that McCann and colleagues (McCann & Pearlman, 1990; McCann, Sakheim, & Pearlman, 1988) have identified as being affected by victimization are also a focus of CPT: safety, trust, power, esteem, and intimacy.

CPT provides exposure to the traumatic memory and training in challenging maladaptive cognitions. This treatment may be better than exposure alone because it also provides corrective information regarding misattributions or other maladaptive beliefs (Resick & Schnicke, 1993). CPT is focused on identifying and modifying "stuckpoints," which are inadequately processed conflicts between prior schema and new information (i.e., the traumatic event). Stuckpoints are also proposed to arise from (a) negative, conflicting schemata imposed by others (victim blame); (b) an avoidant coping style; or (c) no relevant schema in which to store the information.

CPT as described by Resick and Schnicke (1993) can be conducted in either group or individual sessions and can be completed in 12 weekly sessions. The content of treatment includes a cognitive information processing explanation of traumatic event reactions and writing assignments about the meaning of the event. This is followed by education regarding basic feelings and how changes in self-statements can affect emotions. Clients are also taught how to identify the connections among actions, beliefs, and consequences, and are asked to write accounts of the traumatic event and read them repeatedly. Resick and Schnicke point out that writings about the trauma are often more detailed than oral accounts and serve as exposure, which facilitates a decrease of strong negative emotions in a way similar to that described in the section on prolonged imaginal exposure. The accounts also expose stuckpoints. In addition, several of the sessions focus on developing skills to analyze and confront stuckpoints and other maladaptive self-statements regarding the traumatic event. This is followed by a series of sessions that cover the five belief areas proposed by McCann, et al. (1988). The final session is devoted to review and planning for the future.

Multiple Channel Exposure Therapy

MCET was adapted from CPT (Resick & Schnicke, 1993), SIT (Kilpatrick et al., 1982), and mastery of your anxiety and panic (Barlow & Craske, 1988) treatments. The utility of this treatment approach is based on the high prevalence of PTSD and panic attacks, and learning and information processing theories. Generally, cognitive-behavioral treatments for PTSD based on learning and information processing theories are hypothesized to work by exposure to the feared memory of the traumatic event or by exposure to cues (e.g., places, situations, smell, and sounds) that are not in and of themselves dangerous, but which became associated with fear at the time of a traumatic event. During the course of these treatments the patient initially experiences high levels of physiological arousal which, with successful treatment, decrease over the course of repeated sessions until extinction occurs. However, for patients who have panic attacks and who are fearful of the attacks, this may be very overwhelming, and thus not feasible. MCET is unique in that it provides exposure to physiologic arousal symptoms prior to cognitive and behavioral exposure. This is hypothesized to decrease fear of physiologic arousal symptoms experienced in PTSD and panic attacks. Thus, when exposure to traumatic memories and cues is conducted, clients will be less fearful of physiologic reactions (Resnick & Newton, 1992).

MCET is a 12-week treatment that has been conducted in groups and individually. It is applicable for individuals who have experienced many types of traumatic events and are suffering from PTSD and panic attacks as a result of their traumatic experience(s). MCET provides exposure through directly accessing the three channels that have been hypothesized to comprise the fear response system: physiologic, cognitive, and behavioral (Lang, 1977). Exposure to the physiologic channel is conducted through interoceptive exposure to physiologic reactions, a method used by Barlow and Craske (1988) in their "Mastery of Your Anxiety and Panic" for the treatment of PD. The exercises that are used to bring about panic-like sensations include having the client shake his or her head from side to side, tensing muscles, holding his or her breath briefly, spinning in a chair, breathing through a straw, stair stepping, and hyperventilating.

Exposure to the cognitive channel is conducted through writing assignments about the traumatic event. This method of exposure has been used effectively with rape victims by Resick and Schnicke (1992) as a component of CPT. Resick has noted that writing provides much more detail than verbal accounts of traumatic events. The process of writing may also be more engaging and palatable than prolonged exposure (PE) for many victims and allows for confidentiality regarding trauma specifics for each participant in a group setting. Finally, the exposure to the behavioral channel is conducted through in vivo exposure to conditioned cues to the traumatic event. This type of exposure has been used in SIT (Kilpatrick et al., 1982; Resick & Jordan, 1988) for rape victims.

In addition to the exposure components, MCET also provides education about PTSD and panic symptoms and includes several cognitive components to address distorted cognitions about trauma. Clients are taught to look at the evidence for their beliefs and to identify when they are overestimating the risk of a negative outcome, catastrophizing, overgeneralizing, basing their thoughts on feelings instead of facts, and disregarding important aspects of situations. Cognitive skills are employed to assist participants in challenging distorted thinking and to fully process traumatic memories. Worksheets addressing disruptions in beliefs about safety, trust, esteem, and power/competency have been adapted from CPT.

Education, breathing retraining, and cognitive components have also been adapted from current treatments for panic disorder (Mastery of Your Anxiety and Panic; Barlow & Craske, 1988), and PTSD (CPT; Resick & Schnicke, 1993). Because the cause of panic in the case of traumatic events is hypothesized to be different than that of spontaneous panic (Falsetti, Resnick, Dansky, Lydiard, & Kilpatrick, 1995), the conceptualization clients are provided with is different than that of Barlow and Craske (1988). Panic attacks are explained as an unconditioned response to the trauma, that following the trauma become a conditioned response to reminders of the trauma. The educational component contains a greater focus on identification of cognitive, physiologic, behavioral, and situational cues that may have been components of index traumatic events than that included in the Mastery of Your Anxiety and Panic education. Exposure to panic symptoms then serves not only to decrease fear of the symptoms themselves, but also provides exposure to the physiological component of fear associated with trauma, and thereby weakens the association of physiological arousal and the traumatic memory.

EMPIRICAL SUPPORT

Studies that have investigated SIT, PET, CPT, and MCET have supported the efficacy of these treatments. Veronen and Kilpatrick (1983) reported that SIT was effective in treating fear, anxiety, tension, and depression in 15 female rape victims treated with 20 hours of SIT. Unfortunately, there was not a control group in this study for comparison. Veronen and Kilpatrick did attempt a comparison study shortly thereafter utilizing SIT, peer counseling, and systematic desensitization. In this study participants were allowed to choose a treatment. Over half chose not to participate, no one chose systematic desensitization, 11 chose SIT, one did not choose and was assigned SIT, and three others chose peer counseling. The clients who completed SIT improved from pre- to posttreatment, but unfortunately no comparisons among treatments could be conducted.

Foa and associates (1991) compared SIT, exposure treatment, supportive counseling, and a no-treatment control group. All clients were seen for nine 90-minute sessions twice a week. The SIT approach in this study differed from that described by Kilpatrick and colleagues (1982) in that it did not include instructions for in vivo exposure to feared situations. Foa and associates reported that all treatments utilized led to some improvement in anxiety, depression, and PTSD. SIT was indicated to be the most effective treatment for PTSD at immediate follow-up, whereas at a 3.5-month follow-up, clients who had participated in the exposure treatment had fewer PTSD symptoms.

More recently, Foa and associates (1999) conducted another study comparing PET, SIT, and a PET-SIT combination in female assault victims. As in the 1991 study, SIT was modified by excluding the in vivo exposure component, so as not to be confounded with PET. Participants were 96 women who had experienced a physical or sexual assault and met criteria for PTSD. Treatment was conducted individually and consisted of nine twice-weekly sessions. Of the 96 women who participated in the study, 17 dropped out during the course of treatment and 79 completed the study. Treatment effects were analyzed in both the intent-to-treat sample and the completer sample. Results from the intent-to-treat sample indicated that PET was superior to SIT and PET-SIT on posttreatment anxiety and global social adjustment at follow-up and had larger effect sizes on PTSD severity, depression, and anxiety, whereas SIT and PE-SIT did not differ significantly from each other on any outcome measure. Results using only treatment completers indicated that all three active treatments reduced PTSD and depression compared to women randomly assigned to a wait-list control group and that these gains were maintained at 3-, 6- and 12-month follow-ups. There are several alternative explanations for the superiority of PET compared to the other treatments. First, there was a trend toward significance for more women who did not work in the PET-SIT (43%) and SIT (30%) groups compared to the PET (19%) and control groups (8%). It is possible that the women who did not work may have been more functionally impaired in ways that were not assessed and that this interfered with their ability to participate in treatment. Indeed, more women also dropped out from these groups. Alternatively, it is also possible that more women actually got better and dropped out for this reason, thus reducing the success rates of the these treatments compared to SIT in the intent-to-treat analyses. It is also possible that the added load of doing both treatments in the same amount of time did not allow for enough time to develop the coping skills in SIT. Finally, an important component of SIT—in vivo exposure—was left out, which may have decreased the effectiveness of SIT.

Resick, Jordan, Girelli, Hutter, and Marhoefer-Dvorak (1988) compared six 2-hour group sessions of SIT, assertion training, and supportive psychotherapy plus information, and a wait-list control group. They reported that all three treatments were effective in reducing symptoms, with no significant differences among treatments. The clients on the wait-list control did not improve. At a 6-month follow-up, improvement was maintained in relation to rape-related fears, but not on depression, self-esteem, and social fears.

In addition to Foa and colleagues (1991, 1999) comparison studies, other researchers have also indicated the efficacy of flooding therapy. Marks, Lovell, Noshirvani, Livanou, and Thrasher (1998) compared exposure and cognitive restructuring. Marks and associates completed a controlled study with 87 patients comparing PET alone, cognitive restructuring alone, combined PET and cognitive restructuring, and relaxation without prolonged exposure or cognitive restructuring. They found that exposure alone, cognitive restructuring alone, and exposure plus cognitive restructuring all produced marked improvement and were generally superior to relaxation training alone. Therapists conducting the treatment in the study reported that doing the combination treatment was more difficult than doing either alone. Interestingly, combining these two treatments did not appear to enhance treatment effect. However, similar to Foa and colleagues' (1999) study, the combination treatment was given in the same amount of time as the other treatment alone. Thus, patients may not have had enough time to thoroughly integrate all they had learned. Given that these treatments are reporting good end-state functioning in only a portion of patients (Marks et al.: 53% exposure, 32% cognitive restructuring, 32% exposure and cognitive restructuring; and Foa, et al. [1999]: 57% exposure, 42% SIT, 36% PET-SIT), it would seem a worthwhile endeavor to conduct treatment outcome studies with combinations of cognitive and behavioral techniques over a longer period of time to determine if this would improve outcome for a larger number of PTSD sufferers.

Results of CPT, which is primarily a cognitive treatment for PTSD, have been promising. Resick and Schnicke (1992) reported significant improvements with CPT on depression and PTSD measures from pretreatment to 6 months posttreatment for 19 sexual assault survivors who were at least 3 months postrape at the start of treatment. Therapy was conducted in group format over 12 weeks and a wait-list control group was also employed ($n = 20$). Rates of PTSD went from a pretreatment rate of 90% to a posttreatment rate of 0%. Rates of major depression decreased from 62% to 42%. Further evaluation of the treatment indicates usefulness of both group and individual formats, with somewhat higher efficacy for treatment administered in individual sessions (Resick, 1993). A large controlled study is currently underway to further test this treatment.

Falsetti and Resnick are currently completing a 3-year controlled study of M-CET. Falsetti and Resnick (1998) reported on preliminary data from the study on 48 women. Of these 48 women, 20 were randomly assigned to the treatment condition and 28 were randomly assigned to the minimal attention control. Two of the subjects from the treatment condition were excluded at the time of initial evaluation, one due to active substance abuse and one due to suicidality. Seven of the remaining 18 subjects have completed treatment, as well as six subjects who first completed the control condition, with an additional three subjects currently in treatment. Treatment data from one of the six subjects who completed treatment after being a control was dropped because she no longer met criteria for PTSD after completing the control condition. Fifteen of the 28 control subjects had completed the study, with an additional three subjects participating in the control condition at the time of data analysis.

Data analyses were conducted on demographic variables of the randomly assigned treatment group ($n = 7$), randomly assigned control-only group ($n = 10$), and the control-then-treatment group ($n = 5$), to determine if there were any differences among these groups on demographic variables. Results of these analyses indicated there were no differences; thus, the treatment data of the control-then-treatment group were combined with data from treatment group. Results indicated that MCET may be an effective treatment for PTSD with panic attacks. At posttreatment, only 8.3% of subjects in the MCET treatment condition met criteria for PTSD compared to 66.7% of subjects in the minimal-attention control group. Panic attacks and related symptoms also decreased significantly. All subjects were experiencing panic attacks at the initial evaluation. At the post-evaluation, 93.3% of the minimal-attention control group subjects had experienced at least one panic attack in the past month, compared to only 50% of the treatment group. Interference of the panic attacks in the past month was assessed on a 5-point scale (0 to 4). At pretreatment, both groups reported moderate to severe interference. At posttreatment, the control group had not changed, whereas the treatment group mean dropped significantly to below mild. Finally, both groups experienced a decrease in depressive symptoms as measured by the Beck Depression Inventory.

CASE EXAMPLE

As research in the area of trauma related disorders has progressed, it is becoming clear that many victims who develop PTSD also develop comorbid disorders. In addition, many clinicians have criticized the treatment outcome literature because it does not address the complexity of comorbid disorders or of patients who have multiple trauma histories. We present here a case of a woman with a multiple trauma history who has PTSD with comorbid panic attacks and who was successfully treated using MCET.

The Case of Ms. B

Ms. B is a 36-year-old European-American female who reported that she was sexually assaulted from ages 4 to 8 by a cousin and at age 12 by an uncle. At age 33 she was raped and beaten by a stranger. She presented with symptoms of PTSD, including nightmares, flashbacks of the most recent rapist's voice, avoiding thoughts and reminders of the most recent rape, loss of interest in activities, feeling distant and cut off from others, feeling numb, difficulty sleeping, irritability, difficulty concentrating, exaggerated startle response, and being easily startled. She reported having approximately one panic attack a week since the most recent rape 3 years ago. Her panic attacks were often triggered by conditioned cues related to the most recent rape, but some attacks also appeared out of the blue and at night while she was sleeping.

Course of Treatment

Ms. B was part of a larger study and had been randomly assigned to group therapy and then followed for 6 months after completing treatment. Ms. B attended 12 weekly, 90-minute, group therapy sessions. She actively participated in the treatment and completed all homework. The first session focused on psychoeducation about the development of PTSD and panic attacks from a cognitive behavioral perspective. She was able to give several examples of her symptoms and conditioned cues associated with the trauma that she avoided or that caused her to panic. For homework she was asked to write about the meaning of the traumatic events in her life in terms of how these events have affected her and to identify other conditioned cues. She reported having two panic attacks the previous week and the average number of PTSD symptoms reported from the daily PTSD symptom checklist was 10 per day. In Session 2, we reviewed her homework and she shared with the group the ways in which the traumas had affected her. She said that since the most recent rape she often felt weak, inferior, and helpless. She reported that she has difficulty trusting others, that she rarely feels safe, that her self-esteem is low, and that she tries to avoid sex with her husband because it reminds her of the rape. She identified several conditioned cues including the smell of alcohol on a man's breath, intimate touches, music, and someone caressing her hair. During this session she learned a breathing retraining technique and was asked to practice this for homework. She did not have any panic attacks the previous week and her average number of PTSD symptoms remained at 10. At the next session, she reported that the breathing helped to reduce her anxiety. In this session the connection of events, thoughts, feelings, and behaviors was introduced and she easily grasped this concept. In addition, she was asked to identify thoughts that may include overestimations of negative consequences for homework and to complete a worksheet that labeled events, thoughts, and feelings to begin to identify the importance of her interpretations to what her emotions are. She did not have any panic attacks the previous week and her average number of PTSD symptoms again remained at 10.

Session 4 focused on learning to challenge distorted thinking that may have resulted from her trauma history and her current PTSD and panic symptoms using a worksheet developed for this that includes questions such as: What is the evidence for and against this thought? What is the realistic probability? and Are you overgeneralizing from past incidents? She was asked to complete these for homework.

In Session 5, Ms. B reported that she had one panic attack, but the monitoring of her PTSD symptoms indicated they had decreased to an average of 6.5 per day. She completed several events-thoughts-feelings worksheets and shared these with the group. One focused on telling herself that she always had to be on guard. She was able to challenge this thought and modify it to say to herself that while it's okay to be cautious, not everyone is out to harm her and that it is okay to let her guard down in situations that are not objectively dangerous. Modifying this thought resulted in decreased fear and anxiety. In this session, interoceptive exposure to physical sensations associated with panic attacks was introduced. Ms. B found that the exercises that caused her anxiety and were similar to what she experienced when she panicked were shaking her head, breathing through a straw, holding her breath, stair stepping and hyperventilating. We developed a hierarchy and she was instructed to begin practicing the least anxiety-provoking exercises and to work her way up to the most anxiety-provoking exercises. Session six continued on the interoceptive exposure, and writing about the traumas was also introduced. She reported not having any panic attacks the previous week and her PTSD symptoms dropped to a 6.

Session 7 focused on her account of the most recent rape. She was able to share her writing with the group and received support from other group members. She was tearful while reading it and said it had been very difficult to write, but that she felt better after completing the assignment. She reported an increase in PTSD symptoms (8.6) and one panic attack. She was asked to write about a second traumatic event for homework and to continue interoceptive exposure exercises.

Session 8 focused on the second writing assignment; distortions and self-blame about the event were identified, and Ms. B was asked to challenge these thoughts. In addition, how safety beliefs can be affected by trauma was discussed and she was asked to complete cognitive worksheets on safety issues. Her PTSD symptoms decreased to six per day and she did not have any panic attacks.

Sessions 9, 10, and 11 focused on in vivo exposure to trauma and panic-related cues. She developed a fear hierarchy for three target fears: exercising, going out socially, and wearing summer clothing. Since the most recent rape she had stopped exercising because she associated an increased heart rate with panic attacks. She did not go out socially because she was fearful of being attacked again and also fearful of having a panic attack in front of others. She did not wear summer clothing because she was fearful that shorts or a swimming suit would draw the attention of men and make her more vulnerable to another sexual assault. Over the course of these sessions she used both cognitive restructuring skills and exposure to reduce her fear and anxiety related to these. During these sessions she did not have any further panic attacks and her PTSD symptoms continued to decrease (5.4, 5.1, 4.0, respectively). In Session 11 she was asked to write about the meaning of the traumas again to determine if her thinking about these events had changed.

The final session was devoted to reviewing treatment and for comparing the meaning assignments. Ms. B read her most recent meaning assignment and then was given the one she had written after Session 1 for comparison. She noted that she no longer thought she could not trust anyone and she did not think she had to stay on guard at all times. She reported that having an understanding of her symptoms made her less afraid of sexual intimacy with her husband, and that she had a more balanced view of the world compared to her first writing.

Posttreatment evaluation and 3- and 6-month follow-ups indicated that Ms. B no longer met criteria for PTSD and she was no longer having panic attacks. Her initial score on the Modified PTSD Symptom Scale was 77. At posttreatment, her score was 23 and at both 3- and 6-month follow-ups it was 12, which clinically would be considered in the normal range. On the Physical Reactions Scale, measure of panic attack symptoms in the past 2 weeks, her initial score was 52. At posttreatment it was 7, at 3 months it was 3, and at 6 months it was 7, indicating very few panic attack symptoms.

SUMMARY AND CONCLUSION

In summary, considerable progress has been made in the treatment of PTSD using therapies that are either primarily cognitive in nature or that use cognitive components. Many of these treatments have been manualized. Resick and Schnicke (1993) have published a book describing CPT. Falsetti and Resnick (1997b) have developed a patient manual and a therapist manual for research purposes that is also likely to be published in the near future. Foa and colleagues (1994) have also manualized exposure therapy for research purposes. This is still a fairly new area for treatment development and research, however, and much work remains to be done. In particular, a more careful examination of combining cognitive and behavioral components over the course of a longer treatment to determine if such combination would provide a further reduction in symptoms for a larger number of people is needed.

REFERENCES

American Psychiatric Association. (1994). *Diagnostic and statistical manual of mental disorders (4th ed.)* Washington, DC: Author.

Atkeson, B. M., Calhoun, K. S., Resick, P. A., & Ellis, E. M. (1982). Victims of rape: Repeated assessment of depressive symptoms. *Journal of Consulting and Clinical Psychology, 50*, 96–102.

Barlow, D. H., & Craske, M. G. (1988). *Mastery of your anxiety and panic manual.* Albany, NY: Center for Stress and Anxiety Disorders.

Beck, A. T., Ward, C. H., Mendelson, M., Mock, J. E., & Erbaugh, J. K. (1961). An inventory for measuring depression. *Archives of General Psychiatry, 4*, 561–571.

Becker, J. V., Skinner, L. J., Abel, G. G., Axelrod, R., & Cichon, J. (1984). Sexual problems of sexual assault survivors. *Women and Health, 9*, 5–20.

Blake, D. D., Weathers, F. W., Nagy, L. M., Kaloupek, D. G., Klaumizer, G., Charney, D., & Keane, T. M. (1990). A clinician rating scale for assessing current and lifetime PTSD: The CAPS-1. *The Behavior Therapist, 13.* 187–188.

Breslau, N., Davis, G. C., Andreski, P., & Peterson, E. (1991). Traumatic events and posttraumatic stress disorder in an urban population of young adults. *Archives of General Psychiatry, 48*, 216–222.

Calhoun, K. S., & Resick, P. A. (1993). Treatment of PTSD in rape victims. In D. A. Barlow (Ed.), *Clinical handbook of psychological disorders* (pp. 48–98). New York: Guilford Press.

Chemtob, C., Roiblat, H. L., Hamada, R. S., Carlson, J. G., & Twentyman, C. T. (1988). A cognitive action theory of post-traumatic stress disorder. *Journal of Anxiety Disorders, 2,* 253–275.

Derogatis, L. R. (1983). *Symptom Checklist-90-Revised: Administration, scoring and procedures manual-II* (2nd ed.). Baltimore, MD: Clinical Psychometric Research.

Di Nardo, P. A., Barlow, D. H., Cerny, J., Vermilyea, B. B., Vermilyea, J. A., Himada, W., & Waddell, M. (1985). *Anxiety Disorders Interview Schedule—Revised (ADIS-R).* Albany: Phobia and Anxiety Disorders Clinic, State University of New York at Albany.

Dunmore, E., Clark, D. M., & Ehlers, A. (1997). Cognitive factors in persistent versus recovered posttraumatic stress disorder after physical or sexual assault: A pilot study. *Behavioral Cognitive Psychotherapy, 25,* 147–159.

Ehlers, A., & Steil, R. (1995). Maintenance of intrusive memories in posttraumatic stress disorder: A cognitive approach. *Behavioral and Cognitive Psychotherapy, 23,* 217–249.

Ellis, E., Atkeson, B., & Calhoun, K. (1981). An assessment of long-term reaction to rape. *Journal of Abnormal Psychology, 90,* 263–266.

Ewing, J. A. (1984). Detecting alcoholism: The CAGE questionnaire. *Journal of the American Medical Association, 52,* 1905–1907.

Ewing, J. A., & Rouse, B. A. (1970, February). *Identifying the hidden alcoholic.* Paper presented at the 29th International Congress on Alcohol and Drug Dependence, Sydney, Australia.

Fairbank, J. A., & Keane, T. M. (1982). Flooding for combat-related stress disorders: Assessment of anxiety reduction across traumatic memories. *Behavior Therapy, 13,* 499–510.

Falsetti, S. A. (1997). Treatment of PTSD with comorbid panic attacks. *PTSD Clinical Quarterly, 7,* 46–48.

Falsetti, S. A., Johnson, M. R., Ware, M. R., Emmanuel, N. F., Mintzer, O., Book, S., Ballenger, J. C., & Lydiard, R. B. (1996, November). *Trauma and PTSD in a sample seeking treatment for anxiety.* Paper presented at the 12th Annual Meeting of the International Society of Traumatic Stress Studies, San Francisco, CA.

Falsetti, S. A., & Resnick, H. S. (1992). *The Physical Reactions Scale.* Charleston, SC: The National Crime Victims Research and Treatment Center, Medical University of South Carolina.

Falsetti, S. A., & Resnick, H. S. (1997a). Frequency and severity of panic attack symptoms in a treatment seeking sample of trauma victims. *Journal of Traumatic Stress, 10,* 683–689.

Falsetti, S. A., & Resnick, H. S. (1997b). Multiple channel exposure therapy: Patient and therapist's manuals. Charleston, SC: National Crime Victims Research and Treatment Center. Unpublished manuscript.

Falsetti, S. A., & Resnick, H. S. (March, 1998). Preliminary results of a manualized group cognitive behavioral treatment for PTSD with panic attacks. Paper presented at the 18th National Conference of the Anxiety Disorders Association of America, Boston, MA.

Falsetti, S. A., Resnick, H. S., Dansky, B. S., Lydiard, R. B., & Kilpatrick, D. G. (1995). The relationship of stress to panic disorder: Cause or effect? In C. M. Mazure (Ed.), *Does stress cause psychiatric illness?* (pp. 111–148). Washington, DC: American Psychiatric Press.

Falsetti, S. A., Resnick, H. S., Resick, P. A., & Kilpatrick, D. G. (1993). The modified PTSD symptom scale: A brief self-report measure of posttraumatic stress disorder. *The Behavior Therapist, 17,* 161–162.

Falsetti, S. A., & Resick, P. A. (1995). Causal attributions, depression, and post-traumatic stress disorder in victims of crime. *Journal of Applied Social Psychology, 25,* 1027–1042.

Foa, E. B., Dancu, C. V., Hembree, E. A., Jaycox, L. H., Meadows, E. A., & Street, G. P. (1999). A comparison of exposure therapy, stress inoculation training, and their combination for reducing posttraumatic stress disorder in female assault victims. *Journal of Consulting and Clinical Psychology, 67*(2), 194–200.

Foa, E. B., Hearst, D. E., Dancu, C. V., Hembree, E., Jaycox, L. H., & Clark, D. (1994). Cognitive restructuring and prolonged exposure (CR/PE) manual. Unpublished manuscript.

Foa, E. B., Riggs, D. S., Dancu, C. V., & Rothbaum, B. O. (1993). Reliability and validity of a brief instrument for assessing posttraumatic stress disorder. *Journal of Traumatic Stress, 6,* 459–473.

Foa, E. B., & Rothbaum, B. O. (1998). *Treating the trauma of rape.* New York: Guilford Press.

Foa, E. B., Rothbaum, B. O., Riggs, D. S., & Murdock, T. B. (1991). Treatment of posttraumatic stress disorder in rape victims: A comparison between cognitive-behavioral procedures and counseling. *Journal of Consulting and Clinical Psychology, 59,* 715–723.

Foa, E. B., Rothbaum, B. O., & Steketee, G. S. (1993). Treatment of rape victims. *Journal of Interpersonal Violence, 8,* 256–276.

Foa, E. B., Steketee, G., & Olasov-Rothbaum, B. (1989). Behavioral/cognitive conceptualization of post-traumatic stress disorder. *Behavior Therapy, 20,* 155–176.

Frank, E., & Stewart, B. D. (1984). Depressive symptoms in rape victims: A revisit. *Journal of Affective Disorders, 7,* 77–85.

Frazier, P., & Schauben, L. (1994). Causal attributions and recovery from rape and other stressful life events. *Journal of Social and Clinical Psychology, 13,* 1–14.

Hollon, S. D., & Garber, J. (1988). Cognitive therapy. In L. Y. Abramson (Ed.), *Social cognition and clinical psychology: A synthesis* (pp. 204–253). New York: Guilford Press.

Holmes, M. R., & St. Lawrence, J. S. (1983). Treatment of rape-induced trauma: Proposed behavioral conceptualization and review of the literature. *Clinical Psychology Review, 3*, 417–433.

Horowitz, M., Wilner, N., & Alvarez, W. (1979). Impact of Event Scale: Measure of subjective distress. *Psychosomatic Medicine, 41*, 209–218.

Hough, M. (1985). The impact of victimization: Findings from the British Crime Survey. *Victimology, 10*, 498–511.

Janoff-Bulman, R. (1989). Assumptive worlds and the stress of traumatic events: Applications of the schema construct. *Social Cognition, 7*, 113–136.

Keane, T. M., Fairbank, J. A., Caddell, J. M., & Zimering, R. T. (1989). Implosive (flooding) therapy reduces symptoms of PTSD in Vietnam combat veterans. *Behavior Therapy, 20*, 245–260.

Keane, T. M., & Kaloupek, D. G. (1982). Imaginal flooding in the treatment of post-traumatic stress disorder. *Journal of Consulting and Clinical Psychology, 50*, 138–140.

Kilpatrick, D. G. (1988). Rape Aftermath Symptom Test. In M. Hersen & A. S. Bellack (Eds.), *Dictionary of behavioral assessment techniques* (pp. 366–367). New York: Pergamon Press.

Kilpatrick, D. G., Edmunds, C. N., & Seymour, A. (1992). *Rape in America: A report to the nation.* Arlington, VA: National Victim Center.

Kilpatrick, D. G., & Veronen, L. J. (1983). Treatment for rape related problems: Crisis intervention is not enough. In L. H. Cohen, W. L. Claiborn, & G. A. Spector (Eds.), *Crisis intervention* (pp. 165–185). New York: Human Sciences Press.

Kilpatrick, D. G., Veronen, L. J., & Best, C. L. (1985). Factors predicting psychological distress among rape victims. In C. R. Figley (Series Ed.), *Trauma and its wake: Vol. 1. The study and treatment of posttraumatic stress disorder* (pp. 113–141). New York: Brunner/Mazel.

Kilpatrick, D. G., Veronen, L. J., & Resick, P. A. (1982). Psychological sequelae to rape: Assessment and treatment strategies. In D. M. Dolays & R. L. Meredith (Eds.), *Behavioral medicine: Assessment and treatment strategies* (pp. 473–497). New York: Plenum.

Koss, M. P. (1985). The hidden rape victim: Personality, attitudinal, and situational characteristics. *Psychology of Women Quarterly, 9*, 193–212.

Lang, P. J. (1977). Imagery in therapy: An information processing analysis of fear. *Behavior Therapy, 8*, 862–886.

Marks, I., Lovell, K., Noshirvani, H., Livanou, M., & Thrasher, S. (1998). Treatment of posttraumatic stress disorder by exposure and/or cognitive restructuring. *Archives of General Psychiatry, 55*, 317–325.

McCann, L., & Pearlman, L. A. (1990). *Psychological trauma and the adult survivor: Theory, therapy and transformation.* New York: Brunner/Mazel.

McCann, L., Sakheim, D. K., & Pearlman, L. A. (1988). Trauma and victimization: A model of psychological adaptation. *The Counseling Psychologist, 16,* 531–594.

Mechanic, M. B., & Resick, P. A. (1993, October). *The Personal Beliefs and Reactions Scale: Assessing rape-related cognitive schemata.* Paper presented at the 9th Annual Meeting of the International Society of Traumatic Stress Studies, San Antonio, TX.

Meichenbaum, D. (1993). Changing conceptions of cognitive behavior modification: Retrospect and prospect. *Journal of Consulting and Clinical Psychology, 61,* 202–204.

Norris, F. H. (1992). Epidemiology of trauma: Frequency and impact of different potentially traumatic events on different demographic groups. *Journal of Consulting and Clinical Psychology, 60,* 409–418,

Resick, P. A. (1993, January). *Group versus individual format of cognitive processing therapy for posttraumatic stress disorder in sexual assault victims.* Paper presented at the Lake George Research Conference on Posttraumatic Stress Disorder, Bolton Landing, NY.

Resick, P. A. (1989). Victims of sexual assault. In A. Lurigio, R. C. Davis, & W. G. Skogan (Eds.), *Victims in the criminal justice system* (pp. 69–86). Newbury Park, CA: Sage Publications.

Resnick, H. S., Best, C. L., Kilpatrick, D. G., Freedy, J. R., & Falsetti, S. A. (1993). *Trauma Assessment for Adults–Self-Report.* Charleston: The National Crime Victims Research and Treatment Center, Medical University of South Carolina.

Resick, P. A., Calhoun, K. S., Atkeson, B. M., & Ellis, E. M. (1981). Social adjustment in victims of sexual assault. *Journal of Consulting and Clinical Psychology, 49,* 705–712.

Resnick, H. S., & Falsetti, S. A. (1996). Assessment of rape and other civilian trauma-related post-traumatic stress disorder: Emphasis on assessment of potentially traumatic events. In T. W. Miller (Ed.), *Stressful life events* (2nd ed., pp. 235–271). Madison, CT: International Universities Press.

Resick, P. A., Falsetti, S. A., Resnick, H. S., & Kilpatrick, D. G. (1991). *The Modified PTSD Symptom Scale—Self-Report.* St. Louis, MO: University of Missouri; Charleston: Crime Victims Treatment and Research Center, Medical University of South Carolina.

Resick, P. A., & Jordan, C. G. (1988). Group stress inoculation training for victims of sexual assault: A therapist manual. In P. A. Keller & S. R. Heyman (Eds.), *Innovations in clinical practice: A source book: Vol. 7,* pp. 99–111). Sarasota, FL: Professional Resource Exchange.

Resick, P. A., Jordan, C. G., Girelli, S. A., Hutter, C. H., & Marhoefer-Dvorak,

S. (1988). A comparative outcome study of behavioral group therapy for sexual assault victims. *Behavior Therapy, 19,* 385–401.

Resnick, H. S., Kilpatrick, D. G., Dansky, B. S., Saunders, B. E., & Best, C. L. (1993). Prevalence of civilian trauma and PTSD in a representative national sample of women. *Journal of Consulting and Clinical Psychology, 61,* 984–991.

Resnick, H. S., Kilpatrick, D. G., & Lipovsky, J. A. (1991). Assessment of rape-related posttraumatic stress disorder: Stressor and symptom dimensions. *Psychological Assessment, 3,* 561–572.

Resnick, H. S., & Newton, T. (1992). Assessment and treatment of post-traumatic stress disorder in adult survivors of sexual assault. In D. Foy (Ed.), *Treating PTSD* (pp. 99–126). New York: Guilford Press.

Resick, P. A., & Schnicke, M. K. (1990). Treating symptoms in adult victims of sexual assault. *Journal of Interpersonal Violence, 5,* 488–506.

Resick, P. A., & Schnicke, M. K. (1992). Cognitive processing therapy for sexual assault victims. *Journal of Consulting and Clinical Psychology, 60,* 748–756.

Resick, P. A., & Schnicke, M. K. (1993). *Cognitive processing therapy for rape victims: A treatment manual.* Newbury Park, CA: Sage Publications.

Robins, L., Helzer, J., Cottler, L., & Goldring, E. (1988). *NIMH Diagnostic Interview Schedule, Version III Revised (DIS-III-R).* St. Louis, MO: Washington University Press and Medical College of Pennsylvania.

Rothbaum, B. O., Foa, E. B., Riggs, D. S., Murdock, T., & Walsh, W. (1992). A prospective examination of posttraumatic stress disorder in rape victims. *Journal of Traumatic Stress, 5,* 455–475.

Saunders, B. E., Mandoki, K. A., & Kilpatrick, D. G. (1990). Development of a crime-related post-traumatic stress disorder scale within the Symptom Checklist-90-Revised. *Journal of Traumatic Stress, 3,* 439–448.

Seidner, A. L., & Kilpatrick, D. G. (1988). Modified fear survey. In M. Hersen & A. S. Bellack (Eds.), *Dictionary of behavioral assessment techniques* (pp. 307–309). New York: Pergamon Press.

Spitzer, R. L., Williams, J. B., Gibbon, M., & First, M. B. (1990). *Structured clinical interview for DSM-III-R, patient edition.* New York: New York State Psychiatric Institute, Biometrics Research Department.

Stroebel, C. F. (1983). *Quieting reflex training for adults: Personal workbook (or practitioners guide).* New York: DMA Audio Cassette Publications.

Veronen, L. J., & Kilpatrick, D. G. (1983). Stress management for rape victims. In D. Meichenbaum & M. E. Jaremko (Eds.), *Stress reduction and prevention* (pp. 341–374). New York: Plenum Press.

Weissman, M. M., & Paykel, E. S. (1974). *The depressed woman: A study of social relationships.* Chicago: University of Chicago Press.

Part III
New Directions and Developments

8

Anger Management

Eric R. Dahlen and Jerry L. Deffenbacher

Anger is a common emotion (Averill, 1983) that, when mild, serves many positive functions, such as signaling dissatisfaction, motivating corrective action, and energizing adaptive coping behavior (Novaco, 1975). However, when intense or expressed in dysfunctional ways, anger can present serious problems. For some clients, healthy anger is denied or projected onto others. Others experience intense, situation-specific anger arousal (e.g., being criticized, having to wait in line, or having to drive behind a slow driver). Still others experience chronic generalized anger in which they are more easily provoked by a wide range of stimuli (Deffenbacher, 1993). Problematic anger may result in significant impairment across many areas of functioning, as it is associated with reduced social support (Hardy & Smith, 1988), relationship difficulties, alcohol abuse, verbal and physical aggression, coping deficits (Deffenbacher, 1992, 1993), stress and burnout at work (Brondolo et al., 1998), and numerous health problems, such as hypertension and coronary heart disease (Diamond, 1982; Goldstein & Niaura, 1992; Matthews & Haynes, 1986). Thus, it is imperative that clinicians are informed about effective treatments for angry individuals.

Because aggression and violent behavior are conceptually distinct from anger (DiGiuseppe, Eckhardt, Tafrate, & Robin, 1994) and may require somewhat different interventions, this chapter will focus only on anger. Specifically, it will focus on angry adults, a sizable population that suffers from clinically significant anger, which, while rarely leading to violent behavior, results in a myriad of problems for the individual and those with whom he or she interacts.

DIAGNOSTIC CONSIDERATIONS

Despite the many negative consequences of dysfunctional anger, the primary diagnostic system, the *Diagnostic and Statistical Manual of Mental Disorders* (*DSM-IV*; American Psychiatric Association, 1994), provides little help. *DSM-IV* provides a means for classifying persons experiencing significant anxious or depressed mood, but it does not include disorders in which pathologic anger is a necessary or sufficient element. Anger is an important component of several Axis I (e.g., intermittent explosive disorder, depression, and posttraumatic stress disorder) and Axis II disorders (e.g., paranoid, antisocial, borderline, and narcissistic personality disorders), but *DSM-IV* does not help the clinician who is faced with a client for whom angry affect is the primary focus of clinical attention. For example, no diagnostic category in the present system could accurately characterize the client who experiences excessive anger in response to being passed over for a promotion at work, even if it was determined that his or her anger resulted in significant impairment in his or her ability to function. If the angry affect was accompanied by aggressive or otherwise dysfunctional behavior, adjustment disorder with disturbance in conduct might be warranted. However, if significant anger occurs in the absence of aggressive behavior, there is no appropriate diagnosis.

Without established diagnostic criteria, it becomes difficult to establish meaningful clinical samples and compare samples of angry individuals across studies (Deffenbacher, Oetting, & DiGiuseppe, 2000; Tafrate, 1995). Of course, the lack of official diagnostic criteria should in no way imply that there are not a sizable number of persons suffering from clinically meaningful anger that deserve our attention.

To address the absence of such criteria, potential anger disorders have been proposed (see Deffenbacher, 1994; Eckhardt & Deffenbacher, 1995). Specifically, criteria have been developed for five anger disorders: (a) adjustment disorder with angry mood, (b) situational anger disorder without aggression, (c) situational anger disorder with aggression, (d) generalized anger disorder without aggression, and (e) generalized anger disorder with aggression. In order to receive any of these proposed diagnoses, an individual would be required to possess significant angry affect and various combinations of anger-related physiological and cognitive processes. For example, the diagnosis of adjustment disorder with angry mood would fit a number of individuals who have suffered one or more stressors and who are experiencing great anger in the absence of other negative emotions or conduct problems. Situational anger disorders would involve strong, interfering anger reactions in specific circumstances or situations linked by a common theme (e.g., others being disrespectful), and generalized anger disorders would involve frequent, dysfunctional anger across a wide range of situations or life areas. Because of the potential treatment implications, a diagnosis including aggression would be warranted when aggressive behavior was part of the clinical presentation.

A COGNITIVE-BEHAVIORAL MODEL OF ANGER

Anger is an internal, experiential state that includes four related domains: (a) emotional/experiential, (b) physiological arousal, (c) cognitive processes, and (d) behavior (Eckhardt & Deffenbacher, 1995; Edmondson & Conger, 1996) that co-occur and interact with each other such that they are often experienced as a single phenomenon (Deffenbacher, 1999). Emotionally, anger is a feeling state that ranges in intensity from mild annoyance to rage and fury. Physiologically, anger is accompanied by adrenal release, increased muscle tension, and activation of the sympathetic nervous system. Cognitively, pathologic anger involves biased information processing (e.g., the perception that one's personal domain or standards have been violated or that the provoking event is unjustified, preventable, intentional, or worthy of punishment) (Beck, 1976, 1999; Dryden, 1990; Ellis, 1977; Lohr, Hamberger, & Bonge, 1988). Behaviorally, anger may be expressed in a variety of functional (e.g., assertion, limit setting, etc.) and dysfunctional (e.g., verbal and physical aggression, withdrawal, excessive alcohol consumption, reckless driving, defensiveness, etc.) ways.

Integrating the work of several prominent cognitive-behavioral theorists (Beck, 1976, 1999; Ellis, 1977; Lazarus, 1991; Meichenbaum, 1985; Novaco, 1978, 1979), anger can be seen as emerging from the interactions of (a) anger-eliciting stimuli, (b) the person's pre-anger state, and (c) the individual's cognitive appraisals of the eliciting stimuli and of his or her ability to cope with such stimuli. First, anger-eliciting stimuli range from easily identifiable external sources of provocation (e.g., someone cuts in front of the individual standing in line, or a loved one makes a rude comment) to a wide variety of internal stimuli (e.g., memories or images cued by external events as in the case of posttraumatic stress disorder, ruminations about an upcoming event, and other emotions). Second, the pre-anger state includes the individual's (a) immediate cognitive-emotional-physical state at the time of provocation, (b) enduring psychological characteristics, and (c) cultural messages about anger and its expression. Although often overlooked, the first of these is particularly important because excitation from prior anger or any aversive physical or emotional state can increase the probability of subsequent anger (Berkowitz, 1990; Zillman, 1971). Finally, while the pre-anger state includes enduring cognitive and cultural biases, the appraisal process is where the individual interprets the meaning of the anger-eliciting event (primary appraisal) and his or her probability of coping effectively (secondary appraisal). Primary appraisal processes of individuals with dysfunctional anger tend to involve a violation of rigid rules for living; blameful, undeserved attacks on identity; unwarranted blockage of important goals, and the like. In essence, something has or could happen that *should not*. Moreover, anger is likely to escalate to the extent the individual feels overwhelmed and out of control, thinks he or she should not be subject to the situation in the first place, and/or believes that anger and aggression are appropriate, justified responses (secondary appraisals).

EMPIRICALLY SUPPORTED COGNITIVE-BEHAVIORAL TREATMENTS

In spite of the fact that anger has received considerably less attention in the treatment literature than depression or anxiety (Kassinove & Sukhodolsky, 1995), the empirical study of anger management has come a long way since Novaco's (1975) seminal work. Although a few alternatives look promising, such as process-oriented group therapy (Deffenbacher, McNamara, Stark, & Sabadell, 1990b), psychopharmacological treatment (Fava et al., 1991, 1996), and meditation (Dua & Swinden, 1992), a growing body of literature supports the value of cognitive-behavioral interventions. Recent meta-analytic studies have shown effect sizes in the .70 to 1.20 range (Beck & Fernandez, 1998; Edmondson & Conger, 1996; Tafrate, 1995), leading Beck and Fernandez to report that the average client receiving cognitive-behavioral treatment experienced greater anger reduction than 76% of control participants. Moreover, there is empirical support for the following cognitive-behavioral interventions: (a) relaxation coping skills, (b) cognitive interventions (e.g., cognitive restructuring/self-instruction or problem solving), (c) behavioral coping/social skills training, and (d) multicomponent interventions consisting of some combination of cognitive, relaxation, and/or behavioral coping/social skills.

Relaxation Coping Skills

Relaxation-based interventions target heightened emotional and physiological arousal that most often characterizes the experience of anger. Clients are usually trained in progressive relaxation and a range of relaxation coping skills, which are then applied for anger reduction within and between sessions. As clients lower their anger arousal through relaxation, they feel calmer and more in control and are better able to access other behavioral skills and more adaptive problem-solving approaches.

Although Novaco's (1975) landmark study found that relaxation was minimally effective, an adaptation of anxiety management training (Suinn, 1990) to anger has proven much more effective (Deffenbacher, Demm, & Brandon, 1986; Deffenbacher, Filetti, Lynch, Dahlen, & Oetting, 2000;

Deffenbacher, Huff, Lynch, Oetting, & Salvatore, 2000; Deffenbacher & Stark, 1992; Hazaleus & Deffenbacher, 1986). In these studies, relaxation led to significant reductions in trait anger, the frequency and intensity of daily anger, anger from a variety of common provocations, anger in response to participants' most anger-provoking, ongoing personal situation, anger suppression, anger-related physiological arousal, and dysfunctional expression. Relaxation was generally as effective as cognitive interventions and a combination of cognitive and relaxation components (Deffenbacher, Huff, et al., 2000; Deffenbacher, Story, Brandon, Hogg, & Hazaleus, 1988; Deffenbacher & Stark, 1992; Hazaleus & Deffenbacher, 1986; Schlicter & Horan, 1981). In addition, positive treatment effects were maintained at 1-year follow-up (Deffenbacher et al., 1986, 1988; Deffenbacher & Stark, 1992; Hazaleus & Deffenbacher, 1986). Moreover, relaxation interventions increase rapport and reduce client resistance to cognitive change strategies (Deffenbacher & Lynch, 1998), are easy to integrate with other treatment components, and have great flexibility as a component of anger reduction therapy or psychoeducational groups.

Cognitive Interventions

Cognitive interventions target biases in information processing and cognitive appraisal processes. Problematic anger is not seen as originating from external events per se, but from the manner in which these events are interpreted (Beck, 1976, 1999; Deffenbacher, 1996; Ellis, 1977; Lazarus, 1991; Novaco, 1978, 1979). Although mild anger (i.e., short-term frustration or annoyance) is naturally produced by a variety of circumstances, an examination of severe or persistent anger usually implicates certain cognitive factors. That is, the angry individual experiences frustrating events and construes them as intolerable, infuriating violations and reacts emotionally and behaviorally to the construed reality. Cognitive interventions help clients identify distorted patterns of thinking and assist individuals in developing more reality-based, less anger-engendering cognitions that are then rehearsed, refined, and applied in vivo. By changing the manner in which they interpret potential sources of provocation, angry individuals can be helped to lower anger arousal and free up their problem-solving and coping resources. Empirically supported cognitive interventions include cognitive restructuring/self-instruction and problem solving.

Cognitive Restructuring and Self-Instructional Training

Cognitive restructuring, most often associated with the cognitive therapies of Ellis (1962, 1973) and Beck (1976; Beck, Rush, Shaw, & Emery, 1979), involves helping the client question the evidence for particular beliefs, explore alternative ways of construing various phenomena, devise experiments through which beliefs can be tested, and explore the utility of certain thoughts or beliefs on one's experience. In the case of anger, cognitive restructuring involves helping angry clients replace "hot" anger-related cognitions with "cooler" more calming thoughts. Similarly, self-instructional training, a component of stress inoculation training (Meichenbaum, 1972, 1985; Meichenbaum & Turk, 1976), encourages clients to modify their verbal self-talk (e.g., "There's no point getting mad right now," or "Instead of getting angry, I'm going to deal with this constructively").

The efficacy of cognitive restructuring and/or self-instructional training for anger management has been supported in studies of community volunteers (Novaco, 1975; Tafrate & Kassinove, 1998), college students (Dahlen & Deffenbacher, 2000; Deffenbacher et al., 1988; Hazaleus & Deffenbacher, 1986; Moon & Eisler, 1983), child-abusing parents (Whiteman, Fanshel, & Grundy, 1987), and caregivers for people with intellectual and/or physical disabilities (Cary & Dua, 1999). Anger-reduction interventions where cognitive restructuring and/or self-instructional training are central components appear to be as effective as those employing biofeedback (Achmon, Granek, Golomb, & Hart, 1989), relaxation coping skills (Hazaleus & Deffenbacher, 1986), and combined cognitive-relaxation components (Deffenbacher et al., 1988). In addition, positive treatment effects have generally been maintained in long-term follow-ups (e.g., Deffenbacher et al., 1988; Hazaleus & Deffenbacher, 1986).

Problem Solving

Problem-solving approaches, usually based on D'Zurilla and Goldfried's (1971) model, are employed in cases where there are deficits in the ability to guide one's behavior in an appropriate task-oriented manner. These approaches are likely to be most helpful for persons who do not exhibit behavioral skill deficits (e.g., poor social skills) but lack general problem-solving skills with which to assess angering situations and select from among various behavioral coping skills in which they are already proficient (Deffenbacher, 1995). Problem-solving interventions reduce anger by helping clients develop cognitive strategies for approaching and defining provoking events as problems and then generating, evaluating, and implementing solutions in a calm and reasonable manner. Although self-instructional strategies may be conceptually more related to cognitive restructuring than to problem solving, most problem-solving approaches also employ self-instructional statements to guide problem solving (e.g., telling oneself to identify the problem, break it down, and generate and implement partial solutions; reminding oneself that one can often escape from an aversive source of provocation; rewarding oneself for effective coping, etc.). Problem-solving interventions have received support in studies of angry college students (Moon & Eisler, 1983) and adult parents who had either committed child abuse or were identified as being at risk to do so (Whiteman et al., 1987). Controlled studies employing long-term follow-ups have not yet been conducted.

Behavioral Coping/Social Skills Training

Whereas relaxation and cognitive interventions typically focus on reducing anger arousal either directly or through cognitive pathways, behavioral coping and social skills interventions target the manner in which anger is expressed. There are several coping skills that may be relevant to anger management (e.g., parenting, budgeting and financial planning, assertive communication, etc.), depending on the sources of provocation and the nature of skill deficits. However, given that most anger occurs in an interpersonal context (Averill, 1983), interpersonal communication, negotiation, and feedback skills are especially likely to be relevant. For example, someone who is unable to articulate his or her needs effectively may become angry when others repeatedly fail to meet them. In addition, persons with maladaptive anger often express their anger in abrasive, intimidating, and potentially destructive ways (e.g., yelling, saying hurtful things, or physically aggressive behavior). Thus, an angry client might be encouraged to cope with angry feelings by removing him or herself from the source of provocation (i.e., taking a time-out) and/or expressing him/herself in more calm, reciprocal, and respectful ways.

Most behavioral coping and social skills approaches are highly structured, therapist-directed, and use sequential skill training formats. Problematic behaviors are identified along with more adaptive expressive behaviors. A subset of these are discussed, modeled, and rehearsed with feedback. After behaviors are modified to incorporate this feedback, they are rehearsed again and contracted for external application. An alternative approach, termed inductive social skills training, was developed by Deffenbacher and colleagues (Deffenbacher, Thwaites, Wallace, & Oetting, 1994; Deffenbacher, Oetting, Huff, Cornell, & Dallager, 1996). It was based on Beck's cognitive therapy and incorporated the Socratic, inductive style characteristic of Beck's approach. Therapists encouraged clients to identify and explore effective behaviors for coping with anger, and clients developed assertive communication strategies. Client-developed behaviors were rehearsed in session, and collaboratively developed behavioral experiments were encouraged between sessions.

Behavioral coping and social skills training interventions have received support for anger management among male community volunteers (Rimm, Hill, Brown, & Stuart, 1974) and angry college students (e.g., Deffenbacher, Story, Stark, Hogg, & Brandon, 1987; Deffenbacher et al., 1994, 1996; Moon & Eisler, 1983). These behavioral interventions appear to be as effective as cognitive (Moon & Eisler, 1983) or combined cognitive-relaxation treatments (Deffenbacher et al., 1987, 1994). Moreover, behavioral coping and social skills interventions delivered in an inductive, Socratic style have compared favorably to the more structured and therapist-directed behavioral skill-building treatments (Deffenbacher et al., 1994) and to cognitive-relaxation interventions (Deffenbacher et al., 1996). In addition, positive treatment gains have been maintained over long-term follow-up (Deffenbacher, 1988; Deffenbacher et al., 1996; Deffenbacher, Oetting, Huff, & Thwaites, 1995).

Multicomponent Treatments

Given the multidimensional nature of anger, it is not surprising that multicomponent treatments (i.e., interventions that combine various treatment components) have dominated the empirical literature since Novaco's (1975) adaptation of stress inoculation training to anger. Multicomponent approaches are based on the assumption that the combination of several strategies will result in optimal change relative to the individual components. Two of the most frequently researched combined interventions are stress inoculation training and cognitive-relaxation coping skills.

Stress Inoculation Training

Stress inoculation training (SIT; Meichenbaum, 1972, 1985) was originally developed to treat anxiety but was adapted for the treatment of angry persons (Meichenbaum & Turk, 1976; Novaco, 1975, 1978, 1979). SIT is a structured treatment program delivered in three phases. Treatment begins with the cognitive preparation phase in which clients learn a new conceptualization of anger that stresses the role of cognition. In the skill acquisition and rehearsal phase, clients receive a combination of cognitive restructuring/self-instructional training, relaxation, and behavioral coping skills. Finally, clients practice applying the skills they have learned in various contexts during the application and practice phase.

SIT and similar treatment packages that combine cognitive, relaxation, and behavioral coping interventions have received support for anger reduction among college students and community volunteers (Novaco, 1975), adult hypertensive patients (Achmon et al., 1989), highly angry college students (Deffenbacher, McNamara, Stark, & Sabadell, 1990a), aggressive parents (Acton & During, 1992), prison inmates (Smith & Beckner, 1993; Smith, Smith, & Beckner, 1994), male veterans diagnosed with posttraumatic stress disorder (Chemtob, Novaco, Hamada, & Gross, 1997), and male veterans referred for outpatient anger management (Timmons, Oehlert, Sumerall, Timmons, & Borgers, 1997). Positive treatment gains have been maintained at follow-ups of 1 year or more (Chemtob et al., 1997; Deffenbacher et al., 1990a).

Cognitive Relaxation Coping Skills

Cognitive-relaxation coping skills (CRCS) was developed by Deffenbacher and colleagues (1987, 1988) by combining cognitive restructuring with a relaxation-based adaptation of anxiety management training. The primary differences between SIT and CRCS include a reduced emphasis on behavior coping skills in CRCS and procedural differences in how the treatment is conducted. In fact, the relaxation component of CRCS was developed to correct methodological problems in Novaco's (1975) SIT intervention (Deffenbacher & Lynch, 1998). CRCS treatment usually begins with the relaxation component, as there is some evidence to suggest that relaxation may help make cognitive interventions more palatable to clients (Deffenbacher et al., 1988). After clients are trained in progressive muscle relaxation and several specific relaxation coping skills, the focus expands to include cognitive restructuring. Both relaxation and cognitive coping skills are rehearsed to reduce anger elicited (usually by anger imagery) within session. As client self-control increases, the anger arousal level is increased, and the therapist's assistance is decreased. Homework typically involves the application of relaxation and cognitive skills in vivo for anger reduction.

CRCS has received considerable support among highly angry college students (Deffenbacher et al., 1987, 1988, 1990b, 1994, 1996; Deffenbacher & Stark, 1992), angry drivers (Deffenbacher, Huff, et al., 2000; Deffenbacher, Filetti, et al., 2000), and abusive parents or those identified as "high risk" to abuse their children (Whiteman et al., 1987). In addition, treatment gains have been maintained over 12- to 15-month follow-ups (Deffenbacher, 1988; Deffenbacher et al., 1995; Deffenbacher & Stark, 1992). Although common sense suggests that the combination of relaxation and cognitive components would be more efficacious than either treatment component alone, this assumption has not been supported empirically. For example, treatment equivalency has been demonstrated between CRCS and the cognitive (Deffenbacher et al., 1988) and relaxation components alone (Deffenbacher & Stark, 1992; Schlicter & Horan, 1981).

BECK'S COGNITIVE THERAPY APPLIED TO ANGER: A NEW DIRECTION AND CASE STUDY

Cognitive therapy (Beck, 1976; Beck et al., 1979) is an empirically supported intervention for depression (Butler & Beck, 1995; Dobson, 1989; Task Force on Promotion and Dissemination of Psychological Procedures, 1995) and other problems including anxiety, eating disorders, personality disorders, relationship problems, schizophrenia, and substance abuse (Beck, 1993). Although cognitive change is thought to be the primary mechanism of change in cognitive therapy, cognitive therapy emphasizes both cognitive and behavioral change strategies. For example, cognitive therapy for depression often begins with behavioral activation (e.g., activity scheduling and graded task assignments), which has been shown to be as important as cognitive restructuring (Jacobson et al., 1996). Thus, cognitive therapy may be thought of as a multicomponent intervention, emphasizing the importance of clients learning to think about and approach life problems differently.

Until recently, Beck's cognitive therapy had not been applied to anger. An intervention based on the inductive style and behavioral change strategies of Beck's cognitive therapy (i.e., the behavioral component without the cognitive change strategies) lowered anger, led to more controlled anger expression, and was as effective as a structured, therapist-directed behavioral intervention and cognitive-relaxation coping skills (Deffenbacher et al., 1994, 1996). Moreover, gains were maintained in long-term follow-up (Deffenbacher et al., 1995, 1996), suggesting that the behavioral element of cognitive therapy was effective. When Beck's full cognitive therapy (i.e., both cognitive and behavioral components) was applied with generally angry college students, cognitive therapy reduced anger, anger suppression, and outward negative anger expression, and increased positive expression styles; gains were maintained at long-term follow-up; and treatment effect sizes suggested clinically meaningful change (Dahlen & Deffenbacher, 2000; Deffenbacher, Dahlen, Lynch, Morris, & Gowensmith, 2000). The cognitive element alone was effective as well (Dahlen & Deffenbacher, 2000). These studies suggest that cognitive therapy is effective with problematic anger. Below is a case study describing the application of cognitive therapy with a highly angry, aggressive driver.

Assessment and Case Description

Jim is a 29-year-old, single, white, unmarried male who works as a mid-level marketing manager in a large computer firm. The first two sessions were devoted to rapport building and assessment. The presenting concern was frequent, intense anger while driving and associated risky and aggressive behavior. He indicated he had always been an angry, aggressive driver and had over the years received several tickets for speeding. He was concerned that if he did not change, he would lose his driver's license, which would have serious repercussions for his work and lifestyle. In the last year, he had received one ticket for speeding and another for speeding and following too close. In addition, while receiving the second ticket, the officer gave Jim a verbal warning about his anger. He was very concerned about the possibility of losing of his license and reported that he did not like feeling so angry and out of control.

Jim's anger while driving was marked by intense emotionality (angry, furious, pissed) and high levels of physiological arousal marked by a surge of adrenalin; elevated tension in the neck, shoulders, and arms; tension across the stomach, clenched jaws, clenched fists, and a hot sensation in the neck and face. Cognitively, his thinking was characterized by demanding and absolutistic thinking about how others should drive; catastrophization regarding the consequences of being late and being slowed by traffic; inflammatory labeling and cursing; a sense of entitlement, derogation, denigration, and accusation of other drivers; and imagery and thoughts of harm and retaliation towards others. Behaviorally, he engaged in considerable aggressive behavior (e.g., making angry faces at others, yelling at other drivers, hostile gestures such as shaking his fists at or giving the finger to other drivers, tailgating, flashing his lights and honking his horn at, and purposefully impeding others as retaliation and punishment for perceived offenses). He also engaged in many risky driving behaviors (e.g., cutting in and out of traffic, speeding, and running yellow lights).

During the assessment phase, Jim completed the Driving Anger Scale, Anger Situation Rating, Driving Anger Expression Inventory, and the self-monitoring log employed in two recent studies of driving anger reduction (Deffenbacher, Filetti, et al., 2000; Deffenbacher, Huff, et al., 2000). His scores were somewhat higher than those of high-anger drivers on level of driving anger and hostile/aggressive driving anger expression and lower on adaptive/constructive driving anger expression. Based on self-monitoring data, Jim became angry while driving 4.5 times per day with an average daily intensity of 71 (0–100 scale) and averaged 3.5 aggressive and 5.0 risky driving behaviors per day. These figures are also above the means for high-anger drivers. In summary, Jim was a highly angry, aggressive, risk-taking driver whose anger made him feel out of control and put him at risk for vehicular crashes and legal consequences.

Cognitive Therapy

Cognitive therapy was introduced in the third session using an analogy to glasses. It was suggested that thoughts were like the lenses in his glasses. If he had clear lenses, traffic and other drivers might be annoying and frustrating, but tolerable. However, if he had red, angry lenses, he would "see" and respond to things in angry, aggressive ways. Jim was intrigued by the analogy, and provided several recent examples of times when he did not react angrily (clear lenses), comparing them to occasions when he reacted with anger (red lenses). Clear thinking and red, angry thinking were identified and contrasted. Therapy was described in terms of helping him acquire corrective, clear lenses by learning how to think about driving situations differently and develop alternative, calmer ways of handling them. Homework involved self-monitoring all "red" thinking while driving. He did this by dictating his thoughts at the time into a pocket recorder and transcribing them later.

Throughout the next eight sessions of cognitive therapy, the therapist consistently employed Socratic questions. Some were cognitively focused (e.g., "What's another way of looking at that?" "How bad would it be if you were late to that meeting?" "Where's your evidence that the other driver did that on purpose?" "Even if you knew for certain that the other driver did it on purpose to piss you off, what's a 'clear' way of thinking about his or her behavior?"). Others were more behaviorally focused (e.g., "What's another way of handling that?" "If you were 'clear' headed, how might you approach that situation?" "If you were giving your 16-year-old nephew three constructive ways of handling that situation, what would they be?" "What could you do that would interrupt your usual aggressive way of dealing with that? For example, what could you do with your hands to keep from giving him the finger?"). Toward the end of every session, a list of "red" and "clear" thoughts and behaviors from that session were summarized. Usually, about 15 minutes of the session were spent visualizing one or two angering situations from the past week (e.g., someone cutting in too closely), becoming angry again, and then mentally rehearsing "clear" thoughts and behaviors to address that situation. In early sessions, the therapist reminded Jim of specific thoughts and behaviors that he had identified earlier, whereas these prompts were faded out in later sessions, as Jim learned to generate them in the moment.

Issues were also explored with silly humor on occasion. For example, when the client referred to other drivers either as "dumb shits" or "asses," he was asked to define his terms concretely, which led to definitions of retarded fecal material and either a burro or cheeks of the buttocks. The client was then asked to draw a picture of these terms and to visualize them in imagery within the session and whenever he used them to label another driver. Later in therapy when Jim described feeling angry with another driver who was cutting in and out of traffic in a rapid, erratic manner, he was asked to list all the possible reasons why someone might behave in that manner. One of his explanations was that the driver might have a bad case of diarrhea and was desperately searching for a place to get off the road. Jim reported that he would want to slow down and back off so that he did not slip and slide if the other driver had an "accident." The pun was enjoyed and extrapolated into principles and practices of safe driving so that the client did not get caught up in other people's "accidents" or "shit" on the road.

Work within the session was extended by collaboratively developed experiments and homework. For example, starting with the fourth session, the client categorized his thoughts and behaviors as "clear" or "red," and generated at least one "clear" alternative for each "red" thought or behavior. For example, to address anger when in a hurry, the client agreed to plan for a realistic margin of problems on the road during every trip over a 3-week period and then to leave home early enough to include that margin. He reported great relief and calmness as a result of doing this, where his initial prediction was that this would make him even more on edge. In addition, on several occasions, the client agreed to interview his friends regarding their attributions about and ways of coping with specific situations on the road (e.g., what they thought about and did when stuck in heavy traffic or slowed down by an accident or what they thought when someone gave them the finger or yelled at them). This was done to provide him with alternative ways of thinking about or dealing with that situation. He extracted themes from the interviews, and these were discussed in the next session in terms of "clear" thinking and behaving. As a final example, after the sixth session, the client spontaneously started dictating "clear" thoughts and self-instructions for rethinking and behaving alternatively. This was clarified and built in as part of in vivo self-monitoring and application.

Cognitive therapy was conducted in this manner for a total of nine sessions. To address maintenance and relapse prevention, the time interval between the last two sessions was lengthened to 3 weeks in order to provide more opportunities for rehearsal and consolidation. A tenth session 3 months later was established to keep Jim focused on continuing to reduce driving anger. In addition, he continued to self-monitor anger and efforts to change, and these were sent to the therapist every 2 weeks with comments returned to the client via e-mail.

Outcome

Jim reported significantly reduced anger while driving, adding that he felt much calmer and no longer out of control. He reported that he rarely even had the urge to give someone the finger, yell at them, tailgate, or flash his lights, but that when he did, he would "think through the situation clearly," and purposefully engage in alternative behavior identified in therapy. He said that he had changed his driving habits significantly as well, indicating that he routinely tried to leave home a little earlier and that he no longer speeded routinely, or cut in and out of traffic. These reports were supported by psychometric and self-monitoring data collected at 3-month follow-up. Reports on measures of driving anger were slightly below the means for college students. Adaptive/constructive forms of driving anger expression increased, and hostile/aggressive forms decreased. Data from self-monitoring logs revealed only a slight decrease in frequency of being angry (i.e., down from an average of 4.5 times per day to 3.8); however, the intensity was reduced from 71 to 30 (out of 100), a level that the client reported reflected only annoyance. He reported less than one aggressive behavior per day and slightly over one risky behavior. Changes on these instruments are equivalent to or better than average change in relaxation and cognitive-relaxation interventions, suggesting meaningful change relative to other interventions as well. A phone call 1 year following treatment revealed continued anger and aggression reduction and no moving violations.

SUMMARY

The assessment and treatment of pathologic anger has been complicated by conceptual confusion regarding anger and aggression, the widespread popularity of various myths about effective anger management (e.g., cathartic expression effectively reduces anger), and the absence of clear diagnostic guidelines. Fortunately, the clinician now has a variety of empirically supported cognitive-behavioral strategies from which to select in providing treatment to angry adults. Relaxation, cognitive restructuring/problem solving, behavioral coping/social skills, and various multicomponent interventions have led to lasting and clinically meaningful anger reduction across a variety of measures compared to no-treatment controls. For the most part, studies comparing one treatment approach to another have demonstrated equivalence (i.e., treatments are better than no treatment, but one treatment condition is not superior to another). In addition, multicomponent interventions have not fared better than their individual components. Furthermore, symptom-treatment matching has not been supported. Of course, it must be recognized that the vast majority of studies on anger reduction deliver treatment in a group therapy format, and thus, it remains to be determined whether the greater flexibility of individual therapy to tailor treatment to the individual client will prove beneficial. Rather than despair over clear superiority of one treatment over another, we would suggest that clinicians now have an arsenal of empirically supported interventions from which to draw. Based on a collaborative assessment and shared conceptualization, clinicians can suggest and integrate treatment components consistent with this conceptualization. Given its inductive style and emphasis on collaboration, Beck's cognitive therapy seems to fit this description well. Although additional research is needed, preliminary work suggests that cognitive therapy appears promising for anger management.

REFERENCES

Achmon, J., Granek, M., Golomb, M., & Hart, J. (1989). Behavior treatment of essential hypertension: A comparison between cognitive therapy and biofeedback of heart rate. *Psychosomatic Medicine, 51,* 152–164.

Acton, R. G., & During, S. M. (1992). Preliminary results of aggression management training for aggressive parents. *Journal of Interpersonal Violence, 7,* 410–417.

American Psychiatric Association. (1994). *Diagnostic and statistical manual of mental disorders* (4th ed.). Washington, DC: Author.

Averill, J. R. (1983). Studies on anger and aggression: Implications for theories of emotion. *American Psychologist, 38,* 1145–1160.

Beck, A. T. (1976). *Cognitive therapy and the emotional disorders.* New York: International Universities Press.

Beck, A. T. (1993). Cognitive therapy: Past, present, and future. *Journal of Consulting and Clinical Psychology, 61,* 194–198.

Beck, A. T. (1999). *Prisoners of hate: The cognitive basis of anger, hostility, and violence.* New York: Harper Collins.

Beck, R., & Fernandez, E. (1998). Cognitive-behavioral therapy in the treatment of anger: A meta-analysis. *Cognitive Therapy and Research, 22,* 63–74.

Beck, A. T., Rush, A. J., Shaw, B. F., & Emery, G. (1979). *Cognitive therapy of depression.* New York: Guilford Press.

Berkowitz, L. (1990). On information regulation of anger and aggression: A cognitive-neoassociationistic analysis. *American Psychologist, 45,* 494–503.

Brondolo, E., Masheb, R., Stores, J., Stockhammer, T., Tunick, W., Melhado, E., Karlin, W. A., Schwartz, J., Harburg, E., & Contrada, R. J. (1998). Anger-related traits and response to interpersonal conflict among New York City traffic agents. *Journal of Applied Social Psychology, 28,* 2089–2118.

Butler, A. C., & Beck, A. T. (1995). Cognitive therapy for depression. *The Clinical Psychologist, 48,* 3–5.

Cary, M., & Dua, J. (1999). Cognitive-behavioral and systematic desensitization procedures in reducing stress and anger in caregivers for the disabled. *International Journal of Stress Management, 6,* 75–87.

Chemtob, C. M., Novaco, R. W., Hamada, R. S., & Gross, D. M. (1997). Cognitive-behavioral treatment for severe anger in posttraumatic stress disorder. *Journal of Consulting and Clinical Psychology, 65,* 184–189.

Dahlen, E. R., & Deffenbacher, J. L. (2000). A partial component analysis of Beck's cognitive therapy for the treatment of general anger. *Journal of Cognitive Psychotherapy, 14,* 77–95.

Deffenbacher, J. L. (1988). Cognitive-relaxation and social skills treatments of anger: A year later. *Journal of Counseling Psychology, 35,* 234–236.

Deffenbacher, J. L. (1992). Trait anger: Theory, findings, and implications. In C. D. Spielberger & J. N. Butcher (Volume Eds.), *Advances in personality assessment: Vol. 9* (pp. 177–201). Hillsdale, NJ: Lawrence Erlbaum Associates.

Deffenbacher, J. L. (1993). General anger: Characteristics and clinical implications. *Psicologia Conductual, 1,* 49–67.

Deffenbacher, J. L. (1994, August). *Anger and diagnosis: Where has all the anger gone?* Paper presented at the Annual Meeting of the American Psychological Association, Los Angeles, CA.

Deffenbacher, J. L. (1995). Ideal treatment package for adults with anger disorders. In H. Kassinove (Ed.), *Anger disorders: Definition, diagnosis, and treatment* (pp. 151–172). Washington DC: Taylor & Francis.

Deffenbacher, J. L. (1996). Cognitive-behavioral approaches to anger reduction. In K. S. Dobson & K. D. Craig (Eds.), *Advances in cognitive-behavioral therapy.* Thousand Oaks, CA: Sage Publications.

Deffenbacher, J. L. (1999). Cognitive-behavioral conceptualization and treatment of anger. *Journal of Clinical Psychology, 55,* 295–309.

Deffenbacher, J. L., Dahlen, E. R., Lynch, R. S., Morris, C. D., & Gowensmith, W. N. (2000). An application of Beck's cognitive therapy to general anger reduction. *Cognitive Therapy and Research, 24,* 689–697.

Deffenbacher, J. L., Demm, P. M., & Brandon, A. D. (1986). High general anger: Correlates and treatment. *Behavior Research and Therapy, 24,* 481–489.

Deffenbacher, J. L., Filetti, L. B., Lynch, R. S., Dahlen, E. R., & Oetting, E. R. (2000). *Cognitive-behavioral treatment of high anger drivers.* Manuscript submitted for publication.

Deffenbacher, J. L., Huff, M. E., Lynch, R. S., Oetting, E. R., & Salvatore, N. F. (2000). Characteristics and treatment of high anger drivers. *Journal of Counseling Psychology, 47,* 5–17.

Deffenbacher, J. L., & Lynch, R. S. (1998). Cognitive/behavioral intervention for anger reduction. In V. E. Caballo (Volume Ed.), *Manual para el tratamiento cognitivo-conductual de los trastornos psicologicos: Vol. 2* (pp. 639–674). Madrid, Spain: Siglo XXI.

Deffenbacher, J. L., McNamara, K., Stark, R. S., & Sabadell, P. M. (1990a). A combination of cognitive, relaxation, and behavioral coping skills in the reduction of general anger. *Journal of College Student Development, 31,* 351–358.

Deffenbacher, J. L., McNamara, K., Stark, R. S., & Sabadell, P. M. (1990b). A comparison of cognitive-behavioral and process oriented group counseling for general anger reduction. *Journal of Counseling and Development, 69,* 167–172.

Deffenbacher, J. L., Oetting, E. R., & DiGiuseppe, R. (2000). *Principles of empirically supported intervention programs applied to anger management.* Unpublished manuscript.

Deffenbacher, J. L., Oetting, E. R., Huff, M. E., Cornell, G. R., & Dallager, C. J. (1996). Evaluation of two cognitive-behavioral approaches to general anger reduction. *Cognitive Therapy and Research, 20,* 551–573.

Deffenbacher, J. L., Oetting, E. R., Huff, M. E., & Thwaites, G. A. (1995). Fifteen-month follow-up of social skills and cognitive-relaxation approaches to general anger reduction. *Journal of Counseling Psychology, 42*, 400–405.

Deffenbacher, J. L., & Stark, R. S. (1992). Relaxation and cognitive-relaxation treatments of general anger. *Journal of Counseling Psychology, 39*, 158–167.

Deffenbacher, J. L., Story, D. A., Brandon, A. D., Hogg, J. A., & Hazaleus, S. L. (1988). Cognitive and cognitive-relaxation treatments of anger. *Cognitive Therapy and Research, 12*, 167–184.

Deffenbacher, J. L., Story, D. A., Stark, R. S., Hogg, J. A., & Brandon, A. D. (1987). Cognitive-relaxation and social skills interventions in the treatment of general anger. *Journal of Counseling Psychology, 34*, 171–176.

Deffenbacher, J. L., Thwaites, G. A., Wallace, T. L., & Oetting, E. R. (1994). Social skills and cognitive-relaxation approaches to general anger reduction. *Journal of Counseling Psychology, 41*, 386–396.

Diamond, E. L. (1982). The role of anger and hostility in essential hypertension and coronary heart disease. *Psychological Bulletin, 92*, 410–433.

DiGiuseppe, R., Eckhardt, C., Tafrate, R., & Robin, M. (1994). The diagnosis and treatment of anger in a cross-cultural context. *Journal of Social Distress and the Homeless, 3*, 229–261.

Dobson, K. S. (1989). A meta-analysis of the efficacy of cognitive therapy for depression. *Journal of Consulting and Clinical Psychology, 57*, 414–419.

Dryden, W. (1990). *Dealing with anger problems: Rational-emotive therapeutic interventions.* Sarasota, FL: Practitioner's Resource Exchange, Inc.

Dua, J. K., & Swinden, M. L. (1992). Effectiveness of negative-thought-reduction, meditation, and placebo training treatment in reducing anger. *Scandinavian Journal of Psychology, 33*, 135–146.

D'Zurilla, T. J., & Goldfried, M. R. (1971). Problem solving and behavior modification. *Journal of Abnormal Psychology, 78*, 107–126.

Eckhardt, C. I., & Deffenbacher, J. L. (1995). Diagnosis of anger disorders. In H. Kassinove (Ed.), *Anger disorders: Definition, diagnosis, and treatment* (pp. 27–47). Washington, DC: Taylor & Francis.

Edmondson, C. B., & Conger, J. C. (1996). A review of treatment efficacy for individuals with anger problems: Conceptual, assessment, and methodological issues. *Clinical Psychology Review, 16*, 251–275.

Ellis, A. (1962). *Reason and emotion in psychotherapy.* New York: Lyle Stuart.

Ellis, A. (1973). *Humanistic psychology: The rational-emotive approach.* New York: Julian Press.

Ellis, A. (1977). *How to live with—and without—anger.* New York: Reader's Digest Press.

Fava, M., Alpert, J., Nierenberg, A. A., Ghaemi, N., O'Sullivan, R., Tedlow, J., Worthington, J., & Rosenbaum, J. F. (1996). Fluoxetine treatment of anger attacks: A replication study. *Annals of Clinical Psychiatry, 8*, 7–10.

Fava, M., Rosenbaum, J. F., McCarthy, M., Pava, J., Steingard, R., & Bless,

E. (1991). Anger attacks in depressed outpatients and their response to fluoxetine. *Psychopharmacology Bulletin, 27,* 275–279.

Goldstein, M. G., & Niaura, R. (1992). Psychological factors affecting physical conditions: Cardiovascular disease literature review. *Psychosomatics, 33,* 14–145.

Hardy, J. D., & Smith, T. W. (1988). Cynical hostility and vulnerability to disease: Social support, life stress, and physiological response to conflict. *Health Psychology, 7,* 447–459.

Hazaleus, S. L., & Deffenbacher, J. L. (1986). Relaxation and cognitive treatments of anger. *Journal of Consulting and Clinical Psychology, 54,* 222–226.

Jacobson, N. S., Dobson, K. S., Truax, P. A., Addis, M. E., Koerner, K., Gollan, J. K., Gortner, E., & Prince, S. E. (1996). A component analysis of cognitive-behavioral treatment for depression. *Journal of Consulting and Clinical Psychology, 64,* 295–304.

Kassinove, H., & Sukhodolsky, D. G. (1995). Anger disorders: Basic science and practice issues. In H. Kassinove (Ed.), *Anger disorders: Definition, diagnosis, and treatment* (pp. 1–26). Washington, DC: Taylor & Francis.

Lazarus, R. S. (1991). *Emotion and adaptation.* New York: Oxford University Press.

Lohr, J. M., Hamberger, L. J., & Bonge, D. (1988). The nature of irrational beliefs in different personality clusters of spouse abusers. *Journal of Rational-Emotive and Cognitive-Behavior Therapy, 6,* 273–285.

Matthews, K. A., & Haynes, S. G. (1986). Type A behavior pattern and coronary disease risk: Update and critical evaluation. *American Journal of Epidemiology, 123,* 923–960.

Meichenbaum, D. H. (1972). Cognitive modification of test anxious college students. *Journal of Consulting and Clinical Psychology, 39,* 370–380.

Meichenbaum, D. H. (1985). *Stress inoculation training.* New York: Pergamon Press.

Meichenbaum, D. H., & Turk, D. (1976). The cognitive-behavioral management of anxiety, anger, and pain. In P. O. Davidson (Ed.), *The behavioral management of anxiety, depression and pain* (pp. 1–34). New York: Brunner/Mazel.

Moon, J. R., & Eisler, R. M. (1983). Anger control: An experimental comparison of three behavioral treatments. *Behavior Therapy, 14,* 493–505.

Novaco, R. W. (1975). *Anger control: The development and evaluation of an experimental treatment.* Lexington, MA: Lexington Books.

Novaco, R. W. (1978). Anger and coping with stress: Cognitive behavioral interventions. In J. P. Foreyt & D. P. Rathjen (Eds.), *Cognitive behavior therapy: Research and application* (pp. 135–173). New York: Plenum Press.

Novaco, R. W. (1979). The cognitive regulation of anger and stress. In P. C. Kendall & S. D. Hollon (Eds.), *Cognitive-behavioral interventions: Theory, research, and practice* (pp. 241–285). New York: Academic Press.

Rimm, D. C., Hill, G. A., Brown, N. N., & Stuart, J. E. (1974). Group-assertive training in treatment of expression of inappropriate anger. *Psychological Reports, 34,* 791–798.

Schlicter, K. J., & Horan, J. J. (1981). Effects of stress inoculation on the anger and aggression management skills of institutionalized juvenile delinquents. *Cognitive Therapy and Research, 5,* 359–365.

Smith, L. L., & Beckner, B. M. (1993). An anger management workshop for inmates in a medium security facility. *Journal of Offender Rehabilitation, 19,* 103–111.

Smith, L. L., Smith, J. N., & Beckner, B. M. (1994). An anger-management workshop for women inmates. *Families in Society, 75,* 172–175.

Suinn, R. M. (1990). *Anxiety management training: A behavior therapy.* New York: Plenum Press.

Tafrate, R. C. (1995). Evaluation of treatment strategies for adult anger disorders. In H. Kassinove (Ed.), *Anger disorders: Definition, diagnosis, and treatment* (pp. 109–129). Washington, DC: Taylor & Francis.

Tafrate, R. C., & Kassinove, H. (1998). Anger control in men: Barb exposure with rational, irrational, and irrelevant self-statements. *Journal of Cognitive Psychotherapy, 12,* 187–211.

Task Force on Promotion and Dissemination of Psychological Procedures. (1995). Training in and dissemination of empirically-validated psychological treatments: Report and recommendations. *The Clinical Psychologist, 48,* 3–27.

Timmons, P. L., Oehlert, M. E., Sumerall, S. W., Timmons, C. W., & Borgers, S. B. (1997). Stress inoculation training for maladaptive anger: Comparison of group counseling versus computer guidance. *Computers in Human Behavior, 13,* 51–64.

Whiteman, M., Fanshel, D., & Grundy, J. F. (1987). Cognitive-behavioral interventions aimed at anger of parents at risk of child abuse. *Social Work, 32,* 469–474.

Zillman, D. (1971). Excitation transfer in communication-mediated aggressive behavior. *Journal of Experimental Social Psychology, 7,* 419–434.

9

Antisocial Behaviors in Children and Adolescents: Expanding the Cognitive Model

Laura D. Hanish and Patrick H. Tolan

Youth antisocial behaviors such as physical aggression, lying, bullying, vandalism, stealing, use of a weapon, and fire setting are encountered all too frequently by child and family therapists. In fact, they constitute as many as one-half of child and adolescent therapy referrals, with some cases meeting criteria for a diagnosis of conduct disorder and others presenting at subclinical, but still problematic, levels (Kazdin, 1987). Unfortunately, they also tend to be difficult to treat, reflecting the overall stability of these behaviors and their frequent co-occurrence with other problems, such as substance use, school failure, early and risky sexual behavior, victimization, and depression (Caspi & Moffitt, 1995; Dishion, French, & Patterson, 1995; Hanish & Guerra, 2000; Huizinga & Jakob-Chien, 1998). Prognosis is particularly poor for children who possess numerous individual, family, and sociocultural risk factors, who develop antisocial behavior problems early in childhood, and who exhibit multiple and severe forms of antisocial behavior (Caspi & Moffitt, 1995).

The severity of this problem has propelled the search for effective treatments. One of the most recognized interventions is cognitive therapy. Cognitive therapy of antisocial behavior involves modifying the maladaptive social problem-solving patterns and beliefs that often underlie and support children's decisions to engage in antisocial behavior. Clinical research, however, indicates that the effectiveness of cognitive interventions is limited (Guerra & Slaby, 1990; Hudley & Graham, 1993; Kazdin, Bass, Siegel, & Thomas, 1989; Lochman & Lenhart, 1995; Pepler, King, & Byrd, 1991). This is primarily because cognitive therapy targets only one of the many risk factors for antisocial behavior; such a limited focus in unlikely to produce lasting change in children who exhibit the most severe problems and who are in the greatest need of treatment (Reid, 1993; Wasserman & Miller, 1998). Also needed are intervention components that target child behavioral, family, and contextual contributors to antisocial behavior. Indeed, when cognitive treatments are used in combination with other treatment techniques, their effectiveness is increased (Hanish, Tolan, & Guerra, 1996; Kazdin, Siegel, & Bass, 1992; Metropolitan Area Child Study, in press). In this chapter, we describe the utility and limitations of cognitive therapy for antisocial behavior. We suggest that the effectiveness of cognitive treatments is enhanced when they are used together with other treatment modalities that directly target children's behaviors, family interaction patterns, and contextual characteristics. We conclude by illustrating the use of this integrative therapeutic model with a case example.

COGNITIVE TREATMENT OF YOUTH ANTISOCIAL BEHAVIOR: UTILITY AND LIMITATIONS

Cognitive formulations of antisocial behavior, grounded primarily in social cognitive (Bandura, 1986) and social information processing theories (McFall, 1982; Rubin & Krasnor, 1986), have emphasized that children's cognitions, particularly their social cognitions, motivate their aggressive behaviors. The principal tenet of these cognitive models is that antisocial children and adolescents think about social interactions in distorted and maladaptive ways, increasing the likelihood that they will choose to behave aggressively and diminishing the likelihood that they will experience guilt or misgivings. Indeed, research has shown that aggressive youngsters, when faced with a social situation, attend to fewer social cues than do their peers, focusing predominantly on hostile cues and ignoring nonhostile ones (Dodge & Newman, 1981). This selective attention to hostile cues primes aggressive children to interpret social situations as antagonistic, causing them to attribute hostile intent to others' behaviors (Dodge & Frame, 1982; Graham & Hudley, 1994; Slaby & Guerra, 1988). This, in turn, increases the likelihood of selecting and enacting aggressive responses (Dodge, Pettit, McClaskey, & Brown, 1986; Slaby & Guerra, 1988). Moreover, aggressive children and adolescents tend to believe that their behavior is acceptable (Erdley & Asher, 1998; Guerra, Huesmann, & Hanish, 1995; Slaby & Guerra, 1988) and that it will result in valued rewards, such as high self-esteem, social control, and peer approval (Boldizar, Perry, & Perry, 1989; Perry, Perry, & Rasmussen, 1986; Slaby & Guerra, 1988). They also tend to have high self-efficacy for performing aggression coupled with low self-efficacy for inhibiting aggression (Perry et al., 1986).

Although social cognitions are clearly a risk factor for antisocial behavior, they are not the only, nor are they the primary, risk factor. Indeed, research suggests that some antisocial youth are cognitively indistinguishable from their non-antisocial peers (Crick & Dodge, 1996; Rubin, Bream, & Rose-Krasnor, 1991). In a review of predictors of antisocial behavior, Hawkins and colleagues (1998) found that attitudes and beliefs were consistently, but only moderately, correlated with antisocial behavior for males, though they were inconsistently correlated with antisocial behavior for females. Moreover, antisocial behavior depends upon multiple sets of risk factors, including child characteristics (e.g., temperamental and behavioral styles, gender, and cognitions) familial characteristics (e.g., parenting practices, family interactions, and parental beliefs), and contextual characteristics (e.g., peer relations, school experiences, poverty, and exposure to violence; Deater-Deckard, Dodge, Bates, & Pettit, 1998; Dishion et al., 1995; Hawkins et al., 1998). Many of these factors account for more of the variance in child and adolescent behavior problems than do social cognitive factors (Hawkins et al., 1998). In addition, there is mounting evidence to suggest that there are multiple etiologic pathways that lead to youth antisocial behavior and that the presence of multiple risk factors in multiple domains increases the likelihood that a youngster will develop extreme behaviors (Deater-Deckard et al., 1998). Thus, social cognitions may partly explain antisocial behavior for some children, but they do not completely explain antisocial behavior for all children.

In addition, even when children do hold cognitions that contribute to their conduct problems, the origin of these cognitions must be considered in treatment planning. Cognitions supporting aggression do not develop in isolation, but instead emerge in the context of children's developing behaviors and family and social interactions. Normative patterns of child development are a critical influence on the relation between cognition and behavior. Prior to about the middle of elementary school, aggressive behaviors influence the development of related cognitions, but cognitions do not influence the development of aggressive behaviors. It is not until children reach the middle elementary years that children's social cognitive skills have developed sufficiently to permit cognitions to become an important influence on future aggressive behavior (Huesmann & Guerra, 1997). Not only do aggressive cognitions develop from children's existing social behaviors, but aggressive cognitions also develop in the context of interpersonal interactions. Children often acquire the distorted beliefs, values, and information processing patterns that may motivate their antisocial behavior from family members (Barrett, Rapee, Dadds, & Ryan, 1996; Mills & Rubin, 1990). It is not uncommon for the parents of antisocial children to espouse a set of cognitions that support aggression, particularly when the parent also displays antisocial behaviors (Deater-Deckard et al., 1998; Gorman-Smith, Tolan, Loeber, & Henry, 1998; Hawkins et al., 1998). Furthermore, aggressive children who grow up in violent neighborhoods and who affiliate with other aggressive individuals are more likely to be exposed to a set of social norms that promote hostile behaviors (Guerra et al., 1995).

It is not surprising, then, that child-focused cognitive therapies are only minimally effective in treating antisocial behavior. Tests of cognitive interventions in community samples typically produce improvements on some, but not all, outcome indicators (e.g., Hudley & Graham, 1993; Pepler et al., 1991). Behavioral improvements are even less likely to occur for clinical, than for nonclinical, samples. Children who have more severe problems are less likely to respond to treatment (Kazdin & Crowley, 1997; Kendall, Ronan, & Epps, 1991). Moreover, when clinical samples do exhibit behavioral change, the change may be statistically, but not clinically, meaningful, with children frequently continuing to display high rates of antisocial behavior that remain outside of the normative range of functioning (Kazdin et al., 1989). Even when children do exhibit meaningful behavioral change, the changes are often not generalized beyond the treatment and maintained over time (e.g., Guerra & Slaby, 1990; Lochman & Lenhart, 1995).

EXPANDING THE COGNITIVE MODEL IN THE TREATMENT OF YOUTH ANTISOCIAL BEHAVIOR

The primary limitation that plagues cognitive therapy for antisocial behavior is the same limitation that plagues other stand-alone treatments—by focusing on only one risk factor for antisocial behavior this treatment modality is incomplete. However, cognitive therapies have been empirically demonstrated to be a critical aspect of a successful treatment program when used in combination with other treatment modalities that target additional risk factors (Hanish et al., 1996; Kazdin et al., 1992; Metropolitan Area Child Study, 1999). Such an integrated approach is responsive to the research that indicates that antisocial behavior is determined by multiple individual, familial, and contextual risk factors and that children with the most severe behavior problems typically have problems in two or more of these areas (Deater-Deckard et al., 1998; Hawkins et al., 1998). Furthermore, effective treatments for antisocial behavior must include multiple intervention components that target each of the most critical aspects of antisocial behavior: child behavior, family interactions, and contextual characteristics. What follows is a review of the research bearing on each of these factors.

The Role of Child Behavior

Crucial to treatment models is an understanding of the nature and developmental trajectory of antisocial behavior. At its most severe, antisocial behavior begins early in childhood, in the form of aggressive behavior and, to some extent, oppositional behavior (Nagin & Tremblay, 1999). Although aggressive and oppositional behaviors are normative for most children, they usually peak in intensity and frequency at 2 years of age and decline slowly thereafter (Cummings, Iannotti, & Zahn-Waxler, 1989; Keenan & Shaw, 1994; Nagin & Tremblay, 1999). However, for a variety of reasons, some children, approximately 5%, do not follow this normative developmental trajectory; instead, they continue to show elevated levels of aggressive and oppositional behaviors throughout childhood and adolescence (Caspi & Moffitt, 1995; Nagin & Tremblay, 1999). These are the children who are most likely to commit violent and nonviolent offenses, to be diagnosed with conduct disorder, and to be in need of treatment.

From a clinical standpoint, it is important to consider what is causing these children to follow such maladaptive developmental trajectories and to address these factors in treatment. Important considerations include understanding how children's temperament and gender influence their behavior. Temperamental characteristics, such as emotion regulation abilities, are important influences on behavior. The ability to regulate the behavioral and affective expression of emotion is an early developmental predictor of concurrent and subsequent oppositional and aggressive behaviors. Children who are born with easy temperaments and who are skilled at managing their emotions are able to engage in more socially competent behaviors and are more likely to use effective means (e.g., verbal negotiation) to solve their social problems (Eisenberg, Fabes, Karbon et al., 1996). In contrast, children whose temperamental style is more difficult and who are less skilled at managing their affective and behavioral displays are more likely to display socially incompetent and aggressive behaviors and more likely to develop subsequent behavioral problems (Eisenberg, Fabes, Guthrie et al., 1996; Rende, 1993). Thus, such children may also need intervention components that are responsive to their temperamental style and that help children and parents create appropriate environments and cope with temperamental tendencies.

Treatments must also be sensitive to the form and meaning of the child's behavior. Boys and girls display different forms of aggressive behavior. Through the toddler years, there is little difference in the nature of aggressive behavior exhibited by boys and girls (Keenan & Shaw, 1994). As children get older, however, gender differences in conduct problems begin to emerge due to socialization and biological factors (Keenan & Shaw, 1994, 1997). Thus, the nature of aggressive behavior becomes increasingly differentiated for boys and girls. Whereas boys exhibit more physical aggression that is characterized by physical harm, girls exhibit more indirect aggression that is characterized by the destruction of social relationships (Crick & Grotpeter, 1995). By the time children reach adolescence, gender differences in antisocial behavior are even more differentiated, with girls' antisocial behavior often appearing less violent than that of boys, but frequently co-occurring with other problems such as internalizing disorders and teen pregnancy, which may perpetuate antisocial behavior in the next generation (Keenan, Loeber, & Green, 1999). Thus, treatments must also be designed to target the gender-specific forms of antisocial behavior that the child is exhibiting.

Intervention components that target children's behavioral styles may take a variety of forms, depending on the specific needs of the individual. Decisions about which forms are necessary should be made using an ecological framework. Such interventions may involve skill training that teaches youngsters to recognize and regulate their emotions and interact more competently with others. They may also involve behavior modification, using reinforcement and punishment to increase the frequency of positive behaviors and decrease the frequency of negative behaviors. Such behavioral treatments have often been incorporated with cognitive therapies. Other forms of intervention, however, may also be necessary. For instance, when antisocial youth become teen parents, they are likely to benefit from parenting interventions that teach effective means of interacting with children. This is often necessary to reduce the likelihood of intergenerational transmission of antisocial behavior.

The Role of Family Interactions

It is also crucial that interventions for antisocial behavior include a treatment component that addresses family interactions. Children spend much of their time with family members, particularly during early childhood when the behavioral and interactional precursors of later antisocial behavior are often developing (Loeber & Dishion, 1983; Reid & Eddy, 1997). Through parenting styles, socialization practices, and patterns of communication, families can have a tremendous impact on the development of children's behavior. Families of aggressive children tend to experience conflictual, inconsistent, and unsupportive family interactions that contribute to and maintain antisocial behaviors. For instance, parents and children tend to engage in coercive interactions in which family members escalate negative interactions, engaging in increasingly hostile interchanges (Dishion, Patterson, & Kavanagh, 1992; Patterson, 1982). Not only is conflict across generations frequent, but interparental conflict is also common (Hawkins et al., 1998). It is not surprising, therefore, that families of violent and delinquent youths tend to be less cohesive than families of nonviolent and nondelinquent youths (Forgatch & DeGarmo, 1999; Gorman-Smith, Tolan,

Zelli, & Huesmann, 1996). In addition, parents of antisocial children are more likely than other parents to use harsh punishment and to discipline ineffectively and inconsistently, but they are less likely to monitor their children's whereabouts and supervise their activities (Gorman-Smith et al., 1998; Gorman-Smith et al., 1996; Hawkins et al., 1998). These interaction styles afford many opportunities for children to exhibit antisocial behaviors but few opportunities to exhibit positive social behaviors.

Treatments for child antisocial behavior must target these family characteristics when they are evident; if they do not, it is unlikely that the therapy will be effective. Indeed, without intervention, the pattern of maladaptive family interactions that the family has developed will continue to function, thereby maintaining the behavioral status quo and hindering the child's attempts to adopt new positive behaviors and discard antisocial behaviors. The primary foci of family interventions involve teaching parents how to use consistent and appropriate discipline for negative behaviors, how to reinforce positive behaviors, how to monitor their children's activities, how to communicate effectively and warmly with family members, and how to solve family problems (e.g., McMahon, Slough, & Conduct Problems Prevention Research Group, 1996; Tolan & McKay, 1996). These interventions have demonstrated effectiveness in reducing noncompliance and oppositional behavior, aggression, coercive family interactions, arrest rates, and incarceration among youngsters (Bank, Marlowe, Reid, Patterson, & Weinrott, 1991; Dishion & Andrews, 1995; Tolan, Hanish, McKay, & Dickey, 2000; Webster-Stratton, Kolpacoff, & Hollinsworth, 1988). Moreover, in reviews of the literature, several clinical scientists have concluded that family interventions are a necessary component of the most effective interventions for childhood antisocial behavior (Estrada & Pinsof, 1995; Kazdin, 1987; Miller & Prinz, 1990).

In addition to modifying family contexts, parent-focused treatment components can assist parents in modifying their own ineffective problem-solving skills and deviant beliefs and values that contribute to family and child problems (Hanish et al., 1996; Tolan & Gorman-Smith, 1997). Such a treatment component is often necessary to help parents accept and implement changes in the family system (Hanish et al., 1996). This can be particularly useful when the family is experiencing additional problems, such as parental physical or mental illness, parental arrest, marital conflict, stressful circumstances, or poverty because these stressors complicate the family situation and hinder parents' ability to provide effective and responsive parenting, thereby reducing the likelihood that families will respond positively to treatment (Hanish & Tolan, in press; Kazdin & Wassell, 1998; Miller & Prinz, 1990). Thus, interventions that include family and parent change techniques can help the child to acquire new behavioral skills and modify maladaptive cognitions while simultaneously helping the family to accommodate to and encourage the child's changes.

The Role of Context

Effective interventions for youth antisocial behavior must also address the contextual factors that are contributing to the child's behavior. Just as families influence the development of children's antisocial behavior, peers, schools, and communities can also impact conduct problems. Extensive evidence suggests that affiliation with delinquent peer groups increases a child's own delinquent behavior (Dishion, McCord, Poulin, 1999). This effect operates through a process whereby deviant peers reinforce one another for delinquent activity (Dishion et al., 1999). In addition, peers' norms regarding the appropriateness of aggression affect children's behavior; children in peer groups that approve of aggression are more likely to be aggressive themselves (Henry et al., 2000). Moreover, peers and teachers can have additive effects on the development of antisocial behavior. Indeed, children in classrooms in which both peers and teachers punish aggression (through rejection and reprimands, respectively) show smaller increases in aggression over time compared to children in classrooms in which either peers or teachers (but not both) punish aggression (Henry et al., 2000).

Contextual effects are not limited to peers and schools. Youngsters' and families' experiences in the community can also affect the development of antisocial behavior. Those who live in neighborhoods characterized by moderately high levels of poverty and violence are at greater risk for becoming delinquent and violent themselves, in part because they breed isolation from more functional support systems (Sampson & Laub, 1994; Seidman et al., 1998). Moreover, exposure to community violence is a traumatic event that can significantly increase children's externalizing and internalizing behavior problems (Gorman-Smith & Tolan, 1998). The effects of such peer, school, and community contexts are often mediated by families, who have the power to limit, monitor, or modify children's involvement with negative as well as positive contextual systems.

Thus, interventions must also include treatment components that target the contextual factors that support antisocial behavior. Because peers, schools, and communities are systems that are interconnected with children and families, such interventions often work through the family. By assisting the family to make needed changes in the child's social environments, interventions can have a significant and lasting impact on children's antisocial behavior (e.g., multisystemic therapy; Henggeler, Melton, & Smith, 1992). Thus, not only must interventions target the individual child's cognitions and behaviors that contribute to his or her problems, but they must also address family functioning patterns and the contextual factors that maintain the problem behaviors.

THE INTEGRATION OF COGNITIVE, BEHAVIORAL, FAMILY, AND CONTEXTUAL INTERVENTION

Components in Treating Youth Antisocial Behavior

Effective treatment of antisocial behavior in children and adolescents requires the integration of multiple cognitive, behavior, family, and contextual change techniques (Guerra, Eron, Huesmann, Tolan, & Van Acker, 1997; Hanish et al., 1996; Henggeler et al., 1992; Reid, 1993; Wasserman & Miller, 1998). Most often, such interventions are effective when they are implemented within the context of the family. Parents may require individually focused interventions that help them to adapt to, manage, and facilitate changes in the child and contextual systems as well as family-focused interventions that help them to implement new family management techniques. In addition, in this model, alliance with the both the parents and the child is important. Parental alliance is seen as an important precursor to changes in family interactions and child alliance is seen as an important influence on change in child behavior (Tolan et al., 2000). In sum, the integration of cognitive, behavioral, family, and contextual change techniques is central to treating antisocial behavior (Guerra et al., 1997; Henggeler et al., 1992).

Case Example

Assessment

Michael S was a 9-year-old African-American boy who was brought for therapy by his paternal grandmother, Mrs. S. Michael presented with symptoms of both oppositional defiant disorder and conduct disorder. These symptoms included tantrumming; disruptive and noncompliant behavior at home, school, church, and at his after-school club; lying about his whereabouts and activities; physical aggression towards children and adults (including fighting frequently with peers, throwing rocks, bottles, and other objects at passersby in the neighborhood, and physically threatening to stab his grandmother with knives and scissors); running away from home when his grandmother was not watching to wander the neighborhood for several hours before returning; the frequent use of obscene language; and occasional truancy. In addition, Michael regularly engaged in aggressive play, typically enacting aggressive fantasies, and he associated with similarly deviant peers. He also displayed poor academic achievement; testing revealed an IQ score in the borderline range. Assessment of Michael's belief system revealed that he believed himself to be unlovable and that the only way to gain attention and love was to engage in aggressive behavior. In addition, Mrs. S reported that he had been prenatally exposed to multiple substances and had been born with cocaine in his bloodstream. Reportedly, many of these symptoms had been evident since early childhood, and they had increased in severity and intensity with age.

An assessment of the family situation revealed that Mrs. S, who was widowed and in her late sixties, was the primary caretaker and legal guardian for Michael. Michael's father had a history of antisocial behavior, and he had been incarcerated for physical assault with a weapon since Michael was a young child. Michael's mother had abandoned her son shortly after his birth and reportedly abused multiple substances. Neither Michael's father nor his mother maintained regular contact with Michael, with each other, or with Mrs. S. Moreover, whenever interactions between Michael and his parents did occur, they tended to be lacking in warmth and affection. Interactions between Mrs. S and Michael were similarly cold, and Mrs. S often behaved in a rejecting way toward her grandson, ignoring him and sending him away (e.g., to another room to play by himself). Mrs. S and Michael frequently engaged in hostile, coercive interactions, and Mrs. S disciplined Michael inconsistently, using inappropriate and ineffective strategies when attempting to manage his behavior. Her discipline typically consisted of attempts to ignore Michael's behavior and empty threats (that his uncle would beat him if he misbehaved). For instance, on one occasion, Michael ran around the therapy room, throwing toys, pinching adults and pulling hair, and interrupting conversations. During this episode, Mrs. S slumped helplessly in her chair, hopelessly begged Michael to behave himself, turned toward the therapist, and said "See how difficult he is?" Similarly, her attempts to monitor his behavior were also inconsistent and ineffective, as she frequently went to her room leaving Michael to occupy himself.

Assessment also revealed that the family was struggling with numerous other stressors that exacerbated their problems. Mrs. S and Michael lived in a small apartment that was located in an impoverished urban neighborhood characterized by relatively high crime rates and few resources. The family subsisted on a meager income based on a small pension and monthly Social Security checks. Mrs. S reportedly felt a sense of isolation in her community and she perceived little social support. She stated that her daughter and son-in-law (Michael's aunt and uncle) occasionally provided childcare and emotional support, but this was limited by a somewhat strained relationship with her daughter and the fact that it was difficult for Mrs. S to make the trip to her daughter's home (using public transportation) in a different neighborhood. She also identified one friend who occasionally provided instrumental support (e.g., driving her and Michael to therapy sessions when the weather was bad). To complicate the situation, Mrs. S also suffered from cataracts that hindered her vision and heart problems that limited her mobility and agility.

In sum, the assessment revealed that Michael experienced numerous individual, familial, and contextual risk factors for antisocial behavior, with the majority of risk factors centered in the family context (cf. Loeber & Dishion, 1983). The assessment also indicated that Michael was following a developmental trajectory that is characteristic of early onset antisocial behavior. In early onset antisocial behavior, the behavioral precursors of later antisocial behavior in the form of oppositional and defiant behaviors and coercive family interactions, are evident in early childhood. These early problems then develop into increasingly serious symptoms of antisocial behavior as children get older (Lahey, Loeber, Quay, Frick, & Grimm, 1992). In Michael's case, the lying, physical aggression, and truancy, which are characteristic of diagnoses of conduct disorder, had already emerged, and he was at risk for developing other more extreme symptoms of antisocial behavior (Caspi & Moffitt, 1995).

Treatment

Michael was referred to the first author (L. H.) for psychotherapy by his former therapist, who was leaving the mental health clinic where Michael was being seen. A review of his treatment history revealed that he had been attending therapy for the previous 2 years. Michael's former therapist had tried several different forms of treatment, including play therapy, individual cognitive therapy, pharmacotherapy, and ecological interventions that focused on obtaining a more appropriate school placement for Michael; enrolling Michael in an after-school program that provided him with structured, adult-supervised peer activities while simultaneously providing Mrs. S with some relief from childcare; and helping Mrs. S to manage numerous daily stressors that interfered with her ability to parent. Although these treatments had little effect on Michael's behavioral symptoms, they were effective in minimizing some of the nonfamilial risk factors associated with Michael's behavior problems in achieving a positive, trusting, alliance with both Michael and Mrs. S, and in providing Mrs. S with much needed support.

Initial therapy sessions focused on assessment, helping Mrs. S and Michael adapt to the change to a new therapist and building a working alliance. Then, family-focused treatment, with the goals of assisting Mrs. S to discipline consistently, to provide appropriate consequences for misbehavior, to reinforce positive behavior, and to engage in more warm and supportive interactions with her grandson, was implemented. It soon became apparent, however, that Mrs. S held a number of beliefs that interfered with her ability to adopt these new parenting practices. Mrs. S revealed that she believed that Michael was inherently a "bad child" who was incapable of improving his behavior. She responded selectively to his behavioral cues, ignoring his positive behaviors, interpreting his bids for attention as misbehavior, and responding only to his aversive behaviors. She also reported low self-efficacy in relation to managing Michael's behavior and believed that adaptive behavior management practices would be ineffective and would tire her out. Further exploration revealed that these beliefs stemmed, in part, from her feeling angry toward her son and Michael's mother for abandoning him and also toward her late husband, who had compelled her to adopt Michael against her will. Indeed, Mrs. S felt that she did not want her grandson, and she was unwilling to devote much time and energy to raising him.

Given these cognitive and affective impediments to family treatment, the focus of the therapy sessions shifted to helping Mrs. S to recognize and cope with her anger and to identify and modify the cognitions that were interfering with effective parenting. For example, Mrs. S. began to recognize that many of Michael's aversive behaviors reflected his desire for attention, rather than the "bad child" that she previously thought him to be. She also became aware that her anger was more appropriately directed toward her son and daughter-in-law, rather than toward Michael. Subsequently, Mrs. S was able to implement new parenting practices. As she slowly adopted more effective parenting strategies, she started to change her belief that effective parenting is tiresome; instead, she reported feeling more energized. She became more engaged with Michael and responded to his appropriate behaviors with increased warmth. Her behavior management skills improved, and she began to use increasingly effective and consistent discipline techniques. She also began to communicate to Michael that he was loved and wanted. This, in turn, helped to dispel Michael's belief that he was unlovable and unwanted.

As Mrs. S modified her parenting behaviors, Michael's antisocial behaviors diminished. His aggressive and disruptive behaviors decreased, and he ceased threatening his grandmother with weapons. His wandering and lying also decreased, and he became more compliant with Mrs. S's directives. These behavioral changes further motivated increased changes for both Michael and Mrs. S. After having met weekly with the family for 8 months, treatment sessions were reduced in frequency to biweekly and then monthly. At this time, therapy sessions focused on maintaining changes and helping the family to negotiate additional stressors (e.g., helping Mrs. S to make plans for Michael's care should she be incapacitated by her illness).

CONCLUSIONS

Multiple etiologic pathways lead to youth antisocial behavior, making this a complex problem that is difficult to treat. Consequently, different therapies must often be used in combination to produce change; stand-alone therapies that target only one of many risk factors, are limited in effectiveness. Selection of the necessary intervention components should be made on the basis of careful evaluation of the client's strengths and weaknesses; however, assessments should address child cognitive and behavioral factors as well as relevant family and contextual factors (Hanish & Tolan, in press). As demonstrated in our case example, cognitive behavioral treatments that address these additional risk factors significantly improve their utility for changing antisocial behavior.

REFERENCES

Bank, L., Marlowe, H., Reid, J. B., Patterson, G. R., & Weinrott, M R. (1991). A comparative valuation of parent-training interventions for families of chronic delinquents. *Journal of Abnormal Child Psychology, 19*, 15–33.

Barrett, P. M., Rapee, R. M., Dadds, M. R., & Ryan, S. (1996). Family enhancement of cognitive styles in anxious and aggressive children. *Journal of Abnormal Child Psychology, 24*, 187–203.

Boldizar, J. P., Perry, D. G., & Perry, L. C. (1989). Outcome values and aggression. *Child Development, 60*, 571–579.

Caspi, A., & Moffitt, T. E. (1995). The continuity of maladaptive behavior: From description to understanding in the study of antisocial behavior. In D. Cicchetti & D. J. Cohen (Eds.), *Developmental psychopathology: Vol. 2. Risk, disorder, and adaptation* (pp. 472–511). New York: Wiley.

Crick, N. R., & Dodge, K. A. (1996). Social information-processing mechanisms in reactive and proactive aggression. *Child Development, 67*, 993–1002.

Crick, N. R., & Grotpeter, J. K. (1995). Relational aggression, gender, and social-psychological adjustment. *Child Development, 66*, 710–722.

Cummings, E. M., Iannotti, R. J., & Zahn-Waxler, C. (1989). Aggression between peers in early childhood: Individual continuity and developmental change. *Child Development, 60*, 887–895.

Deater-Deckard, K., Dodge, K. A., Bates, J. E., & Pettit, G. S. (1998). Multiple risk factors in the development of externalizing behavior problems: Group and individual differences. *Development and Psychopathology, 10*, 469–493.

Dishion, T. J., & Andrews, D. W. (1995). Preventing escalation in problem behaviors with high-risk young adolescents: Immediate and 1-year outcomes. *Journal of Consulting and Clinical Psychology, 63*, 538–548.

Dishion, T. J., French, D. C., & Patterson, G. R. (1995). The development and ecology of antisocial behavior. In D. Cicchetti & D. J. Cohen (Eds.), *Developmental psychopathology: Vol. 2. Risk, disorder, and adaptation* (pp. 421–471). New York: Wiley.

Dishion, T. J., McCord, J., & Poulin, F. (1999). When interventions harm: Peer groups and problem behavior. *American Psychologist, 54,* 755–764.

Dishion, T. J., Patterson, G. R., & Kavanagh, K. A. (1992). An experimental test of the coercion model: Linking theory, measurement, and intervention. In J. McCord & R. E. Tremblay (Eds.), *Preventing antisocial behavior: Interventions from birth through adolescence* (pp. 253–282). New York: Guilford Press.

Dodge, K. A., & Frame, C. L. (1982). Social cognitive biases and deficits in aggressive boys. *Child Development, 53,* 620–635.

Dodge, K. A., & Newman, J. P. (1981). Biased decision-making processes in aggressive boys. *Journal of Abnormal Psychology, 90,* 375–379.

Dodge, K. A., Pettit, G. S., McClaskey, C. L., & Brown, M. M. (1986). Social competence in children. *Monographs of the Society for Research in Child Development, 51*(2, Serial No. 213).

Eisenberg, N., Fabes, R. A., Guthrie, I. K., Murphy, B. C., Maszk, P., Holmgren, R., & Suh, K. (1996). The relations of regulation and emotionality to problem behavior in elementary school children. *Development and Psychopathology, 8,* 141–162.

Eisenberg, N., Fabes, R. A., Karbon, M., Murphy, B. C., Wosinski, M., Polazzi, L., Carlo, G., & Juhnke, C. (1996). The relations of children's dispositional prosocial behavior to emotionality, regulation, and social functioning. *Child Development, 67,* 974–992.

Erdley, C. A., & Asher, S. R. (1998). Linkages between children's beliefs about the legitimacy of aggression and their behavior. *Social Development, 7,* 321–339.

Estrada, A. U., & Pinsof, W. M. (1995). The effectiveness of family therapies for selected behavioral disorders of childhood. *Journal of Marital and Family Therapy, 21,* 403–440.

Forgatch, M. S., & DeGarmo, D. S. (1999). Two faces of Janus: Cohesion and conflict. In M. Cox & J. Brooks-Gunn (Eds.), *Conflict and cohesion in families: Causes and consequences* (pp. 167–184). Mahwah, NJ: Erlbaum.

Gorman-Smith, D., & Tolan, P. H. (1998). The role of exposure to community violence and developmental problems among inner-city youth. *Development and Psychopathology, 10,* 101–116.

Gorman-Smith, D., Tolan, P. H., Loeber, R., & Henry, D. (1998). The relation of family problems to patterns of delinquent involvement among urban youth. *Journal of Abnormal Child Psychology, 26,* 319–333.

Gorman-Smith, D., Tolan, P. H., Zelli, A., & Huesmann, L. R. (1996). The relation of family functioning to violence among inner-city minority youths. *Journal of Family Psychology, 10,* 115–129.

Graham, S., & Hudley, C. (1994). Attributions of aggressive and nonaggressive African-American male early adolescents: A study of construct accessibility. *Developmental Psychology, 30*, 365–373.

Guerra, N. G., Eron, L. D., Huesmann, L. R., Tolan, P. H., & Van Acker, R. (1997). A cognitive-ecological approach to the prevention and mitigation of violence and aggression in inner-city youth. In D. P. Fry & K. Bjorkqvist (Eds.), *Cultural variation in conflict resolution: Alternatives to violence* (pp. 199–213). Mahwah, NJ: Erlbaum.

Guerra, N. G., Huesmann, L. R., & Hanish, L. D. (1995). The role of normative beliefs in children's social behavior. In M. Clark (Series Ed.) & N. Eisenberg (Vol. Ed.), *Review of personality and social psychology: Vol. 15. Social development* (pp. 140–158). Thousand Oaks, CA: Sage Publications.

Guerra, N. G., & Slaby, R. G. (1990). Cognitive mediators of aggression in adolescent offenders: 2. Intervention. *Developmental Psychology, 26*, 269–277.

Hanish, L. D., & Guerra, N. G. (2000). *A longitudinal analysis of patterns of adjustment following peer victimization.* Manuscript submitted for publication.

Hanish, L. D., & Tolan, P. H. (in press). Patterns of change in family based aggression prevention. *Journal of Marital and Family Therapy.*

Hanish, L. D., Tolan, P. H., & Guerra, N. G. (1996). Treatment of oppositional defiant disorder. In M. A. Reinecke, F. M. Dattilio, & A. Freeman (Eds.), *Cognitive therapy with children and adolescents* (pp. 62–78). New York: Guilford Press.

Hawkins, J. D., Herrenkohl, T., Farrington, D. Pl., Brewer, D., Catalano, R. F., & Harachi, T. W. (1998). A review of predictors of youth violence. In R. Loeber & D. P. Farrington (Eds.), *Serious and violent juvenile offenders: Risk factors and successful interventions* (pp. 106–146). Thousand Oaks, CA: Sage Publications.

Henggeler, S. W., Melton, G. B., & Smith, L. A. (1992). Family preservation using multisystemic therapy: An effective alternative to incarcerating serious juvenile offenders. *Journal of Consulting and Clinical Psychology, 60*, 953–961.

Henry, D., Guerra, N. G., Huesmann, R., Tolan, P. H., Van Acker, R., & Eron, L. (2000). Normative influences on aggression in urban elementary school classrooms. *American Journal of Community Psychology, 28*, 59–81.

Huesmann, L. R., & Guerra, N. G. (1997). Children's normative beliefs about aggression and aggressive behavior. *Journal of Personality and Social Psychology, 72*, 408–419.

Hudley, C., & Graham, S. (1993). An attributional intervention to reduce peer-directed aggression among African-American boys. *Child Development, 64*, 124–138.

Huizinga, D., & Jakob-Chien, C. (1998). The contemporaneous co-occurrence of serious and violent juvenile offending and other problem behaviors. In R. Loeber & D. P. Farrington (Eds.), *Serious and violent juvenile offenders: Risk factors and successful interventions* (pp. 47–67). Thousand Oaks, CA: Sage Publications.

Kazdin, A. E. (1987). Treatment of antisocial behavior in children: Current status and future directions. *Psychological Bulletin, 102,* 187–203.

Kazdin, A. E., Bass, D., Siegel, T., & Thomas, C. (1989). Cognitive-behavioral therapy and relationship therapy in the treatment of children referred for antisocial behavior. *Journal of Consulting and Clinical Psychology, 57,* 522–535.

Kazdin, A. E., & Crowley, M. (1997). Moderators of treatment outcome in cognitively based treatment of antisocial children. *Cognitive Therapy and Research, 21,* 185–207.

Kazdin, A. E., Siegel, T. C., & Bass, D. (1992). Cognitive problem-solving skills training and parent management training in the treatment of antisocial behavior in children. *Journal of Consulting and Clinical Psychology, 60,* 733–747.

Kazdin, A. E., & Wassell, G. (1998). Treatment completion and therapeutic change among children referred for outpatient therapy. *Professional Psychology: Research and Practice, 29,* 332–340.

Keenan, K., Loeber, R., & Green, S. (1999). Conduct disorder in girls: A review of the literature. *Child and Family Psychology Review, 2,* 3–19.

Keenan, K., & Shaw, D. (1994). The development of aggression in toddlers: A study of low income families. *Journal of Abnormal Child Psychology, 22,* 53–78.

Keenan, K., & Shaw, D. (1997). Developmental and social influences in young girls' early problem behavior. *Psychological Bulletin, 121,* 95–113.

Kendall, P. C., Ronan, K. R., & Epps, J. (1991). Aggression in children/adolescents: Cognitive-behavioral treatment perspectives. In D. J. Pepler & K. H. Rubin (Eds.), *The development and treatment of childhood aggression* (pp. 341–360). Hillsdale, NJ: Erlbaum.

Lahey, B. B., Loeber, R., Quay, H. C., Frick, P. J., & Grimm, J. (1992). Oppositional defiant and conduct disorders: Issues to be resolved for DSM-IV. *Journal of the American Academy of Child and Adolescent Psychiatry, 31,* 539–546.

Lochman, J. E., & Lenhart, L. (1995). Cognitive behavioral therapy of aggressive children: Effects of schemas. In H. P. J. G. van Bilsen, P. C. Kendall, & J. H. Slavenburg (Eds.), *Behavioral approaches for children and adolescents: Challenges for the next century* (pp. 145–166). New York: Plenum Press.

Loeber, R., & Dishion, T. (1983). Early predictors of male delinquency: A review. *Psychological Bulletin, 94,* 68–99.

McFall, R. M. (1982). A review and reformulation of the concept of social skills. *Behavioral Assessment, 4,* 1–33.

Metropolitan Area Child Study (in press). *A cognitive-ecological approach to* preventive aggression in urban and inner-city settings: Preliminary outcomes. *Journal of Consulting and Clinical Psychology.*

McMahon, R. J., Slough, N. M., & Conduct Problems Research Group (1996). Family-based intervention in the Fast Track Program. In R. DeV. Peters & R. J. McMahon (Eds.), *Preventing childhood disorders, substance abuse, and delinquency* (pp. 90–109). Thousand Oaks, CA: Sage Publications.

Miller, G. E., & Prinz, R. J. (1990). Enhancement of social learning family interventions for childhood conduct disorder. *Psychological Bulletin, 108*, 291–307.

Mills, R. S. L., & Rubin, K. H. (1990). Parental beliefs about problematic social behaviors in early childhood. *Child Development, 61*, 138–151.

Nagin, D., & Tremblay, R. E. (1999). Trajectories of boys' physical aggression, opposition, and hyperactivity on the path to physically violent and nonviolent juvenile delinquency. *Child Development, 70*, 1181–1196.

Patterson, G. R. (1982). *Coercive family process.* Eugene, OR: Castalia.

Pepler, D. J., King, G., & Byrd, W. (1991). A social-cognitively based social skills training program for aggressive children. In D. J. Pepler & K. H. Rubin (Eds.), *The development and treatment of childhood aggression* (pp. 361–379). Hillsdale, NJ: Erlbaum.

Perry, D. G., Perry, L. C., & Rasmussen, P. (1986). Cognitive social learning mediators of aggression. *Child Development, 57*, 700–711.

Reid, J. B. (1993). Prevention of conduct disorder before and after school entry: Relating interventions to developmental findings. *Development and Psychopathology, 5*, 243–262.

Reid, J. B., & Eddy, J. M. (1997). The prevention of antisocial behavior: Some considerations in the search for effective interventions. In D. M. Stoff, J. Breiling, & J. D. Maser (Eds.), *Handbook of antisocial behavior* (pp. 343–356). New York: Wiley.

Rende, R. D. (1993). Longitudinal relations between temperament traits and behavioral syndromes in middle childhood. *Journal of the American Academy of Child and Adolescent Psychiatry, 32*, 287–290.

Rubin, K. H., Bream, L. A., & Rose-Krasnor, L. (1991). Social problem solving and aggression in childhood. In D. J. Pepler, & K. H. Rubin (Eds.), *The development and treatment of childhood aggression* (pp. 219–248). Hillsdale, NJ: Erlbaum.

Rubin, K. H., & Krasnor, L. R. (1986). Social-cognitive and social behavioral perspectives on problem solving. *Minnesota Symposium on Child Psychology, 18*, 1–68.

Sampson, R. J., & Laub, J. H. (1994). Urban poverty and the family context of delinquence: A new look at structure and process in a classic study. *Child Development, 65*, 523–540.

Seidman, E., Yoshikawa, H., Roberts, A., Chesir-Teran, D., Allen, L., Friedman, J. L., & Aber, J. L. (1998). Structural and experiential neighborhood contexts, developmental stage, and antisocial behavior among urban adolescents in poverty. *Development and Psychopathology, 10,* 259–281.

Slaby, R. G., & Guerra, N. G. (1988). Cognitive mediators of aggression in adolescent offenders: 1. Assessment. *Developmental Psychology, 24,* 580–588.

Tolan, P. H., & Gorman-Smith, D. (1997). Families and the development of urban children. In H. J. Wahlberg, O. Reyes, & R. P. Weissberg (Eds.), *Urban children and youth: Interdisciplinary perspective on policies and programs* (pp. 67–91). Thousand Oaks, CA: Sage Publications.

Tolan, P. H., Hanish, L. D., McKay, M. M., & Dickey, M. H. (2000). *Measuring process in child and family interventions: An example in prevention of aggression.* Manuscript submitted for publication.

Tolan, P. H., & McKay, M. M. (1996). Preventing serious antisocial behavior in inner-city children: An empirically based family prevention program. *Family Relations, 45,* 148–155.

Wasserman, G. A., & Miller, L. S. (1998). The prevention of serious and violent juvenile offending. In R. Loeber & D. P. Farrington (Eds.), *Serious and violent juvenile offenders: Risk factors and successful interventions* (pp. 197–247). Thousand Oaks, CA: Sage Publications.

Webster-Stratton, C., Kolpacoff, M., & Hollinsworth, T. (1988). Self-administered videotape therapy for families with conduct-problem children: Comparison with two cost-effective treatments and a control group. *Journal of Consulting and Clinical Psychology, 56,* 558–566.

10

Eating Disorders: Enhancing Effectiveness Through the Integration of Cultural Factors

Nona L. Wilson and Anne E. Blackhurst

Feminist scholars have criticized the cognitive model of eating disorders for not adequately incorporating cultural issues into conceptualization and treatment of the disorders. The primary point of contention is that the cognitive model emphasizes the individual and the role of idiosyncratic distortions within individual cognitive processes, while largely ignoring broader cultural factors and thus appearing to pathologize women (Bordo, 1993; MacSween, 1993). In contrast, feminist researchers have amassed considerable evidence to support the notion that eating disorders are culturally ensconced problems, arising out of a particular constellation of social factors (Bordo, 1993; Chernin, 1994; Wooley, 1994). And while it is true that cognitive therapy has not made full use of feminist scholarship, a feminist perspective is not incompatible with the cognitive model. The goal then of this chapter is to help bridge, both theoretically and pragmatically, what seems a needless gap between feminist and cognitive approaches. In this chapter, we will argue that clinicians can achieve greater integration of cultural factors into the treatment of bulimia and anorexia while remaining true to the cognitive-behavioral framework.

Drawing from feminist scholarship, we will (a) propose a model for linking individual cognitions to cultural values throughout treatment as a vehicle for cognitive restructuring; (b) demonstrate how characteristic cognitive distortions can be understood as internalized cultural directives; (c) suggest guidelines for assigning, structuring, and processing media-based interventions; and (d) recommend methods for assisting clients in using enhanced cultural criticism skills for relapse prevention. Before proceeding to these issues, however, it is useful to review both cognitive and feminist models of eating disorders.

THE COGNITIVE MODEL

The cognitive model is a mediational model in which emotion and behavior are influenced by cognition. That is, it is the perception of events, not the events themselves, that trigger emotional reactions and help determine behavioral responses. Moreover, the model hypothesizes that distortion—or, as less commonly described, bias—in thinking undergirds all psychological difficulties (Beck, 1995). Cognitive therapy seeks to alleviate disturbance in mood and behavior by modifying cognition. Further, cognitive theory has evolved to the point of identifying the kinds of cognitive distortion or bias that tend to characterize particular problems, and thus offers highly specialized treatment for specific disorders.

Specialized cognitive-behavioral therapy (CBT) for bulimia and anorexia is available in the form of manualized protocols (Fairburn, Marcus, & Wilson, 1993; Garner, Vitousek, & Pike, 1997). The manuals, their rationale, and the clinical and empirical support for them are readily available elsewhere (Garner & Garfinkel, 1997), and the goal here is not to present in detail that material. Rather, our goal is to highlight the ways in which the treatment manuals, specifically—and the cognitive model on which they are based, more broadly—may better integrate a feminist perspective into treatment.

Virtually all approaches to understanding anorexia and bulimia recognize an extreme preoccupation with shape and weight as the core of these disturbances. Fairburn's (Wilson, Fairburn, & Agras, 1997) model is no exception. He identifies concerns about shape and weight as the "central feature" of eating disorders, noting that "most other features can be understood as secondary to them" (Fairburn, 1997, p. 211). But while dieting is understood as secondary to the central concern about shape and weight, the maintenance of eating disorders hinges on extreme and rigid dieting rules and practices. Intense and inflexible dieting goals set in motion a predictable sequence of inevitable dietary transgressions, temporary disinhibition, self-recrimination, and a reactivation of intense and inflexible dieting rules.

Fairburn's (Wilson et al., 1997) treatment manual for bulimia, then, aims not only to regulate eating patterns, but also—and ultimately, more importantly—to modify the central problematic cognitions. The treatment consists of three stages. In the first stage, the client is educated about the cognitive model of the development and maintenance of bulimia, and behavioral techniques are introduced to help normalize eating. In the second stage, such efforts are continued, but the focus shifts to tackling all forms of dieting and to challenging the "thoughts, beliefs, and values" that maintain the problem (Wilson et al., 1997, p. 220). The third and final stage is devoted to relapse prevention.

This approach is not only theoretically sound, but it has also achieved impressive empirical support (Wilson et al., 1997). There can be little doubt that it is indeed "the treatment of choice" for bulimia (Garner et al., 1997). From a feminist perspective, however, it is remarkable that despite the considerable emphasis that Fairburn (2000) places on changing the "value system" that eating-disordered clients have adopted, he never contextualizes their beliefs within the broader culture. He repeatedly comes to the very edge of feminist notions, particularly when advocating that clinicians teach clients to "look at, not through" the value system that perpetuates their disorder, but he consistently fails to take the next step. This is regrettable because decades of feminist cultural criticism offer a keen and piercing vision with which to "look at, not through" value systems.

The treatment manual developed by Garner and colleagues (1997) for anorexia parallels, both conceptually and pragmatically, Fairburn's (Wilson et al., 1997) model for treating bulimia. It is a three-stage treatment, with the first stage geared toward building trust and setting treatment parameters. Stage 2 shifts the focus to cognitive work designed to change beliefs related to food and to broaden the scope of the therapy to address issues such as self-esteem, self-control, and perfectionism. The third and final stage attends to relapse prevention. This manual, however, goes much further in directly addressing cultural issues than does Fairburn's (Wilson et al., 1997) manual.

Clinicians are instructed to begin "challenging cultural values regarding weight and shape" in the very first stage. Furthermore, Garner and colleagues (1997) state that a "central component of cognitive therapy is helping each patient identify and synthesize the personal implications of adopting the prevailing cultural standards related to weight and shape" (p. 120). Thus, their treatment manual identifies cultural values as instrumental in the development and maintenance of anorexia, rather than limiting discussion of the pathogenic process to the client's values. Further, they explicitly direct clinicians to help clients link their individual experiences to the larger culture. Moreover, they acknowledge that "throughout the struggle to recover from their eating disorder, patients are bombarded by media messages glorifying the virtues of dieting and thinness" (p. 120). In doing so, they specify cultural and media messages as clinically relevant issues that should be brought into the therapy process.

Garner and associates suggest "prescribing homework assignments to underscore the cultural pressures on women to diet" (p. 120). They indicate that clients should be encouraged to "gather examples from magazine advertisements promoting unrealistic shapes or equating female worth with physical attractiveness in general and thinness in particular" (p. 120). The intended benefits of such activities are to help clients develop a "healthy sense of indignation" about cultural standards of beauty and to assist clients in reframing the "etiology of the disorder, at least in part, in cultural terms" (p. 120).

Clearly, Garner and associates' treatment manual for anorexia makes a strong case for the importance of addressing cultural issues. Perhaps even more noteworthy, however, is the authors' recognition of how difficult actually doing so is. They warn that treating anorexia involves "swimming against" a "cultural stream" that skews both men's and women's views of women's bodies. And they also recognize that clinicians are not immune to cultural influences. Thus, they wisely caution male clinicians about the importance of being sensitive to prevailing cultural pressures on women, and advise female clinicians to sufficiently free themselves of such pressures so as to avoid unintentionally colluding with clients. Finally, they instruct clinicians to be ever vigilant about ensuring that a clear distinction between criticism of the culture and criticism of the client is maintained.

In their treatment manual for anorexia, Garner and colleagues have outlined what amounts to an ambitious agenda for integrating feminist concepts into CBT. From a feminist conceptual framework, their work is commendable. In order to successfully achieve the treatment goals, clinicians must be sufficiently knowledgeable about the cultural dynamics surrounding eating disorders—and how those issues are both reflected in and shaped by media messages—in order to understand the impact these factors have on individual clients. In addition, clinicians need to structure, assign, and process interventions based on advertising in order to help clients understand the development of their disorder in cultural terms. Along the way, clinicians must facilitate a collaborative critique of cultural values which, for the client, have become cherished, albeit destructive, coping strategies. These are feminist-friendly goals indeed. However, having articulated such goals and having offered cautions about the difficulties of achieving them, the authors provide no further guidance. Attempts to implement Garner and associates' recommendations for critically assessing cultural values without explicit instruction are likely to be a challenge even for seasoned clinicians and may represent a kind of therapeutic gauntlet for novices. Thus, important steps toward integrating cognitive and feminist models may not be taken—or may be misdirected—because needed guidance is missing.

Both Fairburn's (1997) manual for bulimia and Garner and colleagues' (1997) manual for anorexia do not fully realize opportunities to integrate feminist constructs into cognitive therapy. But the manuals, especially Garner et al.'s, open the door to incorporating feminist perspectives. The remainder of this chapter offers a model for more directly uniting CBT and feminist paradigms and provides specific guidelines for doing so. The next step, then, is to discuss key components of a feminist view of eating disorders and their treatment.

FEMINIST PERSPECTIVES ON EATING DISORDERS

Like cognitive behavioral theorists, feminist theorists recognize dieting as a risk factor in the development of eating disorders and attribute widespread dieting to the cultural idealization of thinness. In contrast to most other theoretical approaches, however, feminist scholars concern themselves with the reasons why thinness is so overvalued in women (Wooley, 1995). In short, feminist theorists hold that cultural constructions of gender are central to the understanding and treatment of eating disorders (MacSween, 1993), and they argue that women who develop anorexia or bulimia should not be singled out as pathological (Brown & Jasper, 1993a). Instead, eating disorders are viewed as evidence of pathology in the larger culture—a culture that has historically devalued women, their bodies, their appetites, and their roles in society.

Fear, disgust, and contempt for women and the female body are deeply rooted in Western culture (Wooley, 1994). Unlike men, who have historically been considered rational and logical, women have been deemed impulsive, irrational, and prey to animal urges. Women's bodies, while being a source of attraction and fascination for men, have also been greatly feared, and have been considered uncontrollable, impure, and unclean (Mitchell, 1994). At the same time, women have been defined by their bodies, and their social roles have been identified with and expressed through their bodies: in bearing children, in satisfying men's sexual needs, and in caring for men's and children's emotional and physical needs (Brown & Jasper, 1993b). Although these domestic roles have been idealized in Western culture, they have also been devalued and trivialized.

Furthermore, characterizations of women as weak, incompetent, irrational, and destined by their anatomy for lives of domesticity have served to restrict women's access to more public, highly valued roles (Chernin, 1994). Accordingly, one reason thinness is valued so strongly by women in today's culture is because it offers the possibility of transcending cultural restrictions by creating a body that is less overtly female (Silverstein & Perlick, 1995). Viewed from this perspective, the relentless pursuit of thinness is anything but a shallow, superficial quest to meet the current whims of fashion. It is instead an attempt to create a body deemed worthy of access to opportunities for achievement, accomplishment, and power (Bordo, 1993; Brown & Jasper, 1993b; Chernin, 1994).

In the absence of such opportunities, one of the few sources of power for women in Western culture historically has been the "power" of physical attractiveness (Bloom, 1994; Gutwill, 1994). For although women's natural bodies have been viewed with disgust and contempt, idealized versions of perfect female beauty have held the promise of acceptance, desirability, and power over men. Even today, beauty is considered a central aspect of femininity (Streigel-Moore, 1993). During the second half of the 20th century, idealized images of feminine beauty have been increasingly linked with thinness, while fat has been increasingly linked with a lengthy—and contradictory—list of those "feminine" characteristics that have historically been most feared and denigrated: the all-powerful and controlling mother, female sexuality, lack of willpower, and women's struggles for increased participation in the public sphere (Bordo, 1993; Iggers, 1996; Pipher, 1995; Wolf, 1994; Wooley, 1994). As a result, the thin body so idealized by the fashion and beauty industry is appealing to women on many levels. It is valued not only because it allows women to achieve some measure of power and control in a culture that has historically denied women both, but also because thinness symbolizes the shedding of undesirable, culturally denigrated female characteristics along with their outward representation (Bordo, 1993; Chernin, 1994).

Evidence that most women have internalized the cultural fear and loathing of the natural female body is incontrovertible. One survey of women of all ages found that only 4% felt comfortable about their weight, while the other 96% felt overweight (Pipher, 1995). In another study, 75% of 33,000 women surveyed considered themselves "too fat" despite the fact that only a quarter were considered overweight by the insurance industry's standardized weight charts and 30% were actually underweight (Bordo, 1993). By sixth grade, 79% of girls want to be thinner than they are, and the major worry of 8- to 13-year-old girls is their weight (Pipher, 1995). By college, up to 79% of women experience bulimic episodes (Brown, 1993). Such statistics have led feminist scholars to view body dissatisfaction and weight preoccupation as the norm among girls and women, and anorexia and bulimia as extremes on an almost universal continuum (Brown, 1993; Brown & Jasper 1993a; Hesse-Biber, 1996; Scarano & Kalodner-Martin, 1994).

Closely tied to cultural conceptions of the natural and the idealized female body are equally long-standing, culturally ingrained fears of women's appetites. In fact, a central requirement of femininity has been that women deny their own appetites for physical, intellectual, and emotional nourishment in order to satisfy the needs and desires of others (Bordo, 1993; Brown & Jasper, 1993b; Fursland, 1994). As a result, girls and women learn that if they are to be considered attractive they must contain their appetites. They must not appear too emotionally needy, too powerful, too sexual, too successful, or in any other way "too hungry" (Gutwill, 1994). Women's sexual appetites and their legitimate appetites for power, achievement, and success have been viewed as particularly threatening in our historically male-dominated society—especially during times of rapidly changing gender roles, such as those experienced in America during the past 40 years (Bordo, 1993).

Over the past 4 decades, as women have increasingly pursued their appetites for power and accomplishment in the public sphere, women's containment of their appetites for food has been increasingly associated with femininity, attractiveness and social desirability (Basow & Kobrynowicz, 1990; Bock & Kanarek, 1995). Women who eat smaller meals are perceived as more physically attractive and more socially appealing than women who eat large meals (Basow & Kobrynowicz, 1990), and perceptions of women's femininity and attractiveness increase as their meal size decreases (Bock & Kanarek, 1995). In recent years, low-fat and fat-free foods have joined small-portion sizes and low-calorie foods as symbols of femininity, with women who eat low-fat foods being judged as more attractive, intelligent, and conscientious than women who eat high-fat alternatives (Mooney, DeTore, & Malloy, 1994). Not surprisingly, women internalize cultural expectations about their appetites and typically eat less in situations in which it is important to project an air of femininity and desirability (Pliner & Chaiken, 1990). Maintaining a thin body has thus become valued as an external representation of women's success in achieving control over their unacceptable appetites (Bordo, 1993).

If thinness for women is valued both because it allows women to achieve qualities that have historically been considered masculine (e.g., power, control, and mastery over one's body) *and* because it is associated with the attainment of feminine virtues (e.g., self-restraint, physical attractiveness, and beauty), then it is not surprising that thinness is also valued because it permits women to simultaneously fulfill competing gender role expectations. In fact, according to the feminist model, women's bodies are arenas for the expression of both resistance and conformity to traditional conceptions of femininity (Brown & Jasper, 1993a), and thin bodies are symbolic of the conflicting and competing cultural messages about how women should look and behave (Bloom & Kogel, 1994). While cultural expectations of women's proper roles in society have always been contradictory, they have become particularly conflicting during the last half-century when women have been increasingly expected to succeed in traditionally masculine pursuits while still maintaining feminine traits (Bordo, 1993; Brown & Jasper, 1993b; Streigel-Moore, 1993; Wolf, 1994).

Research supports the feminist contention that weight preoccupation and eating disturbances are associated with gender role conflict. Both the desire to fulfill traditional conceptions of femininity and an internalized devaluation of traditionally feminine traits have been linked to eating disorders. Martz, Handley, and Eisler (1995), for example, found that women with eating disorders reported significantly more stress associated with adherence to rigid feminine gender roles than either a clinical sample of women without eating disorders or a control group of college women without clinical diagnoses. In contrast, Paxton and Sculthorpe (1991) found positive associations between measures of disordered eating and the extent to which a sample of women (n = 149) believed they possessed negative feminine characteristics such as dependency, weakness, anxiety, insecurity, and timidity. At the same time, there is a growing body of research to suggest that women who identify more strongly with masculine characteristics (Paxton & Sculthorpe, 1991) and nontraditional female roles (Johnson & Petrie, 1995; Silverstein, Carpman, Perlick, & Perdue, 1990) are more likely to experience body and eating disturbances. Women who simultaneously desire to be both more masculine and more feminine may be even more susceptible to eating problems (Johnson & Petrie, 1995) and body dissatisfaction (Johnson & Petrie, 1996) than women who desire solely to be more masculine or to be more feminine.

Because feminist scholars view the idealization of thinness and the resulting weight preoccupation and eating disturbances as inexorably linked with limiting and damaging cultural expectations for women, they reject the popular notion that eating disorders are predominantly a product of deleterious media influence (Bordo, 1993; Brown & Jasper, 1993a). However, feminist scholars do acknowledge the media's powerful role in transmitting—and reinforcing—the cultural values, attitudes, and beliefs discussed above (Barthel, 1988; Kilbourne, 1994; McCracken, 1993). In fact, a substantial body of research exists to suggest that there is a direct relationship between media exposure and weight preoccupation, body dissatisfaction, and disordered eating (Stice, Schupak-Neuberg, Shaw, & Stein, 1994).

Women exposed to idealized images of female beauty and thinness subsequently reported that they preferred to weigh less, were less satisfied with their bodies, and were more frustrated about their weight (Turner, Hamilton, Jacobs, Angood, & Dwyer, 1997). The same women were also more preoccupied with the desire to be thin and more afraid of getting fat than were their peers who were randomly assigned to view neutral images. Exposure to idealized images of female beauty also resulted in reduced satisfaction with subjects' own appearance and higher comparison standards for physical attractiveness (Richins, 1991). While some researchers have found similar results regardless of subjects' level of body dissatisfaction or eating disorder symptomatology (Irving, 1990), others have found that women with high levels of body image disturbance (Turner et al., 1997) or eating disorders (Murray, Touyz, & Beumont, 1996) may be especially sensitive to media messages. Thus, although few women escape the harmful effects of media images (Gutwill, 1994), women with eating disorders may be particularly affected. This is an additional reason why exploring media messages and their impact can be so important to recovery and relapse prevention. Given the complex relationship between cultural values and eating disorder symptomatology, however, it is important to have a sound conceptual framework from which to operate before attempting to explore this relationship with clients. A framework for synthesizing CBT and feminist principles is described below.

A UNIFIED CONCEPTUAL FRAMEWORK

The cognitive model proposes understanding individual cognition as a layered phenomenon, consisting of (a) automatic thoughts; (b) intermediate beliefs, rules and assumptions; and (c) core beliefs. The layers differ in nature but each has a reciprocal relation with the others; that is, each layer both supports and is maintained by the other two. This finely nuanced model accounts for the simultaneously mercurial yet stable quality of individual cognitions, and it appreciates the developmental nature of beliefs over the individual's life span. Further, we believe that the model provides an excellent template for understanding and working with long-standing, widespread cultural beliefs and values within CBT, and, more specifically, for examining how those cultural values are contained within contemporary advertisements.

Table 10.1 provides a model for translating the cognitive framework for conceptualizing individual cognition into a cultural conceptualization. Just as individual cognition is layered, so too are culturally endorsed values and beliefs. We maintain that cultural values exist in a stratified, symbiotic system consisting of overt messages, contemporary cultural directives, and core cultural beliefs. To more fully delineate this, it is useful to review a few of the main characteristics of each layer of individual cognition and then describe the parallel traits of each layer of cultural values. Moreover, using a typical food advertisement from a popular women's magazine, we will illustrate how cultural values are present (and powerful) in advertising in a similarly layered fashion.

Automatic Thoughts and Overt Messages

Beck (1995) describes automatic thoughts as a stream of seemingly "spontaneous" thoughts that exists just slightly outside of conscious awareness.

TABLE 10.1 Proposed Framework for Advertising Analysis

Individual Conceptualization	*Cultural Conceptualization*
Automatic thoughts	Overt messages
|	|
|	|
Intermediate rules, assumptions, beliefs	Contemporary cultural directives
|	|
|	|
Core beliefs	Core cultural beliefs

Automatic thoughts are fleeting and often are not completely articulated, occurring rather in a kind of verbal and/or image-based shorthand. Although many people do not fully attend to their automatic thoughts, such thoughts are both powerful and predictable. These rapid, transient thoughts occur almost continuously alongside more manifest cognition and can strongly influence mood and behavior, not only because they are virtually ever present, but also because they are perceived as unpremeditated and therefore "true." Automatic thoughts, however, arise from (and then reinforce) the more stable underlying assumptions, rules, and core beliefs a person holds. They are, therefore, susceptible to the distortions that such assumptions and rules may foster.

Overt cultural messages about the value of thinness for women are characterized by many of the same qualities as automatic thoughts. They are, with just a little effort, easily discernible, and are also often fleeting and not fully or consciously attended to. But despite their ephemeral nature, the impact of these messages should not be overlooked. Overt cultural messages, just like automatic thoughts, occur alongside situations, events, and even media messages, for which the real point is something else. Thus, such messages may not be consciously noticed, but their message may be apprehended nonetheless. Moreover, such messages may actually accrue influence because they are not closely attended to and, therefore, go largely unchallenged.

Overt cultural messages about the importance of thinness (and the taboo of weight and appetite) are ubiquitous, both in words and/or images. Such messages are echoed in the comments of friends and family, dispersed in the text of weight loss commercials and advertisements, and projected through visual media. Kilbourne (1994) indicates that Americans, on average, are exposed to approximately 1,500 ads per day, which perhaps qualifies their messages as an almost omnipresent part of modern life. The vast majority of such ads, in some way, equates thinness with satisfaction.

A recent Kellogg's ad for Special K ("Special K Cereal ad," 1997) demonstrates in several ways the nature of overt cultural messages about weight and shape, and also how such messages are disseminated by the media. Using only the image of a spaghetti-strapped, black evening dress, Kellogg's declares that *"Sometimes what you wear to dinner depends on what you have for breakfast."* The text is a fully articulated message, but the image of the dress serves as a kind of visual shorthand, reinforcing the relationship between glamour and thinness, sexiness and weight loss, and desirability and appearance. Just as with automatic thoughts, such shorthand is effective only because it draws upon well-established, well-understood beliefs, rules, and assumptions, or what, in a broader context, we view as contemporary cultural directives about women's bodies.

Sometimes what you wear to dinner may depend on what you eat for breakfast.

Great Taste Never Looked So Good.

Great toasted taste. 110 calories. And it's fat free. Maybe that's just what your diet and exercise plan needs.

Intermediate Beliefs, Rules and Assumptions and Contemporary Cultural Directives

Intermediate beliefs, according to Beck's cognitive model, represent a level of cognition that is more stable and enduring than automatic thoughts, but that is more easily accessed and more malleable than core beliefs (Beck, 1995). Intermediate beliefs are often unarticulated attitudes, rules, and assumptions that people develop as a result of early life experiences. According to this conceptual model, intermediate beliefs are an adaptive response to the environment, but vary in accuracy and functionality. Of particular import to cognitive therapists, intermediate beliefs not only can be examined but also can be modified. Thus, beliefs that are not wholly true or that are not useful may be adjusted or replaced with alternative beliefs that are more valid and more functional. The more impaired the client— that is, the more distorted, active, and pervasive the belief system—the more difficult it typically is to alter the belief system.

Contemporary cultural directives function in much the same manner as intermediate beliefs, providing a link between overt cultural messages and the deepest cultural beliefs. Contemporary cultural directives to women about weight and shape can be thought of as the expectations, rules, and assumptions of a given era about the appropriate body shape, level of concern about body, and degree of effort to reshape the body women should possess, as well as the prevailing myths about what rewards or punishments await women because of their bodies. Thus, cultural directives can vary from generation to generation. The dominant cultural directives of the 1920s, for example, were geared toward achieving a slim, noncurvaceous body, whereas the cultural injunctions of the 1950s were geared toward highly curvaceous, "hour-glass" figures. But regardless of relatively superficial fluctuations across decades, cultural directives remain—as we shall discuss in the next section—essentially consonant with the underlying core cultural beliefs that give rise to them.

As with individual intermediate beliefs, it is often easier to see distortions in and test contemporary cultural directives when they are in the form of "If . . . then" assumptions, rather than when they are in "rule" form. The rules, for example, that underlie the Special K ad might be particularly difficult for clients with eating disorders to challenge: "Women should eat low-fat foods," or "Only thin women should wear revealing clothes," or "Women should work on their appearance." If approached in this form, "rules" may frustrate both the clinician and client in their attempts to leverage change by contextualizing individual beliefs within the broader culture. When transformed into conditional statements or "If . . . then" assumptions, however, cultural directives are a little more yielding to analysis. Clients may be better able to compare assumptions with the reality of their experiences.

For example, assumptions such as, *"If women work on their appearance, they will be happy,"* or *"If women make themselves pleasing to look at, their social lives will be satisfying,"* are more readily challenged because clients can often find exceptions to them. This is not, however, to suggest that doing so is an easy or quick process.

Cognitive therapy literature attests to the fact that changing individual beliefs (especially beliefs that are pervasive and frequently activated) can be a difficult and slow process. Clinicians, then, should expect that helping clients to recognize the distortion in cultural directives about weight and shape—directives that are widespread and often active—will likewise be a protracted endeavor. This is, in part, because of their link to deeply ingrained and recalcitrant core cultural beliefs and values about women's bodies and their relevance to personal worth.

Core Beliefs and Core Cultural Beliefs

Core beliefs, according to Beck (1995), are the most central ideas one holds about self. These beliefs develop early in life and help to shape subsequent intermediate beliefs and automatic thoughts. Beck suggests that negative core beliefs are typically "global, overgeneralized, and absolute" (Beck, 1995, p. 167). Furthermore, when the core belief is activated, the person is able to process information that supports it, but either distorts or fails to recognize disconfirming information. Negative core beliefs can be organized into two categories: those pertaining to unlovability and those related to incompetence (Beck, 1995).

We propose that core cultural beliefs can be understood in much the same way. Core cultural beliefs about women's bodies can be seen as belonging to the most long-standing and central beliefs about women themselves. Such beliefs can be traced back to Descartes's philosophy that proposed a sharp divide between mind and body, with the mind, reason, intellectual pursuits, and public life associated with maleness. The body, bodily functions, emotion, and private or domestic life are considered as belonging to the female domain (Gilday, 1990). As with core individual beliefs, these core cultural beliefs are clearly "global, overgeneralized, and absolute."

According to Descartes's model, the male and female domains are mutually exclusive and antagonistic, with the male sphere being the valued sphere. Thus, not only are women prohibited access to the culturally valued domain of intellectual pursuits, but the sphere to which they are consigned and in which they are not only permitted but pressured to achieve is debased. The resulting double bind is that mastery of the body and pursuit of beauty ideals become at once women's obligation and cause for their denigration. Even as the culture impedes nonbody-based achievement for women, and even as women's social success depends largely upon beauty, women's serious pursuit of body mastery is trivialized. It is not surprising, then, that many women experience body conflicts and that cultural messages to women about their bodies are often contradictory.

As with core individual beliefs, core cultural beliefs can function as a filter that allows the culture to process information that coincides with these beliefs and that largely screens out contradictory information. Selectively sifting out information considerably slows the change process and this is evident in the tenacity of sex-role stereotypes that continue to persist despite educational, occupational, and sexual advances achieved by women.

The role of early and deeply entrenched cultural beliefs is well documented and discussed in an early section of this chapter. As reviewed there, cultural beliefs help to account for why extreme thinness and dieting for women are so strongly endorsed and how thinness and dieting have come to represent higher-order goals of mastery, achievement, and competence for not only the eating-disordered client but also for the general public. These higher-order goals are, of course, linked to core issues of lovability and competence—about which distortions are discernible in popular advertising.

Much like the process in therapy of peeling back layers through a series of questions designed to uncover meaning, the process of "reading" underlying meaning in advertising requires greater attention to implied messages. The meaning of the overt message "Sometimes what you wear to dinner depends on what you have for breakfast" in the Special K ad can be understood, in part, through contemporary cultural directives such as "Women should work on their appearance." Moreover, the underlying, core cultural beliefs that give arise to that directive can be seen as centering around issues of lovability and competence as expressed through body size and shape: "Thin women are attractive," or "Physically attractive women will be wanted and desired," or "Dieting is an avenue to control and power."

Enduring core cultural beliefs about women's appropriate role and sanctioned avenues to success can be seen, then, to give rise to more variable but related cultural directives about weight and shape. Such directives, in turn, feed overt cultural messages about women's thinness and dieting. This system not only parallels the conceptualization for individual cognition but can be seen to exist around the individual system, helping, in part, to shape and sustain it. Many of the characteristic "cognitive distortions" of eating-disordered clients so closely parallel cultural directives that it is, we argue, clinically useful to link the two conceptually and to help clients explore the potential associations between the two.

COGNITIVE DISTORTION OR CULTURAL DIRECTIVE?

One of the most explicit descriptions of the dysfunctional beliefs or cognitive distortions common to women with eating disorders is provided by Garner and colleagues (1997), who identify four dysfunctional thinking patterns: the anorexic wish, fear of losing control, fear of shape change, and beliefs about food. The anorexic wish is the desire, frequently articulated by anorexic women in therapy, to be free from the food and weight preoccupations, low self-esteem, and emotional disturbances that characterize anorexia while maintaining the anorectic's ultra-thin body. This wish is fueled not only by an overvaluation of thinness *per se*, but also by the anorectic's attempt to fulfill higher-order goals, such as mastery, achievement, competence, and individuality, through the attainment of thinness. Clients' desires to achieve feelings of control and mastery by controlling their food intake also give rise to the second dysfunctional belief identified by Garner and colleagues (1997): fear of losing control. Often fueled by dichotomous thinking (e.g., "If I'm not in complete control, I'll lose all control"), which is a reasoning error common to women with eating disorders (Garner & Bemis, 1982), fear of losing control is also closely tied to the intense fear of weight gain.

In addition to generalized fears of weight gain, women with eating disorders typically fear increases in the size of specific body parts such as their hips, stomachs, and thighs (Wooley, 1994). Frequently exacerbated by reasoning errors such as magnification ("I've gained two pounds so I won't be able to wear shorts anymore"), the fear of shape change is also frequently tied to faulty beliefs about food, and the perceived ability of specific foods to result in immediate weight gain. These dysfunctional beliefs about food are commonly associated with reasoning errors such as superstitious thinking ("If I eat a sweet it will be converted instantly into stomach fat"), and typically categorize certain foods as "forbidden" because of their potential to cause weight gain and other foods as "safe" because they are unlikely to lead to a loss of control or shape change.

As illustrated in the conceptual framework outlined in Table 10.1, a synthesis of CBT and feminist approaches to understanding eating disorders yields a model in which individual women's beliefs, rules, and assumptions about body weight and shape directly parallel cultural beliefs and assumptions about women and their bodies. Indeed, feminist scholars have pointed out that what CBT labels "cognitive distortions" can be reinterpreted as fairly accurate encapsulations of the prevailing cultural directives regarding women's bodies and food consumption (Bordo, 1993). Rather than being "idiosyncratic" (Vitousek, 1995, p. 324) to women with eating disorders, these cognitive schemas represent understandable, albeit problematic, responses to restrictive and conflicting cultural norms. Thus, the cognitive distortions identified by Garner and associates (1997) can be understood as internalized versions of the following cultural directives:

- Women should use dieting as a vehicle for achieving higher order goals, such as achievement, competence, mastery, and individuality.

- Women should carefully regulate their eating, because they can very easily lose control (eating is an all-or-nothing proposition).
- Women should be fearful of, and guard vigilantly against, gaining weight.
- Women should eat only socially sanctioned foods (i.e., those that are low in calories or fat) and avoid high-calorie alternatives.

The feminist cultural analysis we presented earlier in this chapter provided the theoretical basis for understanding how contemporary cultural directives and underlying core cultural values are translated into specific food- and weight-related behaviors. We will now illustrate how such directives are communicated to women by advertisements. A recent ad for Eggo Low Fat Waffles ("Eggo Waffle ad," 1998), for example, draws upon women's fears of shape change as well as dysfunctional beliefs about food by depicting a skimpy, blue and white, polka-dot bikini stretched tightly across a large, round, dimpled waffle. Although the ad caption reads, "When you lose fat, you flaunt it"—a reference to the product's new low-fat status—the imagery is clearly suggestive of a too-tight swimsuit adorning a too-fat woman's body (Wilson & Blackhurst, 1999). Taken together, the text and imagery send a powerful message: Women who eat regular waffles instead of the low-fat variety being advertised are in danger of having their bodies expand to gigantic proportions. The ad also reinforces the pursuit of higher-order goals through the quest for thinness by suggesting that losing fat is cause to "flaunt" one's success at dieting.

When you lose fat, you flaunt it.

Introducing Eggo Low Fat Waffles. Low in fat. As irresistible as ever.

A recent Jell-O advertisement for fat-free, sugar free gelatin ("Jell-O ad," 1997) reinforces fears of losing control and fears of shape change by encouraging women to count the calories in a single bite of chocolate cookie. In fact, the ad—which features a tiny piece of cookie balancing on a ruler designed to emphasize the cookie's diminutive size, and the caption "Presenting the 10 calorie, fat free cookie"—suggests that women should forgo the cookie in favor of the even lower calorie fat free Jell-O product. "Even fat free snacks can be loaded with calories," warns the ad copy, which, together with the image, presents a 10-calorie cup of gelatin as a safer and more desirable alternative to the cookie. Such ads not only encourage restrictive dieting practices among all women, but they also normalize the obsessive calorie counting (as well as ritualistic eating practices, such as weighing and measuring food) characteristic of women with eating disorders.

Finally, a recent ad campaign for ConAgra's Healthy Choice products further illustrates how the dichotomous thinking that underlies dysfunctional beliefs and disturbed eating patterns is encouraged and exploited by advertisers ("Healthy Choice ad," 1996). In the ads, advertisers make use of the dichotomy "red light . . . green light" to signal to women that regular, high-fat pizzas, sandwiches, and entrees ("red light") should be passed up in favor of the low-fat versions marketed by Healthy Choice ("green light"). By using imagery designed to separate food into categories of good and bad, allowable and forbidden, ads such as these encourage women to adopt dichotomous thinking in relation to food, eating, and weight. As a result, the ads tacitly foster women's fears of high-calorie food products and endorse a restrictive, overcontrolled approach to eating.

GOALS FOR THE PROPOSED INTERVENTION

When clinicians have achieved a clear understanding of how cultural value systems give rise to and support the individual belief systems characteristic of clients with eating disorders, and when they have developed the cultural criticism skills necessary to identify the layers of cultural values communicated through advertising, they are then prepared to guide clients through this same process. We propose a three-phase intervention, allowing clients and clinicians to identify and explore the layered meanings associated with weight and shape both at the individual and cultural level. The intervention is based on Beck's Cognitive Conceptualization Diagram (Beck, 1995, p. 139) specifically and, more generally, her recommended strategies for working with the automatic thoughts, intermediate rules and assumptions, and core beliefs that make up clients' cognitive experiences.

The intervention is guided by three forms, each associated with a distinct level of the unified conceptual framework presented above, as well as a distinct phase of the intervention. Each of the forms is designed to be used with examples of contemporary fashion, beauty, and food advertisements, which are collected and analyzed by the client as homework assignments and reviewed during therapy sessions.

One of the primary goals for the intervention is to allow clients to identify and examine the relationships between (a) their own problematic thoughts about their bodies, food, and dieting, and (b) cultural norms about women's bodies and appropriate relationships to food. A central prediction of the cognitive model is that relapse is likely unless clients' concerns about weight and shape are successfully addressed (Fairburn et al., 1993). Helping clients learn to critically evaluate the shape- and weight-related themes in advertisements can facilitate critical analysis of their own shape and weight concerns by encouraging them to look *at* the value system reflected in eating disorders rather than looking at the world *through* that value system (Fairburn, 2000). Because many clients are unskilled at identifying problematic thoughts when they occur, Fairburn and associates (1993) recommend assigning homework that will likely provoke such thoughts so that clients can practice the steps in cognitive restructuring. Instructing clients to review fashion, beauty, and food advertisements can serve this function.

Second, the proposed intervention allows the client to identify and investigate the relationship between (a) contemporary cultural directives about women's bodies and dieting, and (b) long-standing core cultural beliefs about women, their bodies, and their appropriate roles. Underlying clients' problematic thoughts about shape and weight are characteristic attitudes, beliefs, and assumptions such as the belief that their problems will be solved once they reach their ideal weight, the belief that people who are thin are happy and successful, and the belief that all their problems result from their weight (Fairburn et al., 1993). Successful treatment and relapse prevention include subjecting these core beliefs to the same kind of restructuring as problematic thoughts. This is often difficult, however, because such attitudes and beliefs are usually implicit and are typically not fully formed or articulated (Wilson et al., 1997). Because the same or very similar attitudes are pervasive in the advertising media, however, exploring the underlying themes in advertisements can be helpful in training clients to identify and critique their own implicit underlying rules.

A third goal of the proposed intervention is to encourage clients to develop a "healthy indignation" (Garner, 1997, p. 149) about the depiction of women in the media, as well as about the cultural directives and core beliefs undergirding media images. Research has demonstrated that particular strategies of media analysis can help women to challenge the dominant body images portrayed in advertisements and to reframe them to include a wider range of "normal" images (Rabak-Wagener, Eickhoff-Shemek, & Kelly-Vance, 1998). The most effective interventions appear to be those that emphasize the clash between the unrealistic, constructed images of female beauty in the media and the diversity of body sizes and shapes among average American women—as well as the negative effects of restrictive dieting (Levine, Piran, & Stoddard, 1999). In addition, the subscription to both general feminist values (Snyder & Hasbrouck, 1996) and specific feminist views toward physical attractiveness (Dionne, Davis, Fox, & Gurevich, 1995) appears to reduce the impact of factors promoting body dissatisfaction and disturbed eating.

A fourth goal of the proposed intervention is for the clinician to support and encourage clients' potential choice to refrain from consuming appearance-oriented media images such as those in women's magazines. It is important to help clients distinguish between the maladaptive process of distorting information and then avoiding it (such as when clients overestimate their body size and then avoid looking at their bodies, or overestimate the negative social consequences of gaining 2 pounds and then avoid social settings as a result) and the adaptive process of choosing to avoid exposure to information that is already distorted and that helps to maintain their difficulties. To help clients make this distinction, clinicians should review information about the goals and techniques of advertising and point out that the ads are designed to distort reality and make viewers feel anxious (Barthel, 1988; McCracken, 1993). The therapist can also discuss how advertisers distort images through techniques such as air brushing, cropping, and computer graphics—in addition to techniques employed by the models themselves, such as plastic surgery.

Finally, and perhaps most importantly, the proposed intervention is designed to teach and reinforce the skills fundamental to the cognitive model, so that clients can apply them to other media and other settings. Learning to identify and restructure automatic thoughts, intermediate rules and assumptions, and core beliefs is a process central to the success of cognitive behavioral treatment of eating disorders. The proposed intervention is a useful addition to cognitive therapy because it helps clients develop and practice these skills. Also like cognitive therapy, the intervention moves from an initial focus on automatic thoughts to deeper-level beliefs.

Form 1: Attending to Personal Reactions to Advertising

Initially, cognitive therapy emphasizes automatic thoughts. The primary goal near the beginning of therapy is to teach clients how to identify their automatic thoughts and to understand their connection to distressing emotion. Clinicians must guard against moving too quickly to challenge the thoughts. Clients must understand them before they can question them. Thus, there is little or no attempt to challenge the thoughts initially, only to assist clients in more fully attending to them and to recognizing their connection to mood. Clients, in fact, may be encouraged to use the onset of negative emotions as a prompt to attend to their thinking. Further, because automatic thoughts are so quick and often not fully elaborated, clients are encouraged to consider what their thoughts "mean" to them as a way of better accessing the significance of the thought and as a way of uncovering intermediate rules, assumptions, and beliefs.

Form 1, Attending to Personal Reactions to Advertising (see Table 10.2), applies both the conceptual and pragmatic aspects of the cognitive model for working with automatic thoughts to working with the overt messages in advertising. The process follows a series of ordered steps that are detailed on the form. First, clients are asked to select advertisements from popular women's magazines—most usefully, from magazines they regularly view. Then, working with one ad at a time, clients briefly describe the content of the ad. For purposes of illustration, let us consider a recent ad (shown in Figure 10.5) for Baked Lays Potato Chips ("Lays Potato Chips ad," 1997) that features two thin, beautiful fashion models dressed in elegant black evening gowns.

The models are each daintily munching on a single flavor of potato chip, the crumbs from which have fallen lightly down the fronts of their dresses. This image provides the basis for the advertisement's caption, "What will the world's most beautiful women be wearing this year?" The emotional charge for the advertisement is provided by the third "model" featured in the photograph: Miss Piggy (Wilson & Blackhurst, 1999). Also wearing a black evening gown, Miss Piggy is shown devouring "every flavor" of the advertised chips, substantially more of which have fallen down the front of her dress.

Using strategies that they have already practiced in the therapy, clients look at the ad and attempt to access their automatic thoughts in reaction to the text and images contained in it. Clients are encouraged to use emotion as a key to automatic thoughts, if the emotion is easier to identify. There is, of course, a wide range of idiosyncratic responses that clients may have, but one possible response is a temporary elevation in mood. Myers and Biocca (1992) report that after viewing television commercials containing attractiveness messages, young women experience a boost in self-

esteem as a result of accepting the message as a kind of internalized pep talk. One effect of attractiveness messages is to suggest that the kind of beauty depicted is easily attainable, and thus the viewer's resolve to pursue it may be reinforced. Thus, clients' emotions may be mild excitement or elation. The accompanying automatic thoughts might be something such as "Those women are really beautiful because they are thin. I should be— and could be—too." On the other hand, clients may be intimidated by the beautiful, thin models and more readily identify with the devalued "pig" in the ad. They may experience a drop in mood through feelings of shame or self-criticism. Their automatic thoughts may be such thoughts as, "I am such a pig. I am so out of control with my eating. I have got to get back on my diet." Along with noting thoughts and emotions, clients are instructed to record any behavior they initiate after viewing the ad, such as exercising, eating less at the next meal, or purging.

Form 1 seeks to help clients slow down the stream of automatic thoughts in order to better understand what it is they are telling themselves and the significance or impact of such thinking. Thus, clients are directed to con-

TABLE 10.2 Form 1: Attending to Personal Reactions to Advertising

Ad #1	*Ad #2*	*Ad #3*
Automatic thought:	Automatic thought:	Automatic thought:
If true, what does it mean?	If true, what does it mean?	If true, what does it mean?
Emotion:	Emotion:	Emotion:
Behavior:	Behavior:	Behavior:

Conditional assumptions, beliefs, rules (If I . . . then . . .)

Positive assumption:

Negative assumption:

Compensatory Strategies: (What do you have the urge to do when you have the thoughts listed above)?

sider the meaning of the automatic thought by responding to the question, "If true, what does it mean?" Again, the meaning will be determined, in part, by each client's unique life experiences, but automatic thoughts are broadly predictable based on underlying core beliefs (Beck, 1995). For those with eating disorders, the problematic beliefs center around an over-valuation of thinness (Wilson et al., 1997). Thus, the meaning of clients' automatic thoughts to such advertisements will likely involve such beliefs as, "I am not thin enough. I could do more to be thinner. In order to be desirable, I must be thin."

Beck's cognitive conceptualization assists clinicians in understanding the layers of clients' cognitions through an examination of conditional assumptions, beliefs, and rules. This intermediate level of cognition is described as often arising in the form of "If . . . then" constructions. Such assumptions, rules, and beliefs fuel automatic thoughts and link them to core beliefs. Form 1 directs clients to work with the "if . . . then" rules they hold by writing down the rules that are operative in their reactions to advertisements. Clients may do this in two ways—by identifying positive outcomes and/or by identifying negative outcomes that they believe are likely to result from particular food-related behavior. For example, clients may identify such rules as "If I stop eating so much, I will be more attractive" or "If I don't do something about my weight, I am going to be a fat pig."

The final step for this form is to attend to any increased urges that may arise in response to the ad. Clients are instructed to think about whether or not they have a desire to do something when they have the thoughts they've recorded. This portion of Form 1 is based on Beck's (1995) concept of compensatory strategies that are used to guard against having to encounter situations or emotions that agitate negative core beliefs. At this stage clients are not yet overtly exploring core beliefs but such beliefs are present, if only faintly, even at this point. Thus, attending to their impulse to action in the context of thinking helps to reinforce for clients the connection not only between thoughts and feelings, and thoughts and behavior, but also begins to suggest the content of deeper-level cognitions.

Form 1 helps clients to identify their automatic thoughts in reaction to advertising and engaging in this process has several potential benefits. First, clients are aided in their efforts to better attend to their automatic thinking and its link to distressing emotions and problematic behaviors. Thus, some of the primary goals of cognitive therapy are advanced. Further, clients can begin to recognize triggers outside themselves and, as a result, lay the groundwork for (a) developing plans to buffer themselves from contributing factors, and (b) linking their personal beliefs to cultural messages. Thus, some of the goals of feminist therapy are likewise promoted.

There are several important cognitive therapy principles that clinicians must be sure to adhere to when using this form with clients. As with all cognitive therapy interventions, clinicians should clearly explain the rationale for the form in order to ensure that clients are equal participants in the activity and understand its potential benefit. Ideally, when clinicians want to introduce the intervention, they will ask clients to collect several ads as homework and bring them to their next session. Part of the next session, then, would be spent completing the form with one or more ads to ensure that clients understand the process. In addition, clinicians must remember and also stress to the client, that the goal, at this point, is not to question or challenge the automatic thoughts, but rather to identify them. Clients would then work with the forms as homework and process their responses in subsequent sessions.

Form 2: Identifying Cultural Directives

The principles of cognitive therapy suggest that once clients have become skilled in identifying and monitoring their automatic thoughts and understand the connection between such thoughts and both distressing emotions and undesirable behavior, they should begin to challenge and restructure problematic cognitions (Garner et al., 1997; Wilson et al., 1997). This process can be particularly demanding for clients with eating disorders, who often find it especially difficult to submit their overvalued ideas to tests of reasonableness or accuracy (Vitousek, 1995). Allowing clients to examine the logic of these ideas from the perspective of an observer can help both clients and clinicians to successfully navigate this phase of therapy and is the goal of Form 2: Identifying Contemporary Cultural Directives (see Table 10.3).

Form 2 builds upon the activities completed in conjunction with Form 1 and, like Form 1, is designed to be completed in a series of ordered steps. First, clients are asked to return to the same advertisements that formed the basis of their work with Form 1. Again working with the ads one at a time, clients are then asked to record the overt or primary messages in the ads—both those that are communicated by the text of the advertisements and those that are communicated through imagery or a combination of text and graphics. Using the same Lays Baked Potato Chip ad as an example, clients might identify such overt messages as "Beautiful women have thin bodies and dainty appetites," and "Women who give in to their appetites are considered pigs." It is important to note, and clients should be encouraged to consider, the fact that many of the overt messages in advertisements are conflicting. For example, in direct contrast to the overt message that women who fail to control their appetites are pigs, the caption at the bottom of the Lays ad states that "Nobody can eat just one." This message not only suggests that controlling one's appetite is impossible, but it also suggests that part of the product's appeal lies in its ability to make women lose control.

Next, clients are instructed to identify the conditional assumptions, rules, and beliefs that are more implicitly communicated in the ad. As with Form 1, this task is accomplished through the use of both positive and negative "if . . . then" statements. In contrast to Form 1, however, Form 2 instructs clients to identify cultural, rather than personal, "rules"—those rules that are presumed to apply to all women and underlie the overt messages in the ad. Examples from the Lays Potato Chip ad might include "If women eat low-fat foods and control their appetites they will earn social approval," or

TABLE 10.3 Form 2: Identifying Contemporary Cultural Directives

Primary messages in the ad:	*Primary messages in the ad:*	*Primary messages in the ad:*
Imagery:	*Imagery:*	*Imagery:*
Text:	*Text:*	*Text:*
Conditional beliefs (If . . . then . . .)	Conditional beliefs (If . . . then . . .)	Conditional beliefs (If . . . then . . .)
Positive:	Positive:	Positive:
Negative:	Negative:	Negative:
Cultural Directives (circle those that apply)	Cultural Directives (circle those that apply)	Cultural Directives (circle those that apply)
1. Women should use dieting as a vehicle for achieving higher-order goals (e.g., achievement, mastery, competence) 2. Women should carefully regulate their eating, because they can very easily lose control 3. Women should be fearful of, and guard vigilantly against, gaining weight 4. Women should eat only socially sanctioned foods	1. Women should use dieting as a vehicle for achieving higher -order goals (e.g., achievement, mastery, competence) 2. Women should carefully regulate their eating, because they can very easily lose control 3. Women should be fearful of, and guard vigilantly against, gaining weight 4. Women should eat only socially sanctioned foods	1. Women should use dieting as a vehicle for achieving higher-order goals (e.g., achievement, mastery, competence) 2. Women should carefully regulate their eating, because they can very easily lose control 3. Women should be fearful of, and guard vigilantly against, gaining weight 4. Women should eat only socially sanctioned foods
Compensatory strategies suggested by the ad:	Compensatory strategies suggested by the ad:	Compensatory strategies suggested by the ad:

"If women are not careful to control their appetites, then they will be considered fat and ugly." From this point, it should be fairly easy for the client to identify, and circle on the form, those cultural directives explicitly or implicitly communicated by the ad. In the case of the Lays ad, evidence of all four directives can be found in the conditional rules and assumptions identified above.

Finally, clients are instructed to identify the specific activities suggested by the ad as a means of adhering to the cultural rules or directives identified. The Lays Potato Chip ad, for example, suggests that women should eat low-fat foods, carefully control their eating, and equate beauty with thinness and dietary restraint. The prevalence of these kinds of messages in contemporary advertisements presents a ready opportunity for clinicians to review with their clients the cognitive-behavioral model for the maintenance of bulimia nervosa (Fairburn et al., 1993; Wilson et al., 1997). Clinicians can point out how the ads are designed to activate, and validate, extreme concerns about shape and weight and then suggest strict dietary control as a solution to these concerns. It is likely that clients will already be familiar with the role of strict dieting in the CBT model and will understand how dieting perpetuates the binge-purge cycle. This understanding provides an opportunity for clinicians to begin to challenge the logic of the cultural directives identified on Form 2.

Once clients have been introduced to the purposes of completing Form 2, and have gone through the process in session using a recent advertisement as an example, completing the remainder of the form should be assigned as homework. In the following session, clinicians should assist their clients in relating their own problematic thoughts, intermediate assumptions, and core beliefs (as identified on Form 1) to the cultural rules and assumptions pervasive in advertisements. Throughout this process, clinicians should help clients to understand that, while their own problematic thoughts and assumptions are typical of women with eating disorders, such thoughts do not result solely from the disorder. Rather, they derive from rigid adherence to a cultural value system that overvalues thinness in women and denigrates women's natural bodies and normal appetites. This understanding sets the stage for the third and final phase of the intervention, which involves critiquing the core cultural beliefs reflected in advertising as a prelude to examining the pros and cons of adopting these beliefs as a personal value system.

Form 3: Critiquing Core Cultural Beliefs

Having examined a series of ads for the directives they issue about eating attitudes and practices, clients are now ready to consider what those directives mean *about* women. That is, if messages such as "women should use dieting as a vehicle for higher-order goals" or "women should be fearful of, and guard vigilantly against, gaining weight" are true, what does that mean? And if such messages are accepted, what to do they suggest about women's competence and lovability?

Form 3 is organized to assist clients in exploring underlying core cultural beliefs that are implicit in the more overt messages of the ads they have considered (see Table 10.4). The first step is to circle any of the four cultural directives that are present in the ads they have examined. Then, clients are instructed to contemplate the "message beneath" the directives by completing two opposing sentence stems: "Women who are extremely thin and/or dieting are. . . ." and "Women who are not extremely thin and/or are not dieting are . . ." Two boxes containing adjectives associated with positive and negative core beliefs about lovability and competence are provided to help clients find words for what they perceive as the "message beneath" the ads' text and images.

Completing this section of Form 3 serves to make more explicit the repeated association between a whole host of desirable traits such as power, control, success, attractiveness, and worthiness and dieting/thinness. Likewise this section of the form reveals the more negative underside of such messages, which is that they, either overtly or by default, suggest that weight gain and freed female appetites are dangerous because they are associated with failure, loss of control, worthlessness, and incompetence. Such messages will surely resonate with clients as the messages represent exactly the kind of the thinking clients have learned is problematic for them and which they are attempting to overcome.

To help leverage a "healthy indignation" about cultural pressures, the form prompts clients to consider what such messages reveal about core cultural beliefs about women, about long-standing, detrimental stereotypes, and about the potential benefits to advertisers in sending such messages. These questions are designed to help clients stop viewing their own preoccupations with weight and shape as something personal and unique, but rather as a larger, more political depersonalization of women as a group. One the difficulties in treating anorexia in particular is the "special status" it is seen as conferring upon the individual (Bemis, 1982). Unseating such a belief may be easier if the client's perspective is sufficiently broadened to register social and historical issues surrounding body preoccupation for women. Lecturing the client about such issues, of course, is not desirable but guided discovering is a well-established cognitive practice.

The final two questions are geared toward helping clients reflect upon the destructive impact of such messages, both for them individually and for women as a group, and to consider what constructive action can be taken to protect against such messages. Here again, clients are encouraged to link their experiences to the larger experience of women in the culture as a way

TABLE 10.4 Form 3: Critiquing Core Cultural Beliefs in Advertising

Look over the information you've recorded for the ads you've gathered. Circle the cultural directives that are recurring themes in the ads.

The ads I've collected repeatedly send the message that:

1. Women should use dieting as a vehicle for achieving higher-order goals (e.g., achievement, mastery, competence)
2. Women should carefully regulate their eating, because they can very easily lose control
3. Women should be fearful of, and guard vigilantly against, gaining weight
4. Women should eat only socially sanctioned foods

The "message beneath" such messages seems to be that:
Women who are extremely thin and/or dieting are:
Women who are not extremely thin and/or are not dieting are:

Positive traits

Competent: adequate powerful free superior effective strong successful perfect winner independent in control

Lovable: attractive desirable rejected alone wanted cared for good worthy special

Negative traits

Incompetent: inadequate powerless trapped inferior incompetent weak vulnerable failure defective not good enough loser needy out of control

Unlovable: unattractive undesirable rejected alone unwanted uncared for bad worthless different not good enough defective loser

What do such messages reveal about what advertisers are suggesting about women as a group beyond the overt messages about weight and dieting?

How do such messages reflect long-standing cultural beliefs (stereotypes) that have oppressed women as a group?

What benefit is there to advertisers for sending such messages?

How are these messages destructive to you and to women as a group?

What constructive action can you take to protect yourself against such messages?

to diminish feelings of isolation, whether they be a pleasurable sense of uniqueness or a shaming sense of defectiveness. The goal is to help clients understand that however distorted and problematic their thoughts, the thoughts did not originate with them. The distortions that characterize their thinking are endemic to the culture.

By exploring the cultural context surrounding eating attitudes and practices, clients are aided in reframing the etiology of the disorder, at least in part, in cultural terms. Doing so reduces the likelihood that they may mistakenly believe that their problematic thinking reveals some personal defect—a potential risk given the attention paid in therapy to cognition. Analysis of core cultural beliefs may help clients to separate themselves from the disorder and therefore make it less threatening to challenge problematic beliefs. Finally, within the context of reviewing cultural issues, prompting clients to consider what constructive action might be taken may be more likely to elicit initiatives that register as empowering rather than restrictive.

SUMMARY

In this chapter, we have argued for a greater integration of established cognitive-behavioral principles with feminist perspectives on eating disorders. To this end, we have presented a unified conceptual framework linking the layers of individual cognition emphasized in cognitive-behavioral approaches with the layers of cultural values emphasized in feminist models, and demonstrating how the latter give rise to and reinforce the former. Finally, we have used this framework as the basis for proposing guidelines for assigning and processing media-based interventions with clients, as well as for assisting clients in using enhanced cultural criticism skills for relapse prevention.

More than a decade of controlled studies evaluating the effectiveness of cognitive-behavioral therapy for eating disorders has demonstrated that CBT is more effective than, or at least as effective as, any other form of psychotherapy with which it has been compared (Wilson et al., 1997). Nonetheless, short-term relapse rates for clients with bulimia nervosa are as high as 49% for binge eating and 64% for purging (Wilson et al.). Likewise, less than half of the CBT patients evaluated in a long-term follow-up study were free of bulimic symptoms 5.8 years after the cessation of therapy (Fairburn et al., 1991). These statistics demonstrate that, despite the empirically validated effectiveness of CBT, there is considerable room for improvement in treatment outcomes. Achieving greater integration of cultural factors into the conceptualization and treatment of eating disorders, while remaining true to the CBT framework, offers the potential for enhancing treatment outcomes and relapse prevention. It is also consistent with a view of eating disorders as complex, multifaceted disorders requiring the application of a variety of theoretical and treatment perspectives (Garfinkel, 1995). In addition, using media-based interventions to explore the role of cultural influences in the development and maintenance of eating disorders will likely become even more important as media continue to proliferate and increasingly invade nearly every aspect of American life (Kilbourne, 1999). The emergence of advertising outlets such as the Internet and school-based, "educational" TV programming means that children will be exposed to sophisticated advertising techniques at younger ages (Pipher, 1995). Already, advertisers recognize children as an important market segment and spend billions of dollars attempting to influence their purchasing habits (Kilbourne, 1999). By the time children reach adolescence, they will have viewed over 6 million advertisements (Kilbourne, 1994, 1999), most of which will market the "cult of thinness" (Hesse-Biber, 1996, p. 82) along with the advertised products. Teaching the cultural and media criticism skills necessary to resist indoctrination into this damaging cultural value system thus seems critical to the prevention and treatment of eating disorders.

REFERENCES

Barthel, D. (1988). *Putting on appearances: Gender and advertising.* Philadelphia: Temple University Press.
Basow, S., & Kobrynowicz, D. (1990, August). *What is she eating? The effects of meal size on impressions of a female eater.* Paper presented at the Annual Meeting of the American Psychological Association, Boston, MA.
Beck, J. S. (1995). *Cognitive therapy: Basics and beyond.* New York: Guilford Press.
Bemis, K. M. (1983). A comparison of functional relationships in anorexia nervosa and phobia. In P. L. Darby, P. E. Garfinkel, D. M., & D. V. Coscina (Eds.), *Anorexia nervosa: Recent developments in research* (pp. 403–416). New York: Alan R. Liss.
Bloom, C. (1994). Bulimia: A feminist psychoanalytic understanding. In M. Lawrence (Ed.), *Fed up and hungry: Women, oppression, and food* (pp. 102–114). London: The Woman's Press.
Bloom, C., & Kogel, L. (1994). Tracing development: The feeding experience and the body. In C. Bloom, A. Gitter, S. Gutwill, L. Kogel, & L. Zaphiropoulos (Eds.), *Eating problems: A feminist psychoanalytic treatment model* (pp. 40–56). New York: Basic Books.
Bock, B. D., & Kanarek, R. B. (1995). Women and men are what they eat: The effects of gender and reported meal size on perceived characteristics. *Sex Roles, 33*(1/2), 109–119.
Bordo, S. (1993). *Unbearable weight: Feminism, Western culture, and the body.* Berkeley, CA: University of California Press.

Brown, C. (1993). The continuum: Anorexia, bulimia, and weight preoccupation. In C. Brown & K. Jasper (Eds.), *Consuming passions: Feminist approaches to weight preoccupation and eating disorders* (pp. 53–68). Toronto, Ontario: Second Story Press.

Brown, C., & Jasper, K. (1993a). Why weight? Why women? Why now? In C. Brown & K. Jasper (Eds.), *Consuming passions: Feminist approaches to weight preoccupation and eating disorders* (pp. 16–35). Toronto, Ontario: Second Story Press.

Brown, C., & Jasper, K. (1993b). Preface. In C. Brown & K. Jasper (Eds.), *Consuming passions: Feminist approaches to weight preoccupation and eating disorders* (pp. 11–14). Toronto, Ontario: Second Story Press.

Chernin, K. (1994). *The hungry self: Women, eating, and identity.* New York: Harper Collins.

Dionne, M., Davis, C., Fox, J., & Gurevich, M. (1995). Feminist ideology as a predictor of body dissatisfaction in women. *Sex Roles, 33*(3/4), 277–287.

Eggo Waffle ad (1998, February). *Better Homes and Gardens, 75*(2), 11.

Fairburn, C. G. (1997). Eating disorders. In D. M. Clark & C. G. Fairburn (Eds.), *Science and practice of cognitive-behaviour therapy* (pp. 209–241). New York: Oxford University Press.

Fairburn, C. G. (2000, June). *Cognitive therapy for eating disorders.* Pre-conference workshop presented at the International Congress of Cognitive Psychotherapy, Catania, Italy.

Fairburn, C. G., Jones, R., Peveler, R. C., Carr, S. J., Solomon, R. A., O'Connor, M. E., Burton, J., & Hope, R. A. (1991). Three psychological treatments for bulimia nervosa. *Archives of General Psychiatry, 48,* 463–469.

Fairburn, C. G., Marcus, M. D., & Wilson, T. G. (1993). Cognitive-behavioral therapy for binge eating and bulimia nervosa: A comprehensive treatment manual. In C. G. Fairburn & T. G. Wilson (Eds.), *Binge eating: Nature, assessment, and treatment* (pp. 361–404). New York: Guilford Press.

Fursland, A. (1994). Eve was framed: Food and sex and women's shame. In M. Lawrence (Ed.), *Fed up and hungry: Women, oppression, and food* (pp. 15–26). London: Woman's Press.

Garfinkel, P. E. (1995). Foreword. In K. D. Brownell & C. G. Fairburn (Eds.), *Eating disorders and obesity: A comprehensive handbook* (pp. vii–viii). New York: Guilford Press.

Garner, D. M. (1997). Psychoeducational principles in treatment. In D. M. Garner & P. E. Garfinkel (Eds.), *Handbook of treatment for eating disorders* (pp. 145–177). New York: Guilford Press.

Garner, D. M., & Bemis, K. M. (1982). A cognitive-behavioral approach to anorexia nervosa. *Cognitive Therapy and Research, 6,* 123–150.

Garner, D. M., & Garfinkel P. E. (Eds.). 1997. *Handbook for the treatment of eating disorders.* New York: Guilford Press.

Garner, D. M., Vitousek, K. M., & Pike, K. M. (1997). Cognitive-behavioral therapy for anorexia nervosa. In D. M. Garner & P. E. Garfinkel (Eds.), *Handbook of treatment for eating disorders* (pp. 94–144). New York: Guilford Press.

Gilday, K. (Producer). (1990). *The famine within* (Film). (Available from Direct Cinema Limited, P.O. Box 10003, Santa Monica, CA 90410.)

Gutwill, S. (1994). Women's eating problems: Social context and the internalization of culture. In C. Bloom, A. Gitter, S. Gutwill, L. Kogel, & L. Zaphiropoulos (Eds.), *Eating Problems: A feminist psychoanalytic treatment model* (pp. 1–27). New York: Basic Books.

Hesse-Biber, S. (1996). *Am I thin enough yet? The cult of thinness and the commercialization of identity.* New York: Oxford University Press.

Iggers, J. (1996). *The garden of eating: Food, sex, and the hunger for meaning.* New York: Basic Books.

Irving, L. M. (1990). Mirror images: Effects of the standard of beauty on the self- and body-esteem of women exhibiting varying levels of bulimic symptoms. *Journal of Social and Clinical Psychology, 9*(2), 230–242.

Jell-O ad. (1997, February 18), *Family Circle, 110*(3), 52–53.

Johnson, C. E., & Petrie, T. A. (1995). The relationship of gender discrepancy to eating disorder attitudes and behaviors. *Sex Roles, 33*(5/6), 405–416.

Johnson, C. E., & Petrie, T. A. (1996). Relationship of gender discrepancy to psychological correlates of disordered eating in female undergraduates. *Journal of Counseling Psychology, 43*(4), 473–479.

Healthy Choice ad. (1996, November). *Fitness,* p. 49.

Kilbourne, J. (1994). Still killing us softly: Advertising and the obsession with thinness. In P. Fallon, M. Katzman, & S. C. Wooley (Eds.), *Feminist perspectives on eating disorders* (pp. 395–418). New York: Guilford Press.

Kilbourne, J. (1999). *Deadly persuasion: Why women and girls must fight the addictive power of advertising.* New York: Free Press.

Lays Potato Chips ad. (1997, February 10), *Time, 149*(6), 87.

Levine, M. P., Piran, N., & Stoddard, C. (1999). Mission more probable: Media literacy, activism, and advocacy as primary prevention. In N. Piran, M. P. Levine, & C. Steiner-Adair (Eds.), *Preventing eating disorders: A handbook of interventions and special challenges* (pp. 1–25). Philadelphia, PA: Brunner/Mazel.

MacSween, M. (1993). *Anorexic bodies: A feminist and sociological perspective on anorexia nervosa.* London: Routledge.

Martz, D. M., Handley, K. B., & Eisler, R. M. (1995). The relationship between feminine gender role stress, body image, and eating disorders. *Psychology of Women Quarterly, 19*, 493–508.

McCracken, E. (1993). *Decoding women's magazines from Mademoiselle to Ms.* New York: St. Martin's Press.

Mitchell, J. (1994). "Going for the burn" and "pumping iron": What's healthy about the current fitness boom? In M. Lawrence (Ed.), *Fed up and hungry: Women, oppression, and food* (pp. 156–174). London: Woman's Press.

Mooney, K. M., DeTore, J., & Malloy, K. A. (1994). Perceptions of women related to food choice. *Sex Roles, 31*(7/8), 433–442.

Murray, S. H., Touyz, S. W., & Beumont, P. J. V. (1996). Awareness and perceived influence of body ideals in the media: A comparison of eating disorder patients and the general community. *Eating Disorders: The Journal of Treatment and Prevention, 4,* 33–46.

Myers, P. N., & Biocca, F. A. (1992). The elastic body image: The effect of television advertising and programming on body image distortion in young women. *Journal of Communication, 42*(3), 108–133.

Paxton, S. J., & Sculthorpe, A. (1991). Disordered eating and sex role characteristics in young women: Implications for sociocultural theories of disordered eating. *Sex Roles, 24*(9/10), 587–598.

Pipher, M. (1995). *Hunger pains: The modern woman's tragic quest for thinness.* New York: Ballantine Books.

Pliner, P., & Chaiken, S. (1990). Eating, social motives, and self-presentation in women and men. *Journal of Experimental and Social Psychology, 26,* 240–254.

Rabak-Wagener, J., Eickhoff-Shemek, J., & Kelly-Vance, L. (1998). The effect of media analysis on attitudes and behaviors regarding body image among college students. *Journal of American College Health, 47*(1), 29–35.

Richins, M. L. (1991). Social comparison and the idealized images of advertising. *Journal of Consumer Research, 18,* 71–83.

Scarano, G. M., & Kalodner-Martin, C. R. (1994). A description of the continuum of eating disorders: Implications for intervention and research. *Journal of Counseling and Development, 72*(4), 356–361.

Silverstein, B., Carpman, S., Perlick, D., & Perdue, L. (1990). Nontraditional sex role aspirations, gender identity conflict, and disordered eating among college women. *Sex Roles, 23*(11/12), 687–695.

Silverstein, B., & Perlick, D. (1995). *The cost of competence: Why inequality causes depression, eating disorders, and illness in women.* New York: Oxford University Press.

Snyder, R., & Hasbrouck, S. (1996). Feminist identity, gender traits, and symptoms of disturbed eating among college women. *Psychology of Women Quarterly, 20*(4), 593–598.

Special K Cereal ad. (1997, February 1), *Family Circle, 110*(2), 51.

Stice, E., Schupak-Neuberg, A., Shaw, H. E., & Stein, R. I. (1994). Relation of media exposure to eating disorder symptomatology: An examination of mediating mechanisms. *Journal of Abnormal Psychology, 103*(4), 836–840.

Streigel-Moore, R. H. (1993). Etiology of binge eating: A developmental perspective. In C. G. Fairburn & T. G. Wilson (Eds.), *Binge eating: Nature, assessment, and treatment* (pp. 144–172). New York: Guilford Press.

Turner, S. L., Hamilton, H., Jacobs, M., Angood, L. M., & Dwyer, D. H. (1997). The influence of fashion magazines on the body image satisfaction of college women: An exploratory analysis. *Adolescence, 32*(127), 603–614.

Vitousek, K. B. (1995). Cognitive-behavioral therapy for anorexia nervosa. In K. D. Brownell & C. G. Fairburn (Eds.), *Eating disorders and obesity: A comprehensive handbook* (pp. 324–329). New York: Guilford Press.

Wilson, G. T., Fairburn, C. G., & Agras, W. S. (1997). Cognitive-behavioral therapy for bulimia nervosa. In D. M. Garner & P. E. Garfinkel (Eds.), *Handbook of treatment for eating disorders* (pp. 67–93). New York: Guilford Press.

Wilson, N. L., & Blackhurst, A. E. (1999). Food advertising and eating disorders: Marketing body dissatisfaction, the drive for thinness, and dieting in women's magazines. *Journal of Humanistic Counseling, Education, and Development, 38*(2), 111–122.

Wolf, N. (1994). Hunger. In P. Fallon, M. Katzman & S. C. Wooley (Eds.), *Feminist perspectives on eating disorders* (pp. 94–111). New York: Guilford Press.

Wooley, S. C. (1995). Feminist influences on the treatment of eating disorders. In K. D. Brownell & C. G. Fairburn (Eds.), *Eating disorders and obesity: A comprehensive handbook* (pp. 294–298). New York: Guilford Press.

Wooley, W. O. (1994). And man created "woman": Representations of women's bodies in western culture. In P. Fallon, M. Katzman, & S. C. Wooley (Eds.), *Feminist perspectives on eating disorders* (pp. 17–52). New York: Guilford Press.

11

Empirically Supported Treatments: Recent Trends, Current Limitations, and Future Promise

William J. Lyddon and David K. Chatkoff

For decades, one of the most fundamental questions facing psychotherapy researchers has been "Is psychotherapy effective?" With few exceptions (cf. Eysenck, 1952, 1961), the answer to this question has been in the affirmative (Lambert & Bergin, 1994; Smith, Glass, & Miller, 1980). That is, when conceived in its broadest generic sense, psychotherapy has been shown to be effective when compared to either no-treatment or to various other types of control groups (Smith & Glass, 1977). In recent years, however, the psychotherapy field has moved away from demonstrating the efficacy of generic treatments to examining the efficacy of what has been referred to as "prescriptive treatments" (Sperry, Brill, Howard, & Grissom, 1996). Having resolved the original question of whether psychotherapy works at all, the psychotherapy scientific community has begun to address a very different question about the effectiveness of psychotherapy—a question perhaps most consonant with Paul's (1967) oft-quoted query: "What treatment, by whom, is most effective for this individual with that specific problem under which set of circumstances?" (p. 111). As a result, what has emerged in recent years is a focus on the identification and classification of specific treatments that empirically have been shown to be effective for well-defined categories of psychological problems.

RECENT TRENDS AND DEVELOPMENTS

To be sure, the empirically supported treatment (EST) movement has become a movement in the true sense of the word and seems to draw much momentum from several converging economic, political, and professional forces. Some of the more significant forces have been managed health care, the rise of biological psychiatry, the creation of the American Psychological Association's (APA) Task Force on the Promotion and Dissemination of Psychological Procedures, and changing accreditation guidelines for doctoral training programs in applied professional psychology (Waehler, Kalodner, Wampold, & Lichtenberg, 2000).

Managed health care, a social and business phenomenon focused on the evaluation and reduction of service costs, has been a significant factor in the growth of the EST movement. Managed health care groups have a significant investment in the issue of health service accountability. Within medical settings, one solution to this issue has been the development of diagnostic related groups (DRGs), which provide a fixed treatment and payment schedule by diagnosis. The expansion of DRGs beyond the realm of medical problems to that of psychological conditions has become a reality in 21st-century psychological practice. As Henry (1998) suggests, the EST movement is conducive to an increasingly dominant managed health care system—a system that most psychological practitioners view as "intrusive, restrictive, and not in the ultimate best interests of their patients" (p. 131).

The rise of biological psychiatry over the last 40 years has also fueled the EST movement. From the introduction of Valium in 1963—the most widely used anti-anxiety drug ever—to the current widespread use of Ritalin and Prozac in the United States ("Mother's little helper," 1996), psychopharmacological solutions have become synonymous with prescriptive treatment for psychological disorders in contemporary psychiatric contexts. The straightforward prescriptive focus of biological treatment is compatible with managed care and DRG emphases and, as a result, places additional pressure on psychologists to empirically demonstrate the effectiveness of psychosocial treatments (Goldfried & Wolfe, 1996).

Responding in part to the rise of biological psychiatry, Division 12 (Clinical Psychology) of the APA established the Task Force on Promotion and Dissemination of Psychological Procedures. In its first publication the task force stated:

> [I]f the public is to benefit from the availability of effective psychotherapies, and if clinical psychology is to survive in this heyday of biological psychiatry, APA must act to emphasize the strength of what we have to offer—a variety of psychotherapies of proven efficacy. (Task Force on Promotion and Dissemination of Psychological Procedures, 1995, p. 3)

The task force delineated minimum criteria for establishing a psychotherapy as "efficacious" and over the years has produced lists of "approved" ESTs (Chambless et al., 1996; Chambless et al., 1998). It is important to note that the task force was explicit in acknowledging that its criteria were designed to evaluate treatment efficacy, or the internal validity of outcome research that is ideally demonstrated when a particular therapy is shown to work in a well-controlled study. The task force criteria are not concerned with treatment effectiveness. Treatment effectiveness refers to the external validity of a therapy and is based on evidence that a particular therapy works in an applied setting outside of the controlled experimental context. Chambless and Hollon (1998) have listed five criteria for judging treatment efficacy. They point out that the treatment must be found to be either superior to a control group or equivalent to an already established treatment. The study must involve the use of a manual designed for the treatment of specific, well-defined problems. The treatment has to (a) be demonstrated as effective in at least two different studies to be designated as "efficacious" or (b) be demonstrated as effective in one study to be designated as "possibly efficacious." Finally, to be demonstrated as both "efficacious and specific," the treatment must be shown to be superior to either a placebo or an established treatment in at least two different research settings.

A final important development in the EST movement involves the change in the standards for accreditation adopted by the APA Office of Program Consultation and Accreditation in 1996—which for the first time included direct mention of ESTs. These standards serve as the primary accreditation guidelines for doctoral programs in clinical, counseling, and school psychology, and include the guidelines that:

> All students can acquire and demonstrate substantial understanding of and competence in implementing intervention strategies (including training in empirically supported procedures). . . . [The] program requires that its students receive adequate and appropriate practicum experiences through applications of empirically supported intervention procedures. (APA, 1996, pp. 6–7)

In support of these guidelines the Division 12 Task Force recommended that APA site-visit teams make ESTs a high-priority issue by requiring that training in ESTs be a criterion for APA accreditation (Task Force on the Promotion and Dissemination of Psychological Procedures, 1995, p. 3). These training recommendations have been endorsed by others (Crits-Christoph, 1996; Persons, 1995; Wilson, 1995).

The EST movement offers the field of psychotherapy a number of potential benefits. For example, the movement provides an organized way for researchers to disseminate knowledge about the efficacy of many general and specific therapies. Furthermore, standardized treatment manuals associated with the EST movement may improve both the reliability and replicability of clinical research, help clinicians in making treatment decisions, and facilitate the training of future clinicians. However, the most fundamental and important benefit of the EST movement may be that of ethical accountability. As Ingram, Hayes, and Scott (2000) have cogently noted, psychologists and other professionals have an ethical obligation to uphold the public trust and to ensure, as much as possible, that the treatments they offer are fundamentally sound. Thus, they contend that the most basic understanding of the ethics code of the APA places an equal obligation on both researchers and practitioners to use empirically supported treatments to guide their work.

As indicated by the contributions to the present volume, cognitive and cognitive-behavioral researchers and practitioners have been at the forefront of the EST movement, and empirical support for their respective strategies and interventions have been used as evidence for the viability of various cognitive models in the conceptualization and treatment of a wide array of psychological dysfunctions. However, what has not been emphasized nearly as much are some of the inherent limitations associated with the development of ESTs. Thus, as a matter of ethical accountability, it is important to underscore that the public trust is also well served when the limitations of ESTs are acknowledged (Ingram et al., 2000). It is to this topic that we now turn.

SPECIFIC LIMITATIONS OF EMPIRICALLY SUPPORTED TREATMENTS

Two of the most significant limitations of the EST movement involve (a) emphasis on the treatment efficacy model of psychotherapy research and (b) its adoption of the randomized clinical trials methodology used in drug research. While these two limitations are separate issues, they are related to each other because the clinical trials approach to drug studies is based on the efficacy research paradigm. It should be noted, however, that while psychotherapy outcome research is currently based on the efficacy model, this model has not always been the dominant approach in the field. Goldfried and Wolf (1996), for example, describe three generations of psychotherapy outcome studies. During the first generation (the 1950s and 1960s), psychotherapy researchers focused on "whether or not psychotherapy was effective in producing personality change" (p. 1009). The second generation took place during the 1960s and 1970s and was driven in large part by the popularity of behaviorism. During this time researchers began to focus on "which specific procedures are more effective in dealing with a specific clinical problem" (p. 1009). Goldfried and Wolf describe the current Generation III studies as modeled after the randomized clinical trials methodology used in medical and pharmacotherapy research. It is within this Generation III framework that the EST movement has evolved.

Treatment Efficacy and Treatment Effectiveness

As previously mentioned, the EST movement currently emphasizes treatment efficacy (the criterion of internal validity) over that of treatment effectiveness and generalizability to the real world of clinical practice (the criterion of external validity). Seligman (1995) clearly draws attention to the issue of generalizability in his discussion of the methodological differences between *efficacy* and *effectiveness* studies. According to Seligman, efficacy studies reflect the methodology of traditional laboratory research. As a result, they incorporate tight experimental controls, including randomization of participants to treatments, manualized treatment protocols, groups of homogeneous participants comprising single morbidity diagnoses, clearly defined outcome measures based on specific theoretical orientations, and the use of control groups. The purpose of all of these controls and procedures is to reduce confounds to a minimum in order to increase internal validity and the ability to attribute a specific outcome to a specific treatment. In contrast, effectiveness studies focus on the outcomes of psychotherapy in clinical settings. In this format, tight experimental controls give way to a greater emphasis on ecological validity and the way that treatments are actually applied. For example, therapists in clinical settings tend not to adhere to a single manualized treatment and often engage in self-correcting behaviors based on clients' responsiveness to initial treatment interventions. In addition, clients in clinical settings are less homogeneous than those selected for efficacy research, and often exhibit comorbid disorders. Further, in clinical settings treatment goals and outcome measures are often more diverse and in many cases are based on competing interests. For example, different treatment expectations may be held by the client, therapist, and/or third-party payer (Strupp, 1996). In effect, the two research modalities, efficacy and effectiveness, measure different phenomena and provide complementary information to both the researcher and clinician.

The Clinical Trials Method

The efficacy research paradigm is exemplified by the clinical trials method employed in medical drug studies where the objective is to determine the effects of a drug and dose dependence for a specific illness or symptom. For example, suppose one wants to study the efficacy of a new phosphate-binding medication for dialysis patients. In this case, a researcher might select and randomly assign dialysis patients with no comorbid disorders to dose-dependent treatment groups and a control group. Diet and other variables would be controlled to ensure similar phosphate-intake levels and similar dialysis protocols. Blood levels of phosphates would then be measured and compared across groups. The hope would be that the new medication would be shown to significantly reduce blood phosphate levels in some dose-response dependent fashion. This same "clinical trials" approach to psychotherapy would be exemplified by a study in which a researcher selects and randomly assigns patients with major depressive disorder, recurrent, with no comorbid pathology, to "dose-dependent," manualized treatments and a control group. The manualization of the treatments would ensure that each patient within a particular treatment group receives the same treatment just as in drug studies in which all within-group patients receive the same drug. Also similar to drug studies, statistical analyses are performed in order to determine the differences between treatment and control groups on outcome measures, including outcome as a function of dose (e.g., type and/or length of therapy).

While so far this sounds like a reasonable approach to identify empirically supported treatments for both medications and psychotherapy, the question of generalizability has not been addressed. As previously mentioned, research designed to determine how well a particular therapy works outside of the controlled experimental context is referred to as effectiveness research (Seligman, 1995). For example, once a drug has been shown to be significantly related to positive outcomes in the laboratory, it must still be evaluated in the field with patients in actual clinical settings. In clinical settings, patients are more heterogeneous and their problems are often more diverse, comorbid diseases are often present, and goals for acceptable outcomes often fluctuate. Furthermore, even if a manualized treatment is used, the physician may still deviate, intentionally or not, from the strict methodology employed in efficacy studies.

Sources of Error

In comparing the clinical effectiveness of pharmacotherapy and psychotherapy, a significant issue involves the differences in source and magnitude of error variance between these modalities. Psychopharmacology, for example, involves sources of error that can not be controlled for either statistically or experimentally. That is, why are some drugs very effective for some individuals and less effective for others? Why does the same drug, such as Prozac, create sexual difficulties for some individuals but not others? Presumably there are differences in the biochemistry and physiology among these individuals that contribute to these differences. While the exact source of these chemical or structural differences is often unknown, the differences, nonetheless, are sources of error variance. If psychotherapy researchers are to use the clinical drug trials model for psychotherapy research, it may be informative to examine the differences in error variance between the two therapeutic modalities. This examination may shed some light on both the strengths and limitations of applying the clinical drug trials model to psychotherapy research as well as potentially lead to the development of strategies for minimizing error variance.

Ingram, Hayes, and Scott (2000) have recently suggested that the major sources of error variance in clinical research may be classified into three categories: (a) therapist variability, (b) therapy variability, and (c) client variability. According to these authors these categories represent "three interacting sources of variance that may significantly affect the extent to which treatments found effective in research can be generalized to clinical settings" (p. 49). Because the pharmacotherapy model has served as the primary basis for psychotherapy efficacy research, we believe it may be informative to compare psychotherapy and pharmacotherapy with respect to therapist, therapy, and client variability.

Therapist Variability

Therapist variability refers to the fact that therapists differ from one another in terms of their skill, competency, level of training, and an innumerable host of other variables. How much of this variance can be controlled through manualization of treatments has not been adequately researched. If psychotherapy and pharmacotherapy are compared in terms of this source of variance, some significant differences between these two modalities become immediately apparent. While skill, level of competency, and training apply to both pharmacotherapy and psychotherapy, their relative degree of variability may be different. Pharmacotherapy, as a process, represents a paradigm in which the role of the physician is often minimized. The physician's role (after a diagnosis is made to determine which medication is the appropriate treatment) is to prescribe the medication and appropriate dose, provide follow-up, and make medication changes as indicated. Major types of physician variance that bear on the external validity of pharmacotherapy therefore include (a) variability in medication choice and dose prescription, (b) variability in monitoring of effectiveness of the medication, and (c) variability in judgment regarding medication substitution. Turning to the practice of psychotherapy, assuming manualized treatments, the same types of therapist error variance are relevant but we believe there may be significantly different magnitudes for each type. For example, the psychotherapist (after a diagnosis is made for which psychotherapy is the appropriate treatment) must (a) prescribe the appropriate therapeutic modality and dose, (b) make judgments regarding the ongoing effectiveness of therapy, and (c) make appropriate intervention adjustments and/or substitutions, just as the physician does. However, one significant difference between the practice of psychotherapy and the practice of pharmacotherapy is that in psychotherapy the psychotherapist is an integral part of the ongoing treatment. Unlike pharmacotherapy in which there may be relatively long periods of time during which the physician relies on the action of an intervention (i.e., a medication) that operates independently of his/her influence, the psychotherapist cannot be so easily separated from the ongoing treatment. Even among psychotherapists who adhere to the same theoretical orientation or manualized treatment, there are simply more periods of interaction with the client and thus the possibility of increased therapist error variance. Most notable in psychotherapy is the variance in judgments and clinical substitutions. While the physician often has objective physiological measures to guide his or her judgments in determining the appropriate treatment modality, the psychotherapist must rely on subjective reports of the client and descriptive diagnostic categories to a much greater extent. In addition, a physician's decisions to substitute medications are more frequently based on objective measures, thereby reducing variance compared to their psychotherapy counterparts. Finally, as mentioned above, whereas the physician is faced with discrete periods of judgment followed by periods during which the patient is taking medication, the psychotherapist is making judgments every time he or she speaks (or is silent) during the therapeutic session. Clearly this increases the potential for variability among different psychotherapists when compared to physicians and the practice of pharmacotherapy.

Therapy Variability

Therapy variability refers to the fact that a therapy used in a clinical trial and that which is used in clinical practice will vary as a function of how the therapy is actually implemented by different therapists. Once again, when comparing pharmacotherapy and psychotherapy with regard to therapy variability, any assumption that the error variance associated with these two forms of treatment is the same may be unwarranted. For example, pharmacotherapy in clinical practice tends not to vary significantly from the empirically supported procedures established in clinical trials. That is, the process of prescribing a specific medication for a specific symptom or syndrome will vary relatively little between an efficacy study and a clinical setting. By way of contrast, the implementation of a manualized EST may vary considerably between the research and clinical setting. As Ingram and colleagues (2000) point out, ESTs are typically manualized in such a fashion as to permit considerable flexibility. While such flexibility is essential in clinical practice, this feature becomes a significant source of error when attempting to empirically demonstrate the effectiveness of a particular EST with clients treated by practicing therapists.

Client Variability

As emphasized by Ingram and colleagues (2000) and others (Seligman, 1995), clients who seek services in the "real world" of clinical practice are significantly more heterogeneous than those selected for clinical trials in efficacy studies. As mentioned previously, efficacy studies generally are designed to study homogenous samples of individuals who meet the criteria of a single diagnosis. While this is intended to minimize the confounds due to comorbid conditions, it creates a potential problem for generalizing to clinical settings. As Ingram and associates note:

> [I]t is unclear how a treatment that is found to be efficacious for a given disorder may be affected by the fact that other disorders or problems coexist with the target disorder. A client in a clinical setting with one constellation of personality problems in addition to the presenting problems may be affected very differently than another client with similar presenting problems and a different constellation of personality issues. (p. 50)

Returning to our comparison of psychotherapy and pharmacotherapy, comorbidity is a source of error for both forms of treatment. However, comorbidity is arguably less of an issue in pharmacotherapy because different diagnostic categories tend to be better defined by their respective symptom clusters (or syndromes). By way of contrast, diagnostic categories for psychological disorders tend to be much more heterogeneous due to the varying criteria needed to establish a particular diagnosis. For example, two persons diagnosed as depressed may have few or, in some cases, as little as one symptom in common.

Although individual differences in patient/client treatment adherence, biochemistry, and physiology are additional sources of variance for both pharmacotherapy and psychotherapy, the relative contribution of each of these factors to total error variance is unknown. However, because psychotherapy primarily targets psychological functioning and psychological mechanisms of change (as opposed to primarily biological mechanisms of change), outcomes may vary significantly due to the operation of numerous individual difference variables of a *psychological* nature (e.g., client motivation, intelligence capacity for introspection, etc.). Thus, because pharmacotherapy and psychotherapy target different mechanisms to bring about change, it is once again unwarranted to assume the error variance between the two modalities is equivalent.

FUTURE PROMISE OF ESTS: THE NEED FOR A FEEDBACK MECHANISM

One important implication of the previous discussion of the potential differences in error variance between efficacy and effectiveness studies for pharmacotherapy and psychotherapy, is that the current practice of employing the clinical trials methodology associated with drug research to psychotherapy research must be critically examined. Although we have suggested that the sources of therapist, therapy, and client error may be greater for psychotherapy than for pharmacotherapy, there is currently no structured method to evaluate this contention. However, one critical and unacknowledged issue associated with the application of the clinical drug trials method to psychotherapy outcome studies is the fact that psychotherapy research only models part of the clinical drug trials method. One of the most important components of the clinical drug trials research process has not been incorporated into psychotherapy research—that is, a feedback mechanism about the clincial effectiveness of a particular treatment in the field. Pharmacotherapy research, for example, incorporates a feedback mechanism to monitor the external validity of the initial efficacy studies. That is, once the efficacy of a drug is determined in the laboratory and the drug has been approved for clinical applications, its effectiveness and side effects are monitored and measured to empirically study the effectiveness of the drug in actual practice settings. The EST movement (and psychotherapy research in general) does not currently incorporate any such feedback mechanism. Once an efficacy study is completed for a psychotherapeutic modality and is identified as an EST or practice guideline, no organized mechanism is in place to determine the particular intervention's degree of effectiveness in clinical settings. Therefore, there is no corrective feedback process to advise psychotherapists (and researchers) about the effectiveness, possible contraindications, or side effects associated with using the treatment in actual clinical practice. This is the very mechanism that is needed in order to make determinations about the external validity of psychotherapy procedures. The development of a feedback procedure is fundamental to the development of any program, whether it is in health care, business, or science. The failure to include such a mechanism limits not only the ability to determine external validity but also precludes the integration of any continuous quality control process.

In the United States, pharmacotherapy implements this feedback mechanism through the Food and Drug Administration (FDA). One responsibility of the FDA is to evaluate the efficacy of new medications as discussed earlier. Another responsibility, however, is to continue to monitor the effectiveness of the medication in clinical settings. As a result of this feedback mechanism, the FDA has the authority to revoke approval for medications if the effectiveness of the medication is not supported in clinical studies or negative outcomes occur. This has been seen recently in the revocation of Fen-Phen (fenfluramine and phentermine) and Redux (dexfenfluramine) due to adverse side effects that were not detected by the efficacy studies (Food and Drug Administration, 1997; Julien, 1998). Currently, professional psychology does not have any feedback mechanism of this nature in place. While guidelines and criteria have been developed to minimally establish a psychological treatment as efficacious, no review body has been charged with the responsibility to monitor the clinical effectiveness of treatments.

Ultimately, it is the implementation of this feedback process that will provide the field of psychotherapy with the database needed to reduce the overall variance in psychotherapy outcomes. Within this framework, data from clinical settings could be used to refine ESTs through the incorporation of contraindications for specific therapies, alternative therapeutic modalities, and potential side effects. If professional psychology is going to model psychotherapy research after the clinical trials approach, then the field must incorporate this feedback mechanism into the EST process. Ultimately, a regulatory body may need to be formed. This body would be charged with monitoring data on the effectiveness of ESTs (and other psychotherapies) within the "real world" of clinical practice.

As we pointed out at the outset of this chapter, an important (albeit often underemphasized) rationale for the EST movement involves an ethical commitment to ensure that the psychological treatments provided to clients are fundamentally sound (Ingram et al., 2000). While the EST movement's focus on the efficacy of psychotherapy procedures represents an important step toward this goal, a similar empirical focus on psychotherapy effectiveness may ultimately serve to fulfill this important social contract to the public trust.

REFERENCES

American Psychological Association (1996). *Guidelines and principles for accreditation of programs in professional psychology.* Washington, DC: Author.

Chambless, D. L., Baker, M. J., Baucom, D. H., Beutler, L. E., Calhoun, K. S., Crits-Christoph, P., Daiuto, A., DeRubleis, R., Detweiler, J., Haaga, D. A. F., Johnson, S., McCurry, S., Mueser, K. T., Pope, K. S., Sanderson, W. C., Shoham, V., Stickle, T., Williams, D. A., & Woody, S. R. (1998). Update on empirically validated therapies: II. *The Clinical Psychologist, 51*, 3–16.

Chambless, D. L., & Hollon, S. D. (1998). Defining empirically supported therapies. *Journal of Consulting and Clinical Psychology, 66*, 7–18.

Chambless, D. L., Sanderson, W. C., Shoham, V., Bennett Johnson, S., Pope, K. S., Crits-Christoph, P., Baker, M., Johnson, B., Woody, S. R., Sue, S., Beutler, L., Williams, D. A., & McCurry, S. (1996). An update on empirically validated therapies. *The Clinical Psychologist, 49*, 5–18.

Crits-Christoph, P. (1996). The dissemination of efficacious psychological treatments. *Clinical Psychology, Science and Practice, 3*, 260–263.

Eysenck, H. J. (1952). The effects of psychotherapy: An evaluation. *Journal of Consulting Psychology, 16*, 319–324.

Eysenck, H. J. (1961). The effects of psychotherapy. In H. J. Eysenck (Ed.), *Handbook of abnormal psychology* (pp. 697–725). New York: Basic Books.

Food and Drug Administration. (1997, 15 September). *FDA announces withdrawal fenfluramine and dexenfluramine (Fen-Phen)* [On-line]. Available http: www.fda.gov/cder/news/phen/fenphenpr81597.htm

Goldfried, M. R., & Wolfe, B. E. (1996). Psychotherapy practice and research: Repairing a strained alliance. *American Psychologist, 51,* 1007–1016.

Henry, W. (1998). Science, politics, and the politics of science: The use and misuse of empirically validated treatment research. *Psychotherapy Research, 8,* 126–140.

Ingram, R. E., Hayes, A., & Scott, W. (2000). Empirically supported treatments: A critical analysis. In C. R. Snyder & R. E. Ingram (Eds.), *Handbook of psychological change* (pp. 40–60). New York: Wiley.

Julien, R. M. (1998). *A primer of drug action* (8th ed.). New York: W. H. Freeman & Company

Lambert, M. J., & Bergin, A. E. (1994). The effectiveness of psychotherapy. In A. Bergin & S. L. Garfield (Eds.), *Handbook of psychotherapy and behavior change* (4th ed., pp. 143–189). New York: Wiley.

Mother's little helper. (1996, March 18). *Newsweek,* pp. 50–56.

Paul, G. L. (1967). Strategy of outcome research in psychotherapy. *Journal of Consulting Psychology, 31,* 109–118.

Persons, J. B. (1995). Why practicing psychologists are slow to adopt empirically-validated treatments. In S. C. Hayes, V. M. Follette, R. M. Dawes, & K. E. Grady (Eds.), *Scientific standards of psychological practice: Issues and recommendations* (pp. 141–161). Reno, NV: Context Press.

Seligman, M. E. P. (1995). The effectiveness of psychotherapy: The consumer report study. *American Psychologist, 50,* 965–974.

Smith, M. L., & Glass, G. V. (1977). Meta-analysis of psychotherapy outcome studies. *American Psychologist, 32,* 752–760.

Smith, M. L., Glass, G. V., & Miller, T. I. (1980). *The benefits of psychotherapy.* Baltimore: Johns Hopkins University Press.

Sperry, L., Brill, P. L., Howard, K. I., & Grissom, G. R. (1996). *Treatment outcomes in psychotherapy and psychiatric interventions.* New York: Brunner/ Mazel.

Strupp, H. H. (1996). The tripartite model and the consumer reports study. *American Psychologist, 51,* 1017–1024.

Task Force on Promotion and Dissemination of Psychological Procedures (1995). Training in and dissemination of empirically-validated psychological treatments: Report and recommendation. *Clinical Psychologist, 48,* 3–23.

Waehler, C. A., Kalodner, C. R., Wampold, B. E., & Lichtenberg, J. W. (2000). Empirically supported treatments (ESTs) in perspective: Implications for counseling psychology training. *The Counseling Psychologist, 28,* 657–671.

Wilson, G. T. (1995). Empirically validated treatments as a basis for clinical practice: Problems and prospects. In S. C. Hayes, V. M. Follette, R. M. Dawes, & K. E. Grady (Eds.), *Scientific standards of psychological practice: Issues and recommendations* (pp. 163–196). Reno, NV: Context Press.

Index